MANAGEMENT AND MEASUREMENT OF SOFTWARE QUALITY

Management and Measurement of Software Quality

UNICOM

Applied Information Technology

edited by
Mike Kelly

AVEBURY
TECHNICAL

Published by
Avebury Technical
Ashgate Publishing Limited
Gower House
Croft Road
Aldershot
Hants GU11 3HR
England

Ashgate Publishing Company
Old Post Road
Brookfield
Vermont 05036
USA

British Library Cataloguing in Publication Data

Management and Measurement of Software Quality -
(UNICOM Applied Information Technology Series)
I. Kelly, Mike II. Series
005.1

ISBN 0 291 39801 4

Printed in Great Britain at the University Press, Cambridge

Contents

Preface

This collection of papers originally set out to cover *Testing*. Taking into account the emergence of software development as an integrated process, the discipline of testing was viewed in its broader context as an integral part of the measurement and management of quality software systems. This collection brings together some of the current thinking in testing as well as chapters on the more general topic of software measurement and the management of the software development process.

No one (well almost no one) would now question the need for quality in IT systems, both in the products themselves and in the processes used to produce them – and thus ultimately in the resources required to produce them. The desire for quality is one thing, however the practical and successful implementation of quality and quality related systems in IT development organisations is another. This is not to say people are not trying, many are and some have been very successful but we are still a long way from having a nation-wide quality culture, let alone one that is European-wide. Other countries are striving for the same goal and at the time of writing, while the UK is probably pre-eminent on the research side, countries such as Germany tend to be leading in the practical application of Quality concepts and their measurement. They will achieve it long before the UK – do we really want to be a second class nation in terms IT as well as economically? – our leading expertise in this area could be our saving grace but continuing to produce poor quality systems using poor quality development processes will is not help us.

For those familiar with the US SEI work in Process Maturity models, the SEI survey which resulted in around 80% of US organisations being still at level 1 (ie. with chaotic processes and non-existent quality infrastructures) came as a surprise at the time but not in hindsight and most would now agree that the result would certainly not have been any different anywhere else, except, perhaps, for Japan.

Doom and gloom, we hear it all the time – but we can do something about it! All we need is not only to recognise the need for quality but to do something about it. In the long run the specific type of quality system is not important, provided it suits your needs. Most can be tailored to specific requirements and all should be seen as a necessary and desirable help towards continuous improvement in processes and products. Where most quality initiatives fail is in the implementation – they are given lip-service only - they are not controlled, they are not managed and they are not measured.

The word quality itself has many meanings attached to it through the ages and the proliferation of meanings has possibly never been as great as now! But what do we mean when talking of 'Meeting the Customers Requirements'; 'Exceeding the Customers Requirements' (!); 'Conforming with the Standard';

'Meeting the Specification'; etc, etc? All these have been quoted (many times) by developers, users, quality assurers, certification agencies, etc. and all with a confidence very often unmatched by experience! Essentially any definition of quality will suffice in a particular situation *provided it is a definition consistent with the stated business objectives of the organisation concerned and that those objectives (goals) are stated in terms that are verifiable* – i.e. in *Measurable* terms. It seems to me somewhat cliched to restate (inaccurately) the by now well over-used Lord Kelvin saying of 'What you cannot measure, you cannot control' (and subsequently rephrased by every expert in the field!). However the fundamental truth of the statement (however phrased) is inescapable. In which case, given the frequency with which it is stated and the frequency with which everyone in the audience mutters their agreement, is it not time we all started to try to comply with the fundamental principles of measurement?

Developers are often (interminably?) blamed for poor 'quality' of software systems, but who buys these systems? Answer, we all do (of one sort or another – be it an office spreadsheet or a command and control system for a nuclear submarine). Who is responsible therefore for the quality of a system? The developer?, the user?, the purchaser/buyer?, the QA staff (in-house or independent)?, the Standards makers? Obviously everyone has a vested interest in 'quality' and their own concept of quality, so therefore, everyone is responsible for the quality (or lack of) of every system.

The purchaser of shoes which fall apart in a week, or a new dishwasher that breaks all the china has every right to, and always (well nearly always) does complain vociferously to the manufacturer and expects full refund or free replacement. So why is this still a rarity for poor quality software systems? Why does the developer still in general expect the user to pay for debugging (euphemistically called maintenance) and why does the user still do so?! Well, apart from the obvious answer of complacency ('it has always been thus') the reasons are many but essentially: lack of proper controls by all parties concerned in development; lack of understanding by many involved of what is going on; lack of agreement of fully understood specifications (resulting from poorly stated and continuously changing requirements); lack of properly implemented measurement procedures, lack of acceptance of responsibility, etc. Or to put it simply: poor management, poor processes, misunderstood product, unmeasured and NIH!

This book will not answer all the problems – but it will help to point those who wish to improve, in the right direction. The chapters here represent a selection of current thought in the area based on best practice in Europe and state-of-the-art research.

The chapters are arranged in four main groups; the first three deal with measurement and metrics; chapters four, five and six with more general quality aspects; chapters seven to twelve consider specifically the more traditional aspects of testing; chapters thriteen and fourteen present actual case histories and finally chapter fifteen provides an introduction to quantitative usability testing.

In selecting the contributions to this book we have tried to restrict the number of purely academic chapters in order to present practical approaches to and applications of testing and measurement techniques.

Nick Ashley's chapter provides an overview of why we should introduce measurement into the development process and in particular its invaluable and necessary aid to management.

The concept of process improvement is fast gaining acceptance in the IT world. Mike Berwick, with his practical experience as quality manager in a major telecomms company and his work with the UK SPICE initiative (formally Improve IT), gives an overview of the current research in Europe and in particular the role of benchmarking in process improvement.

Ernest Wallmüller as a leading exponent of quality in Germany, presents the experiences of ATAG Informatik in setting up a measurement programme and the role of the ESPRIT project on metrics promotion – AMI.

General quality issues are provided by Darrel Ince of the Open University – one of Europe's best known experts in the quality and metrics field and author of many standard works on the subject.

Frank Elstrom looks at the problems, and ways of overcoming them, encountered in trying to 'sell' quality, while Andrew Johnston of Eurotunnel describes the experience of implementing quality on one of Europe's largest projects.

On the more theoretical side of testing there are chapters from Monika Müllerberg of GMD and Patrick Hall and Robert Hierons of Brunel University.

Dorothy Graham is one of the leading experts in the testing domain and here she presents a method of classifying testing tools for evaluation and procurement purposes, i.e. to make it easier for the prospective user to plough through the minefield of choice and select the right tool for the job.

In addition to including some of the more theoretical approaches to 'traditional' testing we have included chapters by Elliott Manley, a leading consultant in the testing and quality area, Brian Hambling of MEG and Helene Lassalle of Verilog in France who give the ir views on the planning and management of testing based on their extensive industrial experience. In addition two 'case studies' of the actual experience of using testing techniques and tools in industry. Many people use testing techniques and tools – some successfully many not – but few to date have been willing to share their experience. The experiences of Ian Weavers at Standard Chartered Bank and Mark Fewster at Performance Software are different but equally instructive for potential users and developers of tools as well as those who have tried and failed but know they still need to keep trying until they get it right – find the right solution for their particular environment.

Finally the need to evaluate software systems in context is a fundamental tenet of a, till now, often neglected part of the testing process, namely usability evaluation. This is changing – usability evaluation is now being increasingly viewed as not only a vital part of the testing process but a major factor in and beyond software quality assurance in general. For this reason we have included a chapter on recent work in the usability assessment field. Miles Macleod and Nigel Bevan of the National Physical Laboratory provide an overview of the European ESPRIT project MUSiC which has developed tools for the quantitative assessment of the various aspects of usabilty.

Finally my sincere thanks to Unicom for their considerable help (and infinite patience) and to all the authors for their diverse and valuable contributions.

1 Selling Quality: Where is the Buyer?

Frank Ekstrom
Delphi Software Ltd

1.1 BACKGROUND DETAILS

Before discussing the actual 'selling' of quality as a commercial venture, we should ponder over a few points:

- Is software quality improvement really high on the organisational priority list or is it just an intermittent flavour of the month?
- Why is the role of 'quality champion' generally set up as a part-time responsibility, more often than not conflicting with other duties.
- Is fear of change a major constraint in the implanting of short-term quality improvements?
- Would quality exposures reflect on individuals who have now moved up in the organisational authority structure?
- Who in the organisation really wants improved quality and are they willing or able to pay the price?

The opinions and observations put forward in this paper are from the viewpoint of an individual 'selling' quality improvement techniques into the Irish marketplace. Many of the problems and pitfalls would also be encountered by individuals attempting to introduce short-term highly visible improvements into their organisations.

As background information, it is important to describe some of the features of the Irish software market, which is small by European and American standards. The lack of size coupled with isolation from the primary world centres creates a unique set of constraints that must be addressed in the identification of products for the market.

The following are the results of a recent survey of 50 representative Irish organisations.

- **Ownership**
  The majority (94%) are indigenous (wholly or partly Irish owned).
- **Business types**
  Software and systems houses represented 80% of the sample.
- **Years established**
  The representation was youthful, with 40% being 5 years or less in age.

Almost 75% existed for 10 years or less.

- **Company size**
  The Irish company size is generally small with 38% having five or fewer employees. Twenty or fewer employees represents 86% of the sample.

1.2 THE DELPHI QUALITY VENTURE

With eagerness, Delphi Software commence its venture of bringing an improved software quality to the Irish marketplace. With over 50 professional staff and considerable experience in testing, the obstacles appeared to be minor hurdles. After all, had not the initial market surveys indicated that the majority of organisations saw quality improvements as a primary goal! Initial products were identified and developed including Delphi's Early Life Cycle Test Methodology.

The initial thrust was to larger organisations. What initially appeared as a cake walk soon became mired down in the quicksand of bureaucracy and indecisiveness. The obstacles encountered included:

- The decision makers (with budgets) were removed from the problem and had passed the responsibility on.
- The individuals with the problem didn't have time to look effectively for solutions as they were too busy fighting fires.
- A credibility gap arose as to whether an external group could implant quality into what took so long to develop. (Was this fear of exposure?)

Although everyone accepted the initial concepts regarding the introduction of quality standards and techniques, the buyers were thin on the ground.

A rethink was in order regarding the products and the marketplace. The nature of the Delphi business strategy stood out as a major constraint. Delphi supplied high quality personnel to an elite client base generally of a large size. The personnel supplied would generally be on the client site for a lengthy period of time which meant that the actual client base was too small to satisfy the viability of the new venture. Other factors, including the total cost (tangible and intangible) of running in-house courses, also acted as inhibitors.

An internal Delphi review of the industrial position was performed and a strategy was adopted. Prior to the actual 'selling', a solid foundation had to be established. This foundation included:

- **Visibility**
  A much larger operational base had to be established. This was accomplished through mail shots, telephone conversations, and speaking at local quality-related events. Visibility is also required when selling quality within an organisation. The key individuals in the various departments must be aware of your existence and goals.

- **Credibility**
  Credentials must be presented. A lot of leg work was required in order to illustrate the benefits of 'practical quality improvements' to selected key figures.
  The principle used is that it becomes a lot easier to sell to someone you know and who trusts you.
  Effective communication to the key figure is probably the single largest factor in getting started on the quality route. The organisational 'quality champion' must deal directly with the key buyers. Of course there is also the fundamental requirement for senior management support.
- **Marketability**
  A compete revamp of the product offerings was made as a direct result of discussions with potential customers. A series of short (two day maximum) public courses were developed. These were aimed at the various managerial and technical levels within the target organisations.
  It is essential that organisers of internal strategies take careful observation of the 'buyers' requirement and prepare a crisp attack plan.
- **Saleability**
  The actual selling of the newly defined products became the easiest phase. The earlier stages had set the scene. A large base had been set up with personal contacts and the products were an outcome of communication with the real buyers.

The major surprise is that the earlier products were resurrected from the grave. Once the credibility barrier had been broken , customers asked for Delphi support during planning and the early phases of the product cycle. In addition, a set of practical software quality standards has been adopted by a number of Dublin based firms.

1.3 PROBLEMS TO BE OVERCOME

The Delphi story has a happy ending, but who knows what the outcome would have been if a strategy had not been formulated. Quality is a marketable commodity from both within and externally but the people and organisational cultures are the key ingredients.

The injection of quality is needed now and not in a year's time. If your organisation doesn't have time to improve quality due to ongoing deadlines or fire fighting, it never will. It is generally the lack of standards and evaluation techniques that precipitated the current situation.

To achieve a short term quality gain it is essential to understand the organisational culture and how change introduction may affect this culture.

The introduction of quality improvement techniques into new areas goes through three stages:

1 Scepticism

Here a cynical attitude prevails, in that the specific area is either operating effectively or that the function being performed is unique and quality injection would have no effect. It will be felt that just another bureaucratic layer is being piled on.

Communication is the key factor in overcoming this initial stage. In addition, a major change should not be undertaken that would alienate the individuals. It would be much wiser to introduce high impact and visible techniques one step at a time in a controlled fashion. The key personnel in the area should be heavily involved in the transition process. It is imperative that the approach is communicated effectively as secrets (intentional or otherwise) will raise the 'panic' levels.

The quality improvement must be detailed, covering the following as a minimum:

- full description of the improvement
- quality drivers
- constraints
- steps in the improvement process
- who is to do it and when
- how is success measured.

Once the quality improvement process has commenced, we enter the second transitional phase of 'fear'.

2 Fear

Fear can take many shapes depending on the specific improvement process and the organisational culture. It can range from personal exposure through potential redundancy.

Communication is again the best response, coupled with visible proof that the quality improvement will positively increase the profile of the task.

Fear is often visible and vocal, and thus can be addressed with relative ease. The real problem is when the fear is hidden. The hidden anxieties must also be addressed.

This stage generally ends when the quality objective is seen as achieving the defined goals.

At this point the individual(s) will feel that they are part of the 'quality circle' and will then be 'owners' and 'initiators' of good quality practices.

3 Way of life

The ultimate goal is that quality and the ongoing improvement of quality forms the basis of an organisational culture.

A major organisational milestone will have been met when this happens. Don't underestimate the effort required to reach this stage and be mindful that the 'champion of quality' is on the firing line until the goal is reached.

The next section covers a multi-step approach to injecting a short-term quality improvement system.

1.4 RECOMMENDED STRATEGY

The following illustrates a basic approach that will allow the introduction of quality in a controlled, visible and effective manner.

The objective of the eight steps is to achieve meaningful and visible quality 'implants' in a short time-frame. The approach is fully compatible with various certification processes.

The steps are as follows:

Step 1: Find the organisational quality driver

A senior manager in the organisation should have the responsibility of driving 'quality initiatives'. It is essential to start at this level. Credibility and management commitment will be questioned at a later point if you don't.

Discussions should reveal opinions and key strategic areas that need addressing. It is important to identify the key drivers of quality within the organisation.

The primary deliverable from this step is a Quality Policy Statement. The policy statement must be communicated throughout the organisation, thereby identifying the commitment to quality by senior management.

Step 2: Work with the champion of quality

An individual within the organisation will have been delegated the role of delivering the perceived quality system. Most of the interfacing will be done with this individual, but often quality improvements is only a part-time activity. If this is true then a number of constraints will have to be addressed, including time allocation and potential conflicts of interest.

The primary deliverable from this step is an overall strategy which may include the setting up of a Quality Initiative Team. Results of this step should be reviewed by the Quality Senior Manager.

Step 3: Assess the current situation

The purpose of this step is to highlight the quality improvement areas that will provide the greatest benefit.

This is accomplished using a base set list of standards, procedures, etc., coupled with a list of organisational quality drivers.

Each element on the list is evaluated, giving it a rating with regard to potential benefit, constraints, and whether it fits into the organisation's quality drivers. The resulting numeric value gives an initial indication of quality improvement potential.

The five areas receiving the highest rating are selected for a more detailed evaluation.

Step 4: Detailed analysis

The selected five potential quality initiatives are now analysed in a more detailed manner. It is important that an initiative does not impede another initiative or have spin-off consequences.

A crucial factor at this point is the establishment of the implementation method and how the success criteria will be set.

Each of the five will again be given a rating and will be used at a later stage as part of the selection criteria for implementation order.

The deliverable from this step is the logical order of implementation, how implementation is to be achieved, and how success is to be measured.

Step 5: Management evaluation and communication

The findings and recommendations as an outcome of Step 4 are reviewed by the Quality Senior Manager. This will ensure that recommended actions do not conflict with future organisation plans.

The outcome of this step is the final selection and ordering of the quality initiatives that will be 'institutionalised'.

Communication within the organisation is crucial at this point. It will reinforce management's commitment to quality.

Step 6: Pilot scheme implementation

The first initiative implemented will have been selected in Step 5.

The implementation will be according to the preset plan.

Measurements will be taken and analysed throughout the implementation period. This will aid in the fine-tuning that may be required as well as an essential ingredient in the evaluation (Step 7).

Trends will be observed to ensure that interim targets are being met as implementation progresses.

Step 7: Pilot scheme evaluation

A formal review takes place at a point that has been predefined in the implementation plan.

The review will form the cornerstone of all future initiatives. Lessons and exposures identified will be used in future initiative implementations.

Results and future initiative plans are communicated to the organisation.

Step 8: Ongoing initiative introduction

Remaining initiatives are introduced in a staggered fashion.

The key here is 'not to start too much too soon'.

All initiatives will be closely monitored and corrective action will be taken if deviations are observed.

The eight step approach is only a beginning. The achievement of the various initiatives only represents milestones and not the end.

Quality improvement potential is always there, and as each initiative is implemented we find ourselves one step up the ladder as a quality organisation.

2 Some of the Questions to Ask about Quality Assurance

Darrel Ince
Open University

My aim is to examine some of the key areas in software quality assurance by explaining a number of questions which I usually ask when I am called in by a potential software customer to judge the competence of a software developer.

2.1 TRACEABILITY

This is a term used to refer to the fact that there is a direct relationship between the functions in a system and the code that implements the functions. In a system which has a high degree of traceability it should prove possible to point at a module and quickly discover what functions it helps implement.

Traceability is vital in a software system. As an example of its importance consider regression testing. Here, a change is made to a system and the developer wishes to discover what system tests and acceptance tests require to be re-executed. If there was a high degree of traceability then all that is required is to discover the code that was affected by the change and work back to the functions corresponding to the code. Once these functions have been discovered then the system tests corresponding to these functions can be extracted and executed.

2.2 THE TIMING OF THE DEVELOPMENT OF THE SYSTEM AND ACCEPTANCE TESTS

A good software developer will start work on the system and acceptance tests as early as possible after the system specification has been completed. There are a number of reasons for this. First, it enables the project manager to obtain an accurate costing for the testing process, at a comparatively early stage in the software project. Second, it enables the manager to discover whether special-purpose testing tools are required. Third, it enables much better validation of the system specification to take place. Developers have reported to me that their system specifications are of a much higher quality if someone is standing over their analysts asking how to test a particular function expressed in the system specification. Ideally the outline system and acceptance tests should be complete by the time that system design has been finished.

2.3 THE INDEPENDENCE OF QUALITY ASSURANCE STAFF

Quality assurance staff should be as independent as possible from the developmental aspects of the software project. The main reason for this is that the typical project manager's main concerns are with time-scales and budget; in the rush to get a system delivered, little else matters and quality often goes overboard. The staff who carry out quality assurance on a project should be completely divorced from the developmental staff. There are a number of options which can be employed. A good option for a large software developer is to have a quality assurance department which has a separate reporting line almost up to board level. The worst option is for the project manager to carry out the quality assurance function himself. Options which lie in the middle of the spectrum are to have quality assurance specialists attached to a number of projects or to have a nominated member of a project carry out quality assurance.

2.4 THE NOTATION USED FOR THE SYSTEM SPECIFICATION

The system specification is the key document on a software project. The project manager uses it to produce a costing for the project; the designer uses it to develop a system design; the quality assurance staff use it to generate the system tests and acceptance tests; and technical writers consult it when developing user documentation.

It can be seen, then, that any error in the system specification will rebound in four directions. It is, thus, crucial that the medium used to express the system specification is as accurate as possible. There is a broad spectrum of notations ranging from unstructured natural language up to mathematics. While I would expect few people to adopt mathematics, it is worth considering using a graphical notation such as data flow diagrams or, as a minimum, specifying standards which lead to better structured natural language documents. Of all the issues discussed this is probably the most crucial.

2.5 THE USE OF A DEVELOPMENT METHODOLOGY

A development methodology is a set of notations, techniques and tools which take a software developer from the statement of requirements to the final program code. Popular methodologies include Yourdon Structured Development, SSADM, Mascot and JSD. They offer a number of advantages to the software developer in the area of quality assurance.

First, because they are backed up with CASE technology, they enable a highly maintainable system to be developed. Second, they enable the developer to produce systems which have high traceability. Third, they enable a better correspondence between the system design and the system specification to occur. While development methodologies are expense to implement, the quality assurance gains are such that I would expect most software developers to pay back their investment within two years.

2.6 THE APPLICATION OF VALIDATION AND VERIFICATION

Many companies think of validation and verification solely in terms of system and acceptance testing. While these are necessary activities they suffer from a major problem: they occur too late in the software project. They occur at a time when, if major reworking is to occur, then major costs are incurred. It is a general rule that if you can validate or verify something in a software project then do it as early as possible. There are a number of very effective techniques which enable the validation effort to be pushed further towards the front end of a project.

Technical reviews are a meeting in which a number of participants attempt to discover defects in a project document or program code. They can occur as early as the project planning stage, or as late as unit coding. The most effective reviews are the system specification review and the system test specification review.

Another effective technique for checking requirements is prototyping: the development of a working model of a system early in the software project. There are a number of tools which can be used to do this: UNIX, fourth generation languages, application generators and very high-level languages are all good examples. Prototyping enables the customer to experience a potential system first hand, and is an excellent way of eliciting and checking requirements.

2.7 UNIT TESTING AND TARGETS

Unit testing is notoriously badly carried out. Perfunctory unit tests usually result in defective modules being passed forward for system testing with a consequent impact on cost when errors are discovered. One technique which attempts to tighten up on unit testing is to set the testers quantitative targets in terms of test coverage.

There are a number of metrics which can be used to judge the quality of a test suite: statement coverage measures the percentage of statements in a module which have been executed by test data; branch coverage measures the percentage of branches executed; and condition coverage measures the percentage of boolean conditions. Unit tests should be asked as a matter of course to include their coverage metrics in the unit folder for a program unit.

2.8 THE EXPLICATION OF DECISIONS

It is a good principle for staff on a software project to be asked, via standards, to justify their decision. Not only is this a requirement for good quality assurance, but it also sharpens up the activities of the development staff. Typical rationalisations that might be demanded include: asking a system designer to justify his design, asking the project manager to give reasons why he has fixed on a particular cost for a project, and asking a unit tester to justify his choice of test data.

2.9 THE ROLE OF MAINTENANCE

Software maintenance can consume as much as 85% of software budgets. This fact has not yet percolated through to software developers. Few insist on standards and procedures which lead to easily maintainable systems.

We now have a number of techniques – both simple and complex – which enable maintenance to be a much happier process than it once was.

One excellent technique is information hiding: developing a design where the design decisions are hidden beneath low-level modules. Other aids to maintenance include building traceability into a system, using CASE technology, and storing documents and data on-line.

2.10 PROGRAMMING STANDARDS

Although we have de-emphasised the role of programming over the last two decades, it still plays an important part in projects. Certainly, for those companies who use poor design and system specification notations, the program code is the first port of call for the maintainers. It is thus important that programming standards are specified which ensures that modules are readable and maintainable.

There are a number of components of a programming standard; the use of comments to identify a module and provide bureaucratic information, the outlawing of unsafe programming constructs, the specification of upper bounds on the number of global variables, the specification of upper bounds on boolean conditions, and the specification of an upper bound on module size.

A particularly important component of a programming standard is the use of assertions. These are executable statements which describe a relationship between variables at a point in a program which must be true at that point. If an assertion is violated, then an error message is issued. Assertions are particularly useful in system and acceptance testing when they provide much needed visibility.

2.11 THE IMPORTANCE OF INTEGRATION TESTING

Integration testing is the process of building up a system incrementally, a few modules at a time, and applying a test after each integration to check that interfaces are correct. Many companies ignore integration testing or carry it out at the sub-system level. This is a bad mistake.

It is a mistake because it enables the developer to pinpoint errors much more easily than during system and acceptance testing. If an error occurs during integration testing then the culprit is, almost invariably, one of the modules which have just been integrated, or one of the modules in the system which call these modules. If an error occurs in system testing the error could have occurred in any one of the modules of the system. For systems which contain thousands of modules this is exceptionally difficult. By using integration testing the developer is able to pinpoint errors much more quickly. There are a number of integration strategies: top-down, bottom-up and inside-out. What strategy is applied should be determined immediately after the system design has been completed.

2.12 THE ROLE OF CHANGE

Change is routine on software projects. Even as late as system testing the developer is having to change his system specification and system design. It is vitally important that change is properly controlled and monitored. This is the role of configuration management.

A minimum configuration management regime should include: the determination of baselines; a procedure for proposed changes to baselines to be raised; a way of evaluating changes; and a procedure for applying the changes and informing a project when these changes have taken place. Finally, a minimal configuration management regime should include a procedure for circulating updated documentation after change has taken place.

2.13 COINCIDENTAL CORRECTNESS

The term **coincidental correctness** refers to the seemingly successful execution of a test, but with the wrong modules being executed. Normally coincidental correctness occurs during system and acceptance testing. It can be minimised by some very simple precautions. First, the developer should maintain documentation which relates the system tests to the modules which are to be executed when a particular system test is exercised. Second, during integration testing and system testing the developer should instrument his program such that each module issues some statement that it has been executed. During system testing the output from these modules can then be checked against the functions/modules documentation.

2.14 RESPONSE TIME

Response time plays an important part in many real-time and commercial data processing systems. There is a myth that response time can be predicted from a system design. While it is possible to design a system such that the response time is not seriously wrong, most software developers require some tuning on their systems. This tuning should occur before system testing, after some preliminary response time tests have been carried out. An important tool to use for tuning is a program instrumentor. This enables hot spots to be detected and the limited amount of resource available for tuning to be employed effectively.

When you have a system which has response constraints it is important that maintainability, or rather changeability is built into the system; one of the best techniques for ensuring this is information hiding.

2.15 VALIDATING THE RESOURCE ESTIMATE

It is vitally important that the cost estimate for a project is checked. You may be a little mystified by the fact that I have included this in a seminar on quality assurance. The answer is that if you get the resource estimate wrong, then the project manager will almost invariably compromise on some developmental activities such as system testing – leading to a degradation of quality in the final system.

There are a number of ways of checking the estimate: by using difference and similarity comparisons, by using advanced statistical techniques such as the Delphi method, or by using some of the newer metrics-based techniques such as function point analysis.

2.16 CARRYING OUT RISK ANALYSIS

An important activity which needs to be carried out during project planning is risk analysis. The project manager should look at all the factors which could be present in an application which might conceivably lead to problems. There isa whole series of these problems. For example, customer experience with information technology and software development is a major factor. A customer who is unfamiliar with software development may sign-off an inadequate system specification, only to demand major changes during acceptance testing. Another example is the experience of the staff who are carrying out the software development, this will obviously affect the time-scales and budgets of the project.

It is important that the project manager is provided with a checklist of risk factors and provides evidence that he has considered all the items on this list. Moreover, the project manager should provide evidence that the risk analysis has been taken into account when estimating the project. Also, the project manager should provide, as part of the project plan, a description of the main risks, and the strategy that is to be adopted to keep the project on course if these risks materialise as events.

2.17 VERIFICATION AND VALIDATION INDEPENDENCE

The worst person to check a project document or program code is the person who produced it. Developing software products is a process akin to giving birth and, like our attitude to children, we feel that there is nothing wrong in them. A good quality assurance system should encourage the checking of an item by staff who did not develop that item. There are a number of techniques which can be employed for this. First, there is the technical review: a meeting of staff unconnected with an item to be validated who check that item for errors. Second, there is the use of metrics for checking test thoroughness. Third, there are techniques such as mutation testing which enable the developer to gain a good idea of the thoroughness of his test data by artificially inserting errors into a system or part of a system.

2.18 THE USE OF ERROR STATISTICS

It is important that the software developer keep statistics about the level of errors reported in the field and allocate resources to judging the severity of the errors. At designated times during the year, the quality assurance department should attempt to track the reasons for some of these errors, and issue a regular report on defects in the software development regime and the quality system.

2.19 PLANNING AND QUALITY ASSURANCE

The quality of a quality assurance system can be judged by how far into front-end activities it intrudes. Many quality assurance systems tend to concentrate on the programming end of the project, although, increasingly, more and more systems are percolating towards the frontend. However, project planning still remains untouched by many quality systems. This is a tragedy.

It is a tragedy because a poor project plan can ruin a project. As a minimum, a project plan should show all the major events in the system, all the major activities, the level of staff involved, the milestones, the results of the risk analysis, a justification of the project estimate, and should have as a subset the test, verification and validation plan.

2.20 TRAINING

Many companies provide training, directly or indirectly, on technical activities such as programming and analysis. However, when it comes to courses in unit testing, integration testing, test validation, generating test plans, developing system and acceptance tests, and running technical reviews, very little is provided. I would say that money spent on these courses will be at least effective as money spent on more technical courses.

2.21 THE COST OF QUALITY

It is something of a misnomer to talk about quality assurance as a cost. However, a good software developer should be spending between 3% and 7% of project budgets on quality assurance. The amount depends on the nature of the software development carried out. A software developer who constructs the same type of commercial data processing software should find his costs towards the lower end of the scale. However, a software developer who produces a large range of software, some of which is difficult, such as real-time embedded software, should expect the quality assurance costs to be nearer to 7%.

2.22 OVERALL PROJECT COSTS

A good question to ask a software developer is: What proportion of your costs do you spend on the various activities that make up your development effort? Poor software developers will tend to load the back-end activities, incurring costs as high as 40% on programming.

2.23 QUALITY ASSURANCE AND EXTERNAL STANDARDS

External standards can be overrated. However, I would expect any software developer who has a quality system to have at least consulted an external standard during the construction of the quality system. For commercial data processing they should at least have looked at BS5750, and for real-time and defence software they should have examined the MOD DefStan standards and the NATO AQAP standards.

3 Muzzling the Alligators: a Pragmatic Approach to Quality

Andrew K Johnston
Eurotunnel plc

3.1 A CONFLICT OF ADVICE

The newcomer to software quality management is faced with a wealth of advice from all corners and in many formats. Analysis, however, usually reduces the brew quite rapidly to two main components: a lengthy stream of ideas for changing the software production process to improve quality rapidly and easily; and, on the other hand, the concerns of experienced practical software builders that such changes will be unpopular, impractical and ineffective.

While some of these latter concerns can easily (and often correctly) be ascribed to laziness or good old-fashioned Luddism on the developers' part, it is nonetheless true that many of the purveyors of quality have vested interests, or at least axes to grind, and there is a minefield of inappropriate solutions.

Eurotunnel, with its very public commercial and time pressures, provides an interesting case study. The main finding is that to improve quality, one must recognise the real problems which constrain and motivate the developers, and offer practical aid in order to gain acceptance of the quality initiative. Once over this hurdle a slow, practical progression is the only way to keep things improving – too great a change or too academic a basis will alienate the developers, and an evident willingness for the QA staff to 'get their hands dirty' will not only improve relationships, but will uncover problems hidden to more conventional methods.

3.2 MATCHING PROBLEM AND SOLUTION

3.2.1 Following the paper trail

The hapless Quality Manager turns to books, courses and consultants for help. In his enthusiasm to move forward, he may well try to adopt an existing quality system, complete with development method. However, such offerings may have a variety of drawbacks:

- **The paper trail**. Too many quality systems and development methods centre around an endless stream of forms and documents. Since it is easier to prescribe format rather than content, that is what tends to happen. Worse still, many formal quality systems verify only the existence of the paper and the project team's assurance that all is correct, and there is no attempt to independently verify the content. Many projects drown under shelf-feet of expensive but unnecessary and, ultimately, inadequate documentation.
- **The infantry approach**. These failures can occur because most formal development methods are reminiscent of an army advancing, one step at a time, into the enemy's machine-gun fire. The attempts to 'deskill' software development entirely miss the point that it is essentially a skilled activity which will fail if the talent is constrained to an inappropriate lowest common denominator. Obviously, even commandos and special agents require control, but it must be relevant and more sophisticated.
- **Lack of real support for design, build and test**. Commercial methods, training, and standards have failed to keep pace with developing software architectures. Development organisations working with relatively new tools (for example fourth-generation languages and relational databases) may find that the commercial publications lag ten years behind the actual tools and techniques they are using, and that they have two alternatives: do without, or grow their own.
- **Optimism about developer motivation, comprehension and skill**. The average developer is not terribly interested in quality matters. Pride and a keenness to get the job done mean that anything which demonstrably improves the quality or productivity for the same effort is acceptable, anything which involves much extra work probably isn't. Good analytical programming or project management skills are rarely an indicator of facility in design or with written language. Documents on quality often remain unread or wrongly interpreted.
- **Expense**. Some of the these elements are very expensive. While it is true that doing nothing may be even more expensive, making the wrong choice can have a large direct as well as indirect cost, and it is also impossible to put all the elements in place together. In the longer term, it may well be true that 'Quality costs nothing', but that does not take cashflow into account.

This is not to say that all quality initiatives are worthless. Some are of great value, but the steps must be matched to the real problems and the readiness of the environment in order to provide a visible benefit.

3.2.2 A multitude of problems

The developer will typically respond to a quality initiative with 'I haven't got time!' His own immediate problems frequently manifest themselves as a shortage of time, money, or both, and even modest improvements in standards and procedures can fall foul of them. Help must be practical, an answer to the question 'What do I actually **do**?'

Developers within Eurotunnel have faced a number of problems which the books totally fail to mention, and which even carefully crafted standards and procedures may not address. Some are rare, but others are all too common:

- **Missing users!** Eurotunnel is that relative rarity, a new business. Inevitably, it has grown top-down, with the real users of the systems only now being recruited. Thus the systems have been defined in advance of the business, often by hard-pressed senior managers lacking time and the user perspective. This leads naturally to...
- **Unstable requirements.** The requirements have changed and kept on changing. Typically, rather than actual change there has been an unwillingness to commit to a decision, followed by a growth of unexpected detail when the decision is at last taken and understood. The problems are exacerbated by the complex relationship between Eurotunnel and its main contractor, TML, and by the number of other (governmental and financial) bodies who have an interest in the decisions. With the best of intentions, change control procedures are entirely ineffective until a certain critical stability is attained.
- **Geographical, linguistic, and cultural diversity**. Eurotunnel is an Anglo-French company, with software development on at least four separate sites, and users on at least as many more. A policy (occasionally inappropriate) that all major applications should be capable of operation in at least the two main languages causes major problems. The linguistic diversity extends to the development team, and documents may change language mid-document.
- **Pre-standard systems.** Standards and toolset evolve, but leave untouched a growing raft of old systems which predate the improvements. It is unrealistic to try to update these systems, but they typically consume more than their fair share of maintenance resources, and the different practices embodied in them may be at odds with later moves to a more advanced and coherent architecture.
- **Non-standard architectures.** Other systems may not fit at all. Functional fit, price, architecture and quality compete when a solution is chosen. Unfortunately, architecture and quality don't always win, particularly when one is searching for bilingual packages to meet specialist needs. Eurotunnel's standards and procedures may just not cover the chosen solution.
- **Emerging technology.** The opposite of the old system, and a special case of the non-standard architecture, is the case where new tools are adopted very early in order to address particular technical problems, but without the supporting standards and knowledge of the pitfalls required to control such usage.

- **Complex supplier chains and diverse quality approaches.** These problems are bad enough when they affect an internal development. They are exacerbated dramatically in an external development. Naturally, there are problems of formalising and expediting communications, and problems of unstable requirements sour the relationship. The supplier may have a different quality system (or none at all), and may not be willing to improve matters. Worse still is when the supplier depends heavily on a third party (the vendor of the toolset or the 'package'), and is unwilling or unable to exert control on the quality of some of the basic elements of the system.
- **The mythical package.** The belief in a 'package' solution is convenient for supplier and client alike, with the client believing that the use of a package will guarantee quality and shorten time-scales, while the supplier can argue against changes to the functionality or quality, and can retain rights even when most of the source code is rewritten. In reality, these approaches are only valid for a small, horizontal application such as a word processor. The fiction of the package serves only to confuse and obstruct when a larger vertical application is under development. In this case, it may be more appropriate to consider the supplier as producing a custom vehicle from a kit of parts.

3.2.3 The way forward

Pessimistic as this may sound, there are techniques which can be employed in such an environment to good effect. Solutions must be targeted at the developers' problems if they are to gain acceptance, but within an overall framework which avoids wasting effort on piecemeal improvements. The framework must act as a guide and a reference structure rather than a constraint on the introduction of new elements. Thus the adoption of a structured method and the creation of a Quality Manual, probably the key elements of the framework, must be seen as the construction of a scaffold to support the construction of the 'real' tools, not as ends in themselves, and certainly not as a structure from which to hang the Quality Manager.

3.3 SOME SUCCESSES

The development of Eurotunnel's quality system followed very much this pattern. An early decision to adopt Oracle's relational database and 4GL on large minicomputers as the strategic development environment suggested the adoption of Oracle's CASE*Method as the core structured method. Early attempts to build this up into a special 'Eurotunnel Development Method' failed because the aims of the various parties were not sufficiently close – internal and external initiatives were meeting the same problems described above.

The CASE*Method is far from perfect: it lacks any real support for the procurement process (and the customisation of package solutions), the production of documentation and software testing. While Oracle provide good training in analysis and some aspects of design, the later stages are very much at the developer's discretion, and there is no real definition of the deliverables at each stage. However, Eurotunnel decided that whatever the imperfections, rather than risk further false starts, the CASE*Method would provide as good a base as any other, and the missing ingredients would be added to it. Earlier, internal initiatives concentrated on the core development documents and the design and programming standards, while external consultants were invited to build on the same foundation adding support for procurement, documentation, and testing.

Obviously, the quality of any system has to match its environment. It is appropriate to expect a system for a few specialist users, or one in which the quality of data may be suspect, to achieve the same quality as a major core application handling key operational data whose quality must be assured. This concept of 'fitness for purpose', expressed using a 'quality profile', was introduced at an early stage to reflect this need for appropriate quality targets.

The quality system has thus evolved, itself growing and developing. As in any evolution, there have been some failures, and some growths have been limited, but there have also been some significant successes.

3.3.1 Technical standards and templates

The adoption of 'standards' is frequently seen as some sort of constraint on the creativity of the developer. However, if the standards can both reduce the scope for wasted development and ease the solution of difficult problems they will, gradually, be adopted. Adequate technical sophistication is important – if there are just a few apparently random or arbitrary rules they will tend to be ignored, but a comprehensive and coherent set of directives makes more sense. Against this must be set the importance of clarity – all developers are not equal, and too complex a rule set will be difficult for the less able (and may be seen as a burden on the more productive). Comprehensive and regular explanation and training is essential.

The production, to the standards, of both development documents and programs can be considerably improved (in both speed and quality) by the use of templates which provide a standards-compliant starting-point. Developers are grateful not to have to continually re-invent the difficult first steps, and see compliance as a convenient by-product. With a little ingenuity, the more repetitive parts of the production process can be automated, but by making the templates specific to the requirements and standards of the company there is none of the rework cost often associated with traditional 'program generators'.

Eurotunnel's standards, for example, embody a series of fairly complex techniques which allow the production of genuinely bilingual Oracle forms. Without templates and specially-developed tools, these would be ignored or abused, whereas in most cases developers now find the extension of the monolingual system a fairly straightforward process of translation.

There is a regular life cycle for standards and templates: **resistance**, **ignorance** (in which the new standards are ignored), **grudging acceptance**, and finally **enthusiasm**. Moving through the life cycle requires considerable effort from the QA group, but it is rewarded, if successful, by much earlier enthusiasm for the next endeavour. Eurotunnel has now reached the point where developers hound the QA group, chasing standards for new areas of work.

3.3.2 Procurement services

Eurotunnel decided that, given the enormity of the task of establishing all the necessary information systems, coupled with the uncertainty of requirements, it would be a good idea, where possible, to purchase an existing 'package' solution and use that as a basis for further development. In order to ease the procurement process, an external consultancy was contracted to help develop a series of procurement guidelines and procedures, supplemented by template Invitations to Tender and contracts. Since the administration of these required good procedural understanding and an overview of the requirements outside the particular project areas, these tasks were given to the QA group. This job of 'procurement control' has grown, with the result that the QA group now takes a key mediating role in contract negotiations, attempting to marry the requirements of the project, the information services managemen,t and the Eurotunnel procurement officers.

This has been a considerable success, with huge improvements in procurement efficiency. The overall view afforded from such a vantage point has on more than one occasion protected Eurotunnel from exposure to disadvantageous terms, and project managers have been very grateful for the reduced effort on their part required in the contracting phase. Formalised communications embodied in the contract and the procurement procedures reduce the risk of the contract going astray, but it is now acknowledged that these need to be policed more strongly to ensure their adoption even when time pressures act against them.

3.3.3 Email communications

With four development sites and users in several more, electronic communications have been essential. By avoiding procedures based on paper forms, but instead making gradually more sophisticated use of electronic mail, with shared filing systems and document templates, we have managed to keep communication efficient and effective as the business and the information services group have grown dramatically.

3.3.4 Reviews, inspections and audits

There appear to be two schools of thought on the role of the QA group – interventionist and non-interventionist. Eurotunnel's group is strongly in the interventionist school. On the basis that the mere existence of a program or a document in no way ensures its content, we have established a structure in which every document undergoes peer or QA-group review. Similarly, all source code is given a 'safety check' before use against the live databases, and a sample is checked more rigorously as part of any QA audit. These measures have proven very successful, and have regularly alerted information services management to areas in which a particular project is weak. Existing suppliers are now being subjected to the same quality audit process and, although sometimes surprised at the results, most of them seem to regard any criticism as constructive.

The quality audit program has also been extended to prospective suppliers, as a now-regular part of the procurement cycle. Perhaps unsurprisingly, some formally-qualified suppliers (those with, or near to, ISO 9000 certification) have revealed, under questioning, surprising gaps in their quality procedures, whereas, happily, others have satisfied us that without formal certification they have a deep enough understanding of the issues to minimise the risks to successful project completion. In one case the results of the audit were sufficient to change the procurement decision, and in many of the others the project team has been alerted early to risks which in the normal scheme of development might not have been revealed until the project was much further under way.

3.3.5 Centres of technical expertise

Eurotunnel has tried, quite successfully, to take advantage of several new tools and techniques, for example, the newer versions of the Oracle database and SQL*Forms 4GL. The QA group has been keen to get involved early in the introduction of these tools, so that the standards can develop in parallel with the early work, and so that there is a central repository of knowledge about these tools. Developers who see their work being turned directly into standards and templates are keen to share their ideas, and, in turn, the QA group can more effectively support their customers (the developers) by understanding the technical issues.

3.3.6 Testing

Software testing is an area where the theoretical treatment is considerably adrift of the real problems. Books consistently consider only very simple cases, where it is possible to draw, for example, a decision table for all states of the system. The real world is quite different – imagine trying to draw a decision table for the accounting system! Public courses on testing are little better: they typically try to be all things to all men, and again concentrate on over-simplified cases. The purveyors of such courses in the UK seem to have only passing familiarity with databases, and their recommended tools and techniques don't apply to 4GLs.

Having discovered this sorry state of affairs, and aware that our testing was rather rudimentary, Eurotunnel commissioned a group of external consultants to work with us to develop more appropriate test standards. These are slanted directly towards our two main cases: internal development in SQL*Forms, and external developments based on existing software. In the cases of internal developments, a high reliance is placed on structural unit test techniques, and inspections play a key part as a proven, efficient way of finding errors.

Since one of the main problems is the lack of a common basis of understanding about testing, we have also developed a series of training courses for developers, testers, IS managers, and even users. These have been a resounding success, and are sufficiently unusual, with their pragmatic 4GL bias, that we have been able to run them commercially.

However, having the right techniques and skills in place has not, of its own accord, solved some of the underlying problems with testing. The structured testing techniques are much more efficient at finding errors - their aim - but the volume of errors found in substantially complete systems may be so large as to be demoralising, and selling the message that finding and removing errors adds value to the system may prove difficult. Also, despite evidence that in recognised high-quality software environments testing is the dominant part of the software cost (Microsoft, for example, employs roughly five testers for each programmer), there is still resistance in commercial information services environments to accept testing budgets as high even as 30% of total, although that may be necessary to meet the target quality of the system.

Finally, while we have attempted to introduce automated test tools they have met with considerable resistance, and it is now becoming apparent that developers prefer manual testing techniques, finding them easier to apply until the software has attained reasonable stability.

The jury is still out on whether Eurotunnel's testing will ultimately be adequate, but the standards and training initiatives have certainly moved the work from a very raw state into a much more mature one, where the problems are at least understood.

3.3.7 Change control

Eurotunnel, by its nature as a growing, new business, suffers a very high rate of change in requirements. The adoption of prototyping and iterative approaches to capture these requirements means that software changes just as much as the documentation.

It has proven relatively easy to enforce *version* control: documents are registered centrally and changes are well marked, while a system of controlled baselines and separate programmer workspaces, in conjunction with a version control tool for the source code, mean that it is fairly easy to monitor changes to individual software items.

What has not proven so easy is *configuration* control: it is still not always possible to trace changes in software back to documentary changes, and with internal communications, documentation, and source code all in different environments, it is not always easy to build up a picture of all the elements of a system.

It is possible to suggest a life cycle for the ability to handle changes, and progress from one state to the next demands the achievement of a certain critical stability, as well as the attainment of certain techniques and discipline. Initially many projects are **chaotic**, with few rules and no real ability to even detect changes. Sooner or later they should progress to **ordered**, in which rules are applied and changes can be monitored. However, only when the overall configuration is clear and changes can be planned ahead of an urgent requirement can the project be considered truly **controlled**.

Within Eurotunnel, very few projects are still chaotic but, equally, few have yet attained the stability for controlled status, and it is clear that such control cannot successfully be applied artificially before that stability exists.

3.4 THE ROLE OF THE QA GROUP

It can be clearly seen that in order to contribute actively, rather than passively, to the improvement of software quality the QA group has to adopt a more pro-active stance than is traditional. Within Eurotunnel, the function is much more that of a 'development support group', and requires a blend of approaches:

Guru The QA role requires substantial technical knowledge. To effectively support developers, to create effective standards and to administer any central resource of technical information the environment and tools must be well understood.

Policeman It is a mistake to believe that even the best rules will be followed or the best tools used of their own accord. Time pressures, developers' inertia and their desire for creativity will all at one time or another work against the standard approach. It is necessary to detect such departures, evaluate them and their reasons, and decide whether they can be allowed, whether they can be rectified amicably, or whether an issue needs to be escalated for a management decision.

Priest If the QA group is seen as knowledgeable and fair, it will inevitably become an early port of call when differences arise between or within the project teams. It is often possible for the

QA function to defuse the situation and negotiate a reasonable agreement, independent of the differing objectives.

Smith The QA group may be responsible for some of the development, test, or documentation tools. In this case, the ability to tailor tools to the specific requirements of the developers is a considerable advantage.

Auditor It is not possible to assume that just because a document or a piece of software exists, the target quality has been attained. Since quality is the sum of product and process, the QA role has to be able to investigate both, knowing the right questions to ask and being able to evaluate evidence to verify the answers.

Negotiator Inevitably, with the multiple role of assessor of quality, recommender of improvements, and participant in the procurement process, negotiating skills are most important. Where possible, the QA role must be able to relate to differing viewpoints and to find a course of action which will satisfy the requirements of the organisation, while still allowing the individual participants to attain their reasonable objectives.

There is no obvious single route to achieving these abilities. A background in various aspects of software development is essential, and it is obviously a good idea for the group to include a number of individuals with different backgrounds and talents. The 'poacher turned gamekeeper' is a key member, since only by knowing and understanding the pressures on the developer will the QA role be able to help deflect and handle them.

3.5 THE FIRST STEPS FORWARD

There are two common strategies for developments of any kind. The first is to try to provide the maximum product (or improvement) for a fixed cost. This tends to lead to an overall plan in which a number of higher-cost or higher-risk elements have been included. Frequently, these elements will then get a disproportionate share of the effort.

The alternative strategy is to look at all the possible components, and to try to evaluate their cost, risk, and benefit. Each can then be assigned a notional 'value':

$$\text{value} = (\text{benefit}) / (\text{cost} * \text{risk})$$

it is then straightforward to plan to implement the highest value elements first, and the lower value elements later. This has the clear advantage that the users can see an earlier return on their investment, and that the development can be modified or even stopped at a later date but some clear benefit will have been achieved.

This is therefore a very good strategy for the implementation of a quality system:

- Firstly, recognise that the customers, the end-users of QA are the developers themselves. They will be unwilling or unable to implement any change which does not provide a clear return on their investment (of effort).
- Assess the problems currently faced by the developers. Are there any which admit a simple solution? If so, early provision of such a solution will win friends and encourage the adoption of later ideas.
- Find a framework into which the various initiatives can fit. If one exists, it will be easy to understand how the different elements relate to each other. Without such a framework, management may not understand and support individual changes.
- Evaluate the cost, risk, and benefit of each change. While a new method or expensive tool may sound very good, if it has little direct benefit, if the amount of change required to current practices is significant (which will increase the cost), or if the level of current understanding in the organisation is not high enough (so that the risk is high) then the value of the introduction will be too low. Be cynical, and ask the developers and their managers to add their assessment of benefit, cost, and risk.
- Finally, dare to be different! What works in one organisation won't necessarily work in another. Theoretical approaches to subjects such as testing lag behind developments in the toolset, and the old methods may have to change. The received wisdom is that the QA organisation should sit apart and monitor paperwork – in practice there is much more to be done.

Improving quality is a slow, and sometimes painful process. There is no magic wand, no silver bullet. All parties must be pragmatic, and must not underestimate the time and effort required. Gradual changes carefully designed to bring defined benefits are the best approach, and must match the culture and status of the organisation. The guiding principle must be 'highest benefit, simplest first'.

4 Measurement as a Management Tool

Nicholas Ashley
Brameur Ltd

A science is as mature as its measurement tools.
Louis Pasteur

4.1 INTRODUCTION

How much will it cost to develop? What is the chance of finishing 20% under budget? Will it be ready on time? How effective are our formal reviews and our test strategy at finding defects? How reliable will it be? What are the most time-consuming development activities? Are open plan offices detrimental to staff productivity?

When these questions, and others like them, are asked by software development managers, they all too often fail to get satisfactory answers. In order to help managers manage they need quantifiable answers to these types of questions. In other words they need to set up a measurement programme to provide this information. But what needs to be done? A check list for setting up a measurement programme should include the following questions.

- Are the goals of the measurement programme aligned to the business goals and stated in quantifiable terms?
- Have we put into place all the infrastructure to support the measurement programme?
- Will it identify where improvements are needed?
- Do the staff know why we are running a measurement programme and what is expected of them?
- What type of training should they be given?
- Are we able to measure the success of the measurement programme?

These questions, and others like them, need to be addressed by teams faced with the difficult job of setting up and running a software measurement programme.

Until recently, an organisation wishing to set up a software engineering measurement programme had little guidance on what to do and usually had unrealistic expectations of the benefits. This led to a climate of scepticism by software managers to the relevance and benefits of measurement.
Now consider the following questions:

- Why do misunderstandings so often occur between customers and

contractors?
- What is software quality?
- Are poor cost estimates a fact of life or is there a way to produce accurate estimates?
- How is it possible to improve the productivity of software development teams without reducing the quality of the systems they produce?
- Are the claims made by tool manufacturers based on hard evidence?

How often have you seen requirements where customers fail to specify what they want in measurable terms but instead use vague terms like user-friendly and highly reliable? Is it any wonder that misunderstandings occur between customers and contractors which often result in unpleasant surprises for users.

Software quality is probably the most misunderstood term used by the software industry. Software developers turn to new tools and methods in the hope of improving software quality while users complain bitterly about 'poor quality'. The fact is that software developers and users have little idea of how to define quality, let alone measure it.

If anyone thinks cost estimation is not important, just consider that some software houses are getting into serious financial difficulties and even facing bankruptcy because they have underestimated the price of fixed-price contracts. For example, a British software house share price fell by 73% in 1990 when they announced losses of £15 million on three fixed-price contracts. In contrast, customers have learnt the hard way that the cheapest bid can often turn out to be the most expensive.

Managers often complain about poor productivity, yet are unable to quantify their development team's productivity and do very little to improve the situation. One of the main ways to improve productivity is to improve the development processes.

We have all come across manufacturers making claims about how their tool requires no formal training, will increase productivity by 30% and improve reliability by 25%. Have you ever thought where they got these figures from. We are usually never told how these results were obtained. It is a pretty safe bet to assume you would not be able to achieve these claims in your work environment, assuming you knew how to go about measuring them.

This booklet shows how to overcome these problems and promotes the use of measurement as *a vital tool for management in helping to improve their business.*

4.1.1 What can measurement do for me?

Before managers provide financial support for setting up a measurement programme, they want answers to three questions, namely:

- What are the benefits?

- When will I see the benefits?
- How much is it going to cost?

Essentially measurement can be used to help produce software systems which meet the customers expectations to time and budget. In other words measurement can be used to generate quantifiable information to help enable managers to manage, in particular to help answer the following questions:

- Where are we?
- Where do we want to go?
- How do we get there?
- Are we getting there?
- Have we got there?
- How do we compare?
- How well do we use our resources?

4.1.2 Main goal

The main goal of this booklet is to motivate managers to use measurement to*understand, control and then improve software development.*

But before introducing changes it is necessary to identify where changes are needed and understand why changes are needed. However, there is little point in introducing changes if you do not have a means of assessing their impact.

This booklet does not extol the virtues of software measurement in isolation but advocates that it should be viewed as part of the whole development process. It advocates using measurement to help software managers and software engineers do their job better. In particular, measurement should be used to:

- enable managers to state their strategic goals in quantitative terms
- improve communications between a customer and contractor
- provide quantifiable information to aid in decision-making and risk analysis
- provide visibility of the development process
- enable managers to operate in a problem prevention mode
- support project planning and monitoring activities.

Essentially this booklet provides answers to the following questions:

- What are the problems faced by software developers?
- Can measurement help to prevent software development problems?
- Is it possible to specify software quality in testable terms?
- How can measurement be used as a management tool?
- What are companies doing with regard to using measurement?
- What is needed to be done to enable a company to use measurement as a

management tool and how much will it cost?

At this point it is worth emphasising that *measurement is basically about applying common sense.*

4.2 PROBLEMS WITH SOFTWARE DEVELOPMENT

This section describes the problems faced by software developers and discusses the main causes of these problems.

The main problems associated with software development are:

- cost overruns
- late delivery
- non conformance to the functional requirements
- 'poor' quality of the delivered product
- 'low' productivity of the development process
- 'high' corrective maintenance costs.

If all these problems sound depressingly familiar we should bear in mind that these are no different to the problems faced by other industries. For example, the Channel Tunnel is a project which has gone over budget.

4.2.1 Main cause of problems

Recent studies of software organisations have shown that the key problems they face are not technical but managerial. *The critical needs of software organisations concern improving management methods.*

A survey carried out in 1989 by Watts S. Humphrey [1] in the USA on 200 software organisations showed that 80% of the organisations adopt an ad hoc approach to software development. The majority of the other 20% of the organisations have established only the basics of project controls, project management and quality assurance.

When asked to name their key problems, few software professionals even mention technology. Their major concerns are:

- open ended requirements
- uncontrolled change
- arbitrary schedules
- insufficient time allowed for testing
- the quality of their products
- inadequate training
- low productivity
- unmanaged system standards.

Watts Humphrey [1] has devised a framework to describe the maturity of an organisation's software development process, known as the SEI Capability Maturity Model. The bottom of the scale represents organisations using an *ad hoc* approach to software development. The top of the scale represents organisations who have a stable development process which is monitored and is continuously being optimised using a measurement infrastructure.

> *Understanding that there are different stages of maturity and knowing where your organisation is and where it can aim to be is the first step to establishing a controllable software process that can continuously be improved.*

The main causes of software development problems are:

- Paying insufficient attention to user needs.
- Not stating the requirements in testable terms, especially the quality attributes, can lead to:
  - lack of clear objectives for the project
  - misunderstanding between customer and contractor
  - difficulty in performing acceptance testing.
- Unrealistic estimates of costs and schedules may result in a project manager having to cut corners, for example, by reducing the amount of planned effort for testing.
- Lack of management control due to poor visibility of potential problems and non adherence to procedures. In general, this will result in management acting in a problem recovery mode rather than a problem prevention mode. Invariably, misdirected management effort results in low productivity.
- Making critical decisions that are not based on quantifiable information, such as when to stop testing and declare the system dependable, is a recipe for disaster. For example, as a minimum, every path in the code should have been tested at least once.
- Not assessing the risks, such as the impact of the constraints and the likelihood of losing key personnel.
- Allowing the requirements to change during development without analysing fully the impact of the changes on the costs and schedules
- Not giving the customer visibility of the proposed technical design solution.
- Paying insufficient attention to the impact of the system on its environment.

4.3 HOW MEASUREMENT CAN HELP PREVENT PROBLEMS

This section describes how measurement can help to solve and, more importantly, **prevent** the problems faced by software developers. It also briefly describes how software measurements can be classified into resource measures, process measures, and product measures.

The first step to understanding and improving software development is to *treat software development as a process that can be controlled, measured and improved.*

The main ways measurement can help to prevent problems in software development are by:

- Providing a key to understanding software development by making it more visible and minimising surprises by identifying problems early on.
- Improving communications by helping to reduce misunderstandings. For example, by replacing vague statements such as user friendly or highly reliable with quantifiable statements that are testable such as,

'a user familiar with the manual system will require
two days training to be able to operate the system
at the rate of processing 10 transactions per hour'.

- Identifying where improvements need to be made in the development process.
- Assessing the impact of changes. It is no good introducing changes if you do not have a means of assessing whether they are improving the situation or making it worse.
- Enabling the efficient introduction of new technology by understanding the development environment.
- Enabling planning of projects in advance by providing justifiable estimates of cost and schedules based on validated historical data.
- Providing quantifiable evidence to support decisions such as when to stop testing and declare the software dependable.
- Enabling managers to monitor and control software development by providing quantifiable information such as spend to date, and effort to complete.
- Assessing the reliability of a software system in order to certify it. It should be noted that the number of defects found during development does not give an indication of how many remain. Users are interested in how long a system will operate before it fails and the impact of the failures. To quote Harlan Mills [3]:
  'Increasing inter-fail times represents progress towards a reliable
  product, whereas increasing defect discovery may be a symptom of
  an unreliable product'.

4.3.1 Questions that measurement can help answer

Questions that measurement can help to answer include:

- Which companies should be invited to tender? Procurers of software systems are starting to introduce the use of measurement to determine which vendors to invite to tender and in tender evaluation. Vendors that cannot justify their costs and schedules in quantifiable terms may not be considered as suitable to enter contract negotiations with. This is apart from whether they are technically competent or not. Procurers have learnt the hard way that the cheapest bid can often turn out to be the most expensive.
  Perhaps it is best summed up by the US astronaut waiting to be blasted off to the moon who remarked to the control tower, 'I can't help feeling I am sitting on top of the cheapest tender'.
- How much will it cost to complete?
- When will it be ready?
- Is the system maintainable? The most successful commercial telecommunications circuit switch in the world during the 1970s and early 1980s (in terms of operational reliability and world wide sales) was unable to be adapted for military use because the software was badly structured. It took two years and £3 million pounds to come to this conclusion. This cost could have been avoided if the complexity of the source code had been measured.
- What is the probability of finishing 20% over budget? A cost estimate should have the property that there is an equal chance of the actual cost being above or below the estimated cost. Unfortunately all too often the estimate is based on the unrealistic assumption that nothing will go wrong.
- What development activities are most time consuming? A company was concerned about productivity and wanted to know what development activities were most time-consuming. The company initiated a measurement programme which revealed that the three most time-consuming activities were defect removal, meetings and travelling to meetings.
- How effective are formal reviews at finding defects? It is always possible to do more inspections, reviews and conduct more dynamic testing. Measurement provides the data that is necessary to understand the costs and benefits of performing inspections, reviews and tests.
- How well did the test routines exercise the code?
- Are high corrective-maintenance costs due to the test strategy? Measurement can help to determine if there is a correlation between the number of failures during operational use and the number of defects found by testing during development. It may be the case that more defects are being found during testing because the test strategy has been improved.
- Are independent test teams more effective at finding defects than the designers and coders of a system?
- Are open plan offices detrimental to staff productivity compared to providing staff with individual offices? IBM conducted a study on how the

work environment affects the performance of an individual. They compared the productivity of project teams working in open plan offices and project teams having individual offices with separate meeting rooms. The findings of the experiment convinced them of the need to provide project staff with individual offices.

4.3.2 Objective measurement and standards

It is not possible to measure anything objectively until it has been defined in quantifiable terms. By objectively is meant that the result of the measurement process must be independent of the person carrying it out.

Measurement standards are essential to enable objective assessments of the size of a software system, the productivity of a development team, the reliability of a software product, etc. At present, there are only a few international software engineering measurement standards such as the IEEE Standard Dictionary Of Measures to Produce Reliable Software. However, various government bodies in Europe, USA and Japan are actively involved in defining measurement standards, especially in the area of software quality attributes. These standards are seen as an essential aid in the process of certifying software products.

4.3.3 Classification of measures

Having briefly described how measurement can prevent problems, we now briefly discuss how measurements can be classified into resource measures, process measures and product measures and to give examples of what can be measured.

Software measurement can be applied to all aspects of software development and software products. For most software projects, the main attributes that require measuring are:

- the size of the system
- cost in terms of effort
- schedules
- risks
- reliability of the product.

Every task can be modelled as the resources needed to perform the task, the process used to carry out the task and the products produced by the task. This applies to any task such as writing a report, conducting a review or transforming a software design into a software system. Using this model it is possible to categorise measurements as either a resource measurement, process measurement or a product measurement, see figure 1.

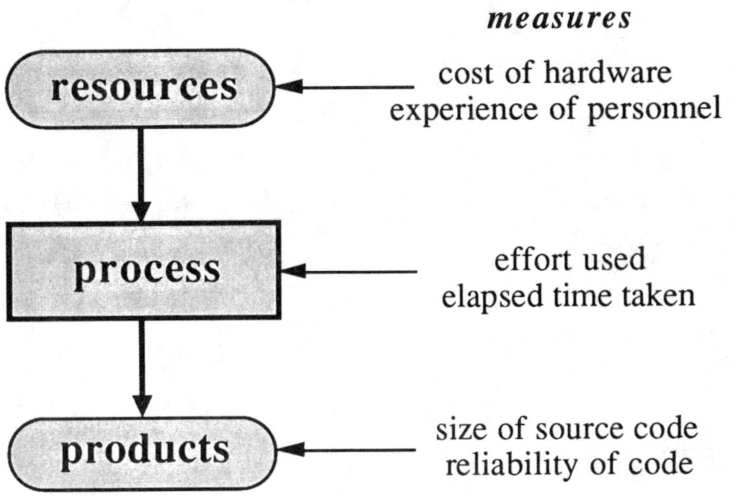

Figure 4.1 Classification of measures

These three categories are now briefly described.

Resource Measures refer to the resources needed to perform the development (hardware, software tools, office space, staff). Resource attributes that can be measured include:

- cost of hardware
- experience of personnel.

Process Measures refer to the **processes** used to develop the system (designing, coding, testing, etc.). Process attributes that can be measured include:

- elapsed time taken to complete a task
- effort used in performing a task
- defect removal efficiency.

Product Measures refer to the **products** that are produced from the software process (such as source code, user manual, test reports etc). Product attributes that can be measured include:

- size of the source code
- reliability of the system
- usability of the system.

The main quantitative indicators of a software project are:

- cost
- effort
- time
- stability
- risk.

The main quantitative indicators of a software product are:

- cost of ownership
- reliability
- usability
- maintainability
- etc.

4.4 SPECIFYING AND MEASURING SOFTWARE QUALITY

This section discusses how to specify and measure software quality.

Software quality means different things to different people. If you asked ten users and software developers what software quality means you would probably get back ten different answers. Typical high-level notions of quality are:

- conformance to requirements
- degree of user satisfaction
- degree of excellence
- reliability
- exceeding the customer's expectations
- fitness for purpose
- cost of rework
- value for money.

Katsuyuki Yasuda of Hitachi Information Systems sums up the main principle behind software quality: Meeting the needs of the user is the ultimate determinant of quality.

4.4.1 Quality from the user viewpoint

At system handover, the customer wants answers to two key questions, namely:

- Does it do what I want?
- How well does it do what I want?

If these questions were not considered in detail when the requirements were produced, then it is unlikely that the system will satisfy customer needs. To help avoid this situation, these two key questions need to be refined into a set of quantifiable statements. Before we go any further we should make it clear that there does not exist a quality benchmark against which a software system can be compared to determine its quality.

When users are asked what is wrong with their software systems their main complaints are that:

- it doesn't do what was wanted
- it breaks down too many times
- it takes too long to recover from breakdowns
- it's slow to respond to users commands
- the interface is not intuitive
- the error messages are uninformative
- the training facilities are inadequate
- the user manuals are difficult to read
- it is difficult to make changes.

4.4.2 What is software quality?

Unfortunately, there is no simple answer, even though the word quality has become common place, and some would say devalued, through advertising hype and slogans expounded by quality gurus, such as: *quality is free*; *zero defects*; *right first time*; *fitness for purpose.*

4.4.3 Does quality = absence of errors?

The answer is no. A necessary condition for a software system to be regarded as a quality product by the user is that it is available to be used when it is needed. However, absence of errors is not a sufficient condition for guaranteeing quality (whatever that may be). To quote Gerald Weinberg [2]: 'Though copious errors guarantees worthlessness, having zero errors guarantees nothing at all about the value of software.'

4.4.4 Does software quality = conformance to requirements?

The answer is no. A common definition of quality is conformance to requirements. According to this definition, if a system conforms to its requirements then it is regarded as a quality system. This is not a definition of quality since, amongst other things, it takes no account of the quality of the requirements. Conformance to requirements means precisely what it says. So why use another word. There is more to quality than conformance to requirements. We illustrate this point with an example:

Consider a software system that conforms to the following requirement: *The system shall have no more than 10 breakdowns per day and it shall take no more than two hours to repair each one*. By most people's standards a system that had up to 10 breakdowns per day and where each breakdown took up to two hours to repair would be practically unusable and hence of extremely poor quality, where quality here is defined as reliability.

If you consider the various notions of what developers and users mean by quality it becomes apparent that software quality is specific to an application or operational environment.

What therefore is this elusive concept called software quality? When defining the requirements for a software system it is necessary to specify what it is meant to do (usually referred to as the functional requirements) and how well it does it (usually referred to as the quality requirements).

In order to talk about software quality and to be able to measure software quality, it first needs to be defined in an objective way. However, in general, it is inappropriate to provide a generic definition because the quality aspects of one system may be different to the quality aspects of another system. For example, in choosing a car there is not one particular thing called quality, although for most people a Rolls Royce would be an example of a quality car. For one driver quality means only having to service the car every 10,000 miles while for another driver quality may be a car that has a leather interior, a wooden dash board and be capable of going from 0 to 60mph in 7 seconds.

The quality of a software system should be expressed as a subset of attributes, which are appropriate to a particular application and its environment. For example:

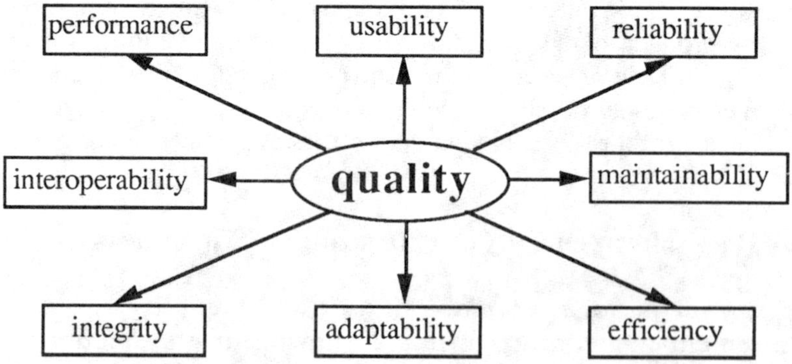

It should be noted that these attributes will need to go through various refinements to form a set of sub-attributes which can be expressed in a quantifiable form. These attributes should then be weighted to reflect their importance. Only then will the customer and the contractor be in a position to be in full agreement about what is required and the quality of the software system can be assessed during acceptance testing.

Having decided which quality attributes are appropriate, it is necessary to refine each attribute into a set of measurable sub-attributes. For example, some of the measurable sub-attributes of usability are:

- effort to learn to use the system
- effort to install the system
- effort to prepare inputs
- effort to learn to maintain the system
- response time to user commands
- skill level required to use the system.

Again not all these measurable sub-attributes may be applicable to a particular application.

The main point about software quality is that it is not absolute, it means different things to different people.

4.5 HOW TO USE MEASUREMENT AS A MANAGEMENT TOOL

This section describes how measurement should be used as a management tool to:

- improve the software development process
- specify the quality attributes of a software system by providing an example for specifying reliability
- determine what information managers and software engineers need in order to help them do their job better and how to get that information.

It should be emphasised that there is no universal set of measures that are applicable to all projects and all project environments. Organisations need to experiment to see what works for their projects and their environment.

The philosophy underlying the use of measurement as a management tool to improve the software development process is to:

- measure what you are doing
- introduce changes
- measure again to determine whether the changes are having the desired effect.

This approach can be formalised into the following steps. First, use measurement to identify where things have gone wrong or need improving. Then understand why things have gone wrong or need improving. For example, it may be thought that the cause of low productivity is a lack of appropriate software tool support. Next, determine the priorities for implementing changes and improvements and produce a plan to accomplish these priorities. Then implement an evolutionary improvement and enhancement programme. Note that it is important to introduce changes gradually and not to try and do everything at once, because if there are too many changes it is very difficult to know which changes are improving the situation. Next, use measurement to determine how well improvements and enhancements are working. Now start all over again because process improvement is a continuous activity.

Figure 4.2 depicts an improvement cycle which can be used during all stages of development and operational use.

The overriding messages are:

- you cannot expect to improve something unless you know what it is you are trying to improve
- understand and control before trying to make improvements
- process improvement is a continuous activity

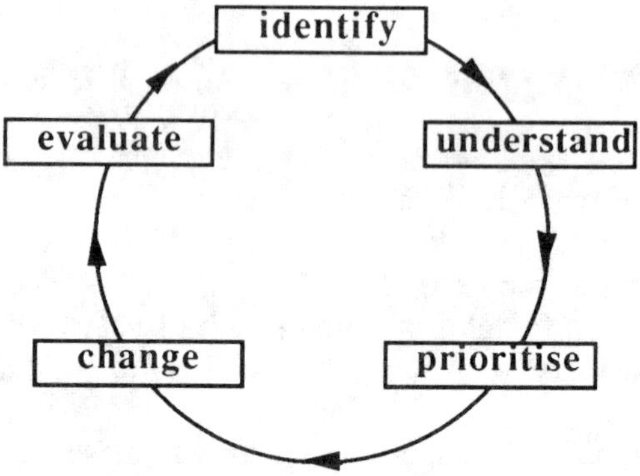

Figure 4.2 Improvement cycle

It should be noted that, in general, it is not much good performing measurements after a problem has occurred. It would be like taking the pulse rate and blood pressure of a dead person. These two measurements may indicate that a person was dead but they would not tell you the cause of death.

4.5.1 GQM approach

We now describe how to determine what information managers and software engineers want in order to help them do their job better and how to get that information. The method described is the GQM (Goal, Question, Measure) top-down approach to software measurement. This approach was developed by

Victor Basili (University of Maryland), originally for analysing defects for a set of NASA projects. The GQM philosophy of software measurement uses a top down approach and consists of:

- determining qualitative goals in terms of:
  - what is wanted
  - who wants it
  - why it is wanted
  - when it is wanted
- refining the goals into a set of questions that require quantifiable answers
- refining the questions into a set of measurable attributes (measures for data collection) which attempt to answer the questions
- using the measures to:
  - quantify your goals
  - determine where changes are needed to meet your goals
  - determine the impact of the changes (is the goal being met?).

Some attributes of software development, such as productivity, are dependent on many factors which are specific to a particular development environment. Two of the main strengths of the GQM approach are that it does not rely on any standard measures and that it can cope with any environment.

4.5.2 Example of applying the GQM technique

Consider the qualitative goal: to improve the accuracy of our cost estimates.

The GQM approach can be used to transform this qualitative goal into a quantitative goal. The first step is to refine this high-level goal into a set of questions that require quantifiable answers:

- Is a documented cost estimation process used?
- Is a cost estimation tool used and if so has it been calibrated to a particular development environment?
- What is the present accuracy?
- Is the accuracy of the estimates improving over time?
- What data is collected?
- Does validated historical data exist relating to previous estimates and actuals of completed projects?
- Over what period of time is the accuracy of the estimates to be improved?
- What is the experience of the estimators?

Using the answers to these and similar questions, it should be possible to produce a quantifiable goal, such as: Within nine months of implementing a formal cost estimation process, produce estimates of effort from a requirement that are within 30% of the actual effort, in 90% of the cases.

Having transformed the qualitative goal into a quantitative goal, the next step is to use the GQM approach to devise a set of measures to determine if the goal has been met.

4.5.3 Characteristics of goals

The main characteristics of an organisation's goals should be that they are

- unambiguous and stated in testable terms, so that people responsible for implementing changes to meet the goals and assessing whether the goals have been met know what is expected of them
- tailored to the specific needs of the customer, company, project manager, etc.
- related to the business objectives of the company.

Furthermore, goals should be regularly reassessed to take account of improvements in the efficiency of a process, increased experience of development teams, new tools, etc.

4.5.4 Typical Goals

Examples of qualitative and quantitative goals are:

- *goals of a company*
  - develop an orderly process that enables staff to operate efficiently
  - improve the development process in order to increase productivity by 10% per year
  - improve its ability to produce quantifiably reliable products more quickly and cheaper
  - halve the cost of operational corrective maintenance in two years
  - achieve a tenfold improvement in post-release defect density in the next five years
  - generate cost estimates that are correct to within 15% of the actual costs before development commences
- *goal of a quality manager*
  - determine the effectiveness of the quality management system
  - determine the cost of defect removal by the various tests, reviews and inspections for each category of defect.

4.6 SOFTWARE MEASUREMENT IN PRACTICE

This section discusses the pioneers who are well on the way to establishing a measurement infrastructure to control and optimise software development. The message here is: Where the leaders go the rest need to follow if they want to stay in business.

The US aerospace industry and military community initiated work in the field of quality measurement in 1971. The Japanese computer manufacturers and IBM were the first companies to measure quality attributes of a software system. Hitachi started their first software factory in 1969. The leading measurement practitioners are:

- Europe – Siemens, BT, ICL, Inland Revenue, TUV Essen
- USA – Hewlett Packard, IBM, US Air Force, NASA, AT&T
- Japan – Fujitsu, Hitachi, Mitsubishi, NEC, Toshiba.

Europe is ahead of the USA and Japan in conducting research in software engineering measurement. The largest European companies are slightly behind the largest US and Japanese companies in applying measurement to understand, control and improve software development. However, Europe is in the process of catching up. This view is supported by the number and popularity of commercially run measurement workshops and seminars that are being organised in the UK, France and Germany.

In Europe measurement tends to be project based rather than company-wide based whereas in Japan the leading edge companies use measurement on a company-wide basis. Leading Japanese companies such as Hitachi and NEC concentrate on improving reliability before productivity as their philosophy is best summed up by the IT manager of Hitachi who stated: *There is no point in producing unreliable software more quickly.*

Those companies who use measurement as a management tool tailor measures to suit their particular development processes and development environments.

The main areas where measurement is used are in estimating costs and schedules, measuring staff productivity and predicting the reliability of a product by collecting data on defects and their causes.

The main goals of those companies that are thinking about setting up a measurement programme are improving cost estimates and reliability.

Companies who have encountered problems in setting up and running measurement programmes cited the following reasons for their problems:

- lack of management commitment
- insufficient resources were available
- management had unrealistic expectations of the benefits
- not providing feedback to staff
- trying to do too much too soon.

In the past little use of measurement was made by software purchasers. For example, most software vendors who submitted proposals were not obliged to provide quantifiable evidence to support their costs, schedules and quality requirements. However, this situation is changing rapidly.

4.6.1 Hewlett Packard

The Hewlett Packard experience of setting up a software measurement programme revealed that:

- establishing a company-wide software measurement programme takes a great deal of hard work
- you must wait at least three years before broad organisaational trends are available
- standards are essential to establish a common vehicle for communication throughout a company.

Hewlett Packard collects data for a variety of purposes, such as determining the:

- efficiency of the development process
- cost to fix post-release defects
- size of systems in terms of non-comment source statements
- effort spent during each phase of development
- productivity of development teams.

The main benefits to Hewlett Packard are:

- a better understanding of the software development process
- a way to measure progress
- making software management more objective and less subjective
- producing better estimates of costs and schedules
- eliminating fundamental causes of defects
- encouraging the definition of a long-term software development strategy based upon a measured understanding of current practices and needs.

4.7 HOW TO SET UP A MEASUREMENT PROGRAMME

This section provides an overview of what an organisation needs to do to set up and run a measurement programme together with an indication of how much it will cost.

Howard Rubens an influential software consultant, reports of evidence that 300 major US IT companies (meaning that they have at least 100 IT staff) have implemented measurement programmes, up to 1990. Of these there have been 60 documented successes, where Rubens defines success as:

- measurement programme results are used in decision making
- they are communicated and accepted outside IT department
- the programme lasts longer than two years.

The main reasons for the failures were:

- Too often management were not committed to the programme.
- Not having clearly defined quantifiable goals for the programme.
- The programmes were not treated as a project. The approach was *ad hoc* with insufficient resources, no clear direction or time-scales.
- Reports generated by the measurement programme failed to generate management action.
- No criteria were defined to assess the success of the measurement programme. Consequently management were unclear of whether the measurement programme was providing tangible benefits.
- Management had unrealistic expectations of the benefits.
- Too often the measurement programme failed to implement a mechanism to provide feedback to the staff/project teams being measured and staff involved with measuring.

The most important aspects of setting up and running a measurement programme are to:

- define quantifiable goals for the measurement programme
- obtain the commitment and funding from senior management
- treat the implementation like a project
- develop an infrastructure to support the programme
- explain to staff what is going on and get their cooperation
- use an evolutionary approach
- provide feedback to development staff.

Figure 4.3 depicts the main tasks that need to be carried out in order to set up a measurement programme.

To obtain long term commitment and funding from senior management it is necessary to demonstrate the benefits of using measurement. Management needs to be convinced that measurement will improve their business, in other words improve the 'bottom line'. This can be achieved by using measurement to demonstrate the validity of what they intuitively believe.

5 Optimising the Development and Test Process

Mike Berwick
Brameur Ltd

5.1 INTRODUCTION

Phrases like 'To stand still is to die', and 'No Company Is Safe' (Tom Peters, *Thriving on Chaos*, Pan, 1987), reflect the realisation that organisations must change to survive, and change almost constantly. The IT industry is more aware of this than perhaps others due to the rapid advances on the technology front and ever increasing customer expectations. Adapting to new practices may well be vital, but where do we start?

The maxim 'the quality of software products depends upon the quality of the process that produces them' guides us a little, but what process is required and what activities does this process need to contain to meet our needs? (We will accept for brevity the premise that a process will include a number of related tasks or activities, such as a particular development and test method.) To summarise:

- What are the appropriate processes (and activities) for a particular project or business?
- Are these activities operating at peak performance?

The key words here are *appropriate* and*performance.*

The consultant, Dr Robb Wilmot, at a recent Prime Computer seminar, reminded his audience that all the technology we require to make major changes to the way we work is here now: networking; CASE; test coverage and analysis tools It is all available in abundance. The onus on improvement is squarely upon all staff, from the project staff to the senior management of the company. However, it is clear that what may be *appropriate* for one particular company or project will likely not be so for another.

Many organisations accept they require the support of measurement to judge process *performance* to manage the business properly. This subject is widely studied, particularly how to measure current products and processes [1]. With such measurements we can trap poor quality, also monitor, adjust and tune the current process. What is not visible from many measurement programmes in current use is:

- How capable are our own ways of working compared to others (e.g. Are we testing effectively?)?
- What investment and changes are needed for future projects?
- Where are the risks in introducing change to our current practices?
- Are subcontractors able to adapt along with us?

Leading software development organisations undertake continual internal process capability assessments, driven by business needs, customer expectations and technology change. Successful optimisation occurs through selective, incremental process improvements to achieve gains in product quality and productivity.

5.1.1 Process capability assessments

Assessments are based upon selected studies of industrial best practices supplemented by studies of any suitable work within the organisation (e.g. recently completed and selected current projects), while considering any changes anticipated for future work. There will also be concerns about the confidentiality of assessment results and the validity of the measurements used when comparing organisations and projects.

5.1.2 Investment decisions

A development organisation may also wish to internally evaluate processes to determine, for example, the risks in undertaking a new test strategy. Other risk reduction activities, such as those in support of significant IT investments such as CASE (Computer Assisted Software Engineering) and CAST (Computer Assisted Software Testing), can benefit from this assessment approach. In these instances studies of the software engineering process are intended to identify weaknesses, particularly in process stability across projects, and to see that there is a clear understanding of the process prior to any investment being made.

5.2 PROCESS BENCHMARKING

The need for process assessment can therefore be considered to be for one of two reasons. Either the prime interest is for internal improvement , or it is for the risk evaluation of an organisation or project (which may be a subcontractor activity) in support of current or future work. Both are to achieve process optimal performance that continues to satisfy the business objectives. Process benchmarking is directed at the project level. Selective studies of activities across projects provide for the evaluation of an organisation. Project evaluation roll-up to organisation level needs very careful analysis, as projects are rarely at the same point in the life cycle and are often producing dissimilar products using varied skills and methods.

Process assessment for the purpose of process capability improvement or capability evaluation have different objectives. The assessment methodology, described here as 'process benchmarking', is the same for both; the results are applied to satisfy the different needs.

Process bBenchmarking looks at both the *completeness* and *effectiveness* of the process in comparison with selected best practices. By this means the *optimisation* of a process's activities or tasks can be obtained with regard to the specific needs of the business.

The name 'process benchmarking' emphasises the fundamental assessment activity, that of undertaking comparisons external to the company (and maybe the IT industry). Another necessity for continual success is generating the co-operation of all in the organisation; of particular need is managing the impact of change, vital for maintaining optimal process performance in the future.

The definition of 'benchmarking' needs to be clearly understood throughout the organisation since it is easy to dismiss the activity as not much more than the collation of some market research data with what can be gleaned from trade journals.

5.2.1 Method overview

We can usefully consider the assessment method as four linked steps that, cycled together, provide the structure for continual improvements to maintain an optimal process for the business. We will then discuss the method in more detail.

5.2.1.1 Step 1

The significant steps commence with the provision of a clear view of business commitment to continuous improvement: IT business in particular needs definition and target setting. This directs the assessment and supports improvement introduction, as there will inevitably be changes to current working practices that may impact on a project's perceived performance in the short term. Increased training and other overhead costs would be likely with any significant change. For example, an increased use of test stages would require more testing and analysis effor; also increases in defect detection rate may distort the quality statistics.

5.2.1.2 Step 2

The next step is Key Issue selection by senior management, often using Meta Planning or other group activities, to generate the initial commitment by all groups likely to be affected. The key issue(s) are to provide clear linkages to the business needs of the IT function.

5.2.1.3 Step 3

The guidance is now available for targeted studies ('benchmarking') of organisations and projects, culminating in a best practice profile specific for the business. This may be as selective as required, to target, for example, test process activities or assess the whole software engineering life cycle process.

5.2.1.4 Step 4

From this profile, an assessment of actual process capability is made. Comparisons between the target and actual profiles show the most significant gap(s) to be targeted for improvement on this occasion.

5.2.1.5 Verification and validation

Verification tracking of each assessment activity provides stimulus to the acceptance of changing work practices, while validation gives traceability to the business needs and enables the support that is vital for continual process optimisation.

5.2.2 Business needs

Considering the method in more detail, selecting the IT related objectives from well-defined business objectives is central to the method's success. The issues to be addressed are best obtained by group discussions at board and senior management levels. The ability to trace improvement initiatives and process improvement measurements back to specific business goals is vital support to continuing commitment, while visible and early results emanating from the changes provide further support.

The benefits of shared commitment have already been seen by some companies in substantial productivity and profit improvements [2]. Rank Xerox, Motorola and IBM are among those who undertake regular process assessment and capability evaluations [3].

By including the process assessment method in well-thought-out company codes of practice, managers and staff can commit to a future of combining process change while retaining the necessary stability to meet the short-term targets.

5.2.3 Key issue selection

Key areas of interest are selected from the business needs using tangible criteria.

Those well understood as measurable entities include:

- Quality costs: 'reduce by 80% in 9 months'
- Time to market: '18 months maximum within 6 months'.

There are other issues that may be considered to be more relevant for comparison such as:

- Staff utilisation: 'staff training increase by 60% in 6 months'
- New technology introduction: '50% projects using CAST in 12 months'.

The selection depends upon the organisation and the purpose of the assessment. All key issues require measurable criteria to be established. While four key iIssues are the maximum experienced by the author, often one, at least initially, is more practical.

5.2.4 Completeness

Beyond quality audits, the need to assess process capability by measuring the attainment of project and organisational goals as a process can be 'complete but costly'.

These activities are complementary:f assuring the continuation of a QMS through adherence to quality standards, although a stabilising influence, not identify whether an activity is appropriate for the business. For example, a paper-based test generating activity and a CAST activity can both withstand a quality audit, but enquires of 'process completeness' would probe suitability for the project, including the stage in its life cycle (paper-based at prototype stage may be acceptable best practice but not later), business need and so forth.

The measure of completeness is whether the defined tasks for the process are performed as required for that project. Dr Wilmot's realism summarises what we all feel, that adopting new technology, or at least new technology that will yield *major* benefits, will inevitably impact short-term budgets and deadlines. The short-term cost is almost always significant and always a hurdle to improvement introduction.

5.2.5 Effectiveness

Increasingly, it appears that too many quality improvement programmes (QIP) are ineffective, meaning the processes and activities introduced or altered by the QIP are not performing as expected. In a recent report from McKinsley & Company (Harvard Business Review, February 1992), a disturbingly large number of companies have quality management programmes that are failing to show signs of meaningful business impact. Senior Managers are expressing reservations about the eventual impact of their quality activities while maintaining their public commitment to see them through. More than half of the companies interviewed stated that their quality programmes have stalled or even failed.

What is the reason for this state of affairs? While there are many factors, there are perceived to be two causes that are frequently present. First is the 'blind pursuit' of QIP or total quality (TQM) programmes: 'what is working for others must work as well for us'.

What is wanted is a clear direction that does not use a lack of adequate progress as a reason or excuse to abandon the TQM initiative. Dr D Youll, Quality Director, Unisys Europe and Africa, summed up the approach when discussing a global view of process assessment at a recent IEE colloquium. He described TQM as 'a journey not a stopping-off point', requiring the selection of good processes and tasks with step-wise change that moves incrementally towards the 'institutionalisation' of standards within the organisation.

For effective TQM, the pursuit of a wide-ranging quality improvement programme can be a false goal, and its ill-planned pursuit distracting and even dangerous to the business need. The value from embarking on a particular improvement programme should be carefully considered by management in the light of a company's competitive situation, strategy and overall needs.

Solution – *a Business Need focus is central to any improvement strategy.*

The second contributor to ineffectiveness is that many stalled TQM programmes lack a results orientation. It is seen that many quality programmes are centred on a 'just do it' approach, in the blind hope that results will follow, rather than as a path to supportable results. All too often correlation with results is not important, and not looked for.

Solution – *Selected measurement methods are necessary for process assessment.*

Effectiveness is established through measuring quantifiable attributes. These are linked to success factors using the Goal Question Metric method. Comparisons with other organisations are used to assist target settings. Where a Metrics programme is operating there may be some useful data available already. The specific needs for process optimising are to monitor the altered processes for predicted performance improvements, and the remaining activities for adverse effects to the way of working due to the disturbances following the changes.

5.2.6 Optimisation

Completeness and effectiveness measures are orthogonal (Figure 5.1). Combined, they provide a good guide to optimal process performance. The introduction of Fagan Inspections in all projects ('our competitors do it') may well reduce effectiveness where stable processes are not used across projects, severely limiting the value of the analysis of results.

Removal of some inspection stages, say at code level, will reduce the 'richness' of the inspection activity while maintaining its overall completeness where error detection is not adversely affected (e.g. design phase detection rate very high). Effectiveness and overall optimisation may well increase due to the reduced process effort.

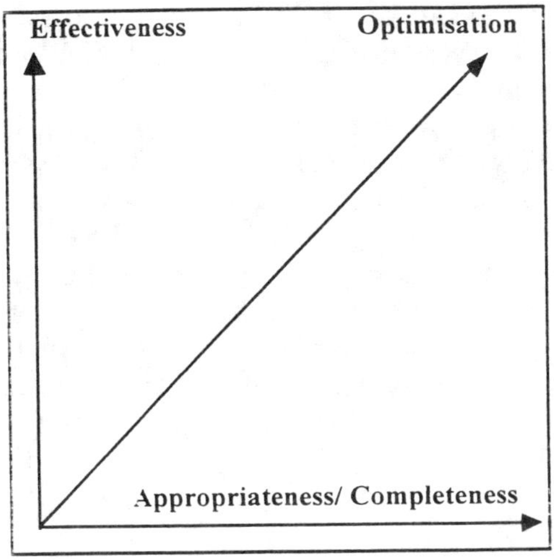

Figure 5.1 Completeness/effectiveness ratio

5.2.7 Assessor selection

Consistent and optimal project performance requires the enthusiastic involvement of all staff. This is best achieved with the participation of small groups undertaking well-defined, short-duration tasks. There is considerable benefit from using those staff to carry out the assessments and evaluations who will be involved in implementing changes to the processes. This will allow 'problem ownership' to be more easily accepted within the organisation. This often leads to early improvement initiatives that result from their direct participation in comparing peer groups. The use of existing team-building structures, such as skill centres and process improvement teams, have also been most effective.

The need for continual re-evaluation further emphasises the advantages of using predominantly project- and business-centred staff. They can readily develop synergy through their day-to-day working and are likely to be available to advise and train further assessors and instigate further detailed studies as required..

5.2.8 Best practice profile

With the purpose of process assessment being a guide and support to process improvements, the best possible practices need to be studied and their relevance to the organisation assessed. There are currently many schemes, operated by companies and procurement agencies in the USA and Britain, that undertake process assessments using models that describe 'best practices' evolved for their particular purpose of assessing organisations [4] [5]. The studies by the assessor groups are mainly combinations of documentary studies, seminar attendances and discussions with customers and internal staff with experience of other companies' work methods.

Following these studies of the selected best practices, success factors related to the key issues are defined as benchmarks. This provides a profile, from which can be selected the processes and the activities contained within them, that are important for the particular study. Success factors per key issue is often a many-to-many relationship, the number (maybe four per activity) is dependant more upon the extent of the life cycle under study.

From assessing the processes, improvements can be planned or, for evaluations of organisational capability, risks assessed and inputs to implementation plans enhanced. Measurements to monitor the processes to be changing or affected by change would then be selected and resources committed.

5.2.9 Gap analysis

The most popular method of assessing completeness is with the guidance of questionnaires that are focused on establishing the presence and breadth of the application of a desired capability. For example, test-plan-related questions may probe the presence of test plans at appropriate stages of the life cycle, as shown to be needed from earlier studies of best practices, and also the planning for training or assurance of skill levels to carry out the tests. Further questions will prompt the assessor to establish whether test planning effectiveness is monitored during the project and improvement feedback also occurs.

An example of an effectiveness-based improvement has been the introduction of 'Software Reuse' in an international telecommunications company. Quality and performance level improvements of over 40%, similar to Japanese and USA leading edge IT companies, have been obtained. Studies established that while the quality of new software products was not significantly better than that obtained from their own comparable projects, the regular inclusion of 80% of reuse code from dedicated 'project groups' into every delivered product provided the further testing of reuse programmes yielded significant results. Supported by the results from a pilot implementation, the setting up of a dedicated reuse production team was justified.

5.2.10 Comparing Across Cultures

The method accommodates the different needs and practices of various IT sectors of the industry and the cultural differences when comparing, for example, businesses in Europe and the USA, and particularly Japan and Europe, with their different work ethics. There should not be the expectation that the results of one area of study will be directly comparable with those of another.

This is a recognised problem when studying 'soft systems' [6]. This is not to say that there are no sensible levels for comparison. The customer is interested in time to market and quality irrespective of the cultural influences upon the process or the product or service supplied. Similar areas can often be found that can be compared, using adjustments to the profiles where appropriate.

5.2.11 Results as profiles

The results of best practice (target) and actual profiles are best shown graphically and should be clearly supported with evidence on how the target profile was obtained. A valid profile can be achieved by applying the same measurement criteria to a model of selected best practices collated by the process benchmarking teams. The significant gaps then show the major strengths, weaknesses and risks.

Recommendations for change can be usefully described by identifying incremental improvement for every selected process as milestone events within an Improvement Plan, written in conjunction with the groups that will be impacted by the proposed change. It takes many months, even years, to make many process improvements effective; early visibility of progress is therefore needed to underpin the acceptance of a continual assessment.

Some profiles can be best presentated with the use of a Kiviat diagram with each axis assigned to a key issue. Figure 5.2 shows an example of such a presentation that is very popular as it clearly shows eight 'Vital Few' high-risk areas (Success Factors). The intent is for the profile to move to a more balanced shape as improvement initiatives become inserted into common practice and only then focus on the centre. Another graphical representation in popular use is the histogram, often used to show the more subjective measures along with box plots and scatter graphs, useful to study trends.

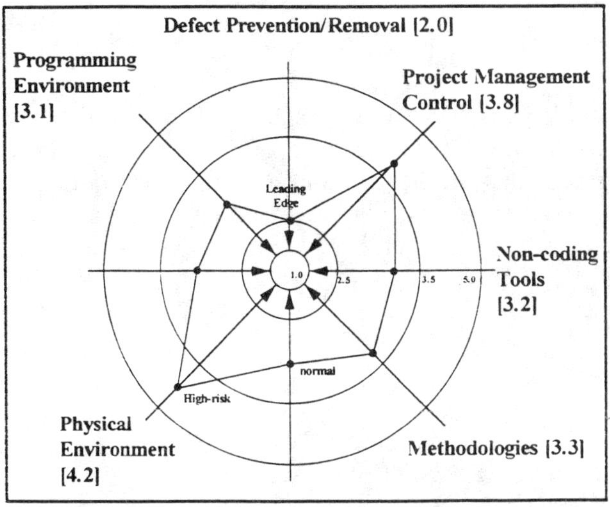

Figure 5.2 Example target and actual profiles

5.3 DO CURRENT STANDARDS HELP ?

Process assessment is supportive of quality atandards, particularly the ISO 9000 series of standards and other (ISO) engineering standards such as the (draft) 'Information Technology Software Life cycle Process' (ISO/IEC JTC1/SC7 N914, September 1991).

Quality standards such as those in the ISO 9000 series are aimed at the assurance of quality, and as such are useful in providing comparisons where the same assessors (or those similarly trained, such as expected from the UK Tick IT scheme) have undertaken quality assessments in related sectors of the industry. The value of these comparisons is limited for our purpose as the necessary quality criterion is for a complete process with feedback and change mechanisms to assure the continual production of products with adequate quality. These prescriptive standards are not designed for assessments to compare or improve processes.

There can be value in selectively drawing on these standards as required where they are seen to be valid to the business, as they provide valuable descriptions of good practice albeit often in a generic sense. Some assessment processes (Bell, Canada and The Scottish Development Agency for example) refer selectively but extensively to IEEE, ISO and other standards. They are used in 'completeness' type measures. As organisations and projects become more sophisticated or 'mature' in their software engineering capability, these and other models often refer to further standards, both definitive and de facto (e.g. Fagan Inspections), as they define incremental institutionalisation of the process and likely result in more consistent product quality within a stable process.

5.4 SUBCONTRACTOR EVALUATION

Here, a necessarily generic view is taken of what are to be selected as best practices. This will mean some aspects of the target profile may pertain to engineering methods that are not appropriate to be incorporated in the standard practice of a particular business. The proposed ISO standard is expected to have generic guidelines, and although expected to be widely applicable, it is envisaged that supplementary guides may still be needed and supported at national, industry sector and organisation levels. The inclusion of subcontractor staff in the evaluation is highly recommended for the reasons of synergy previously mentioned.

5.5 CONFIDENTIALITY AND COMPARISONS

With the results of assessments relate to specified 'business needs', the usefulness to other than the assessors and the project or organisation studied is questionable and is of very little direct value to others, due to the profile shaping that has occurred. Further, such visibility may pose a danger to future co-operation of those involved within the organisation on future assessments.

5.6 ASSESSMENT FREQUENCY

The key issues may be stable over a number of years (perhaps five) unless business strategy changes. For example success factors may well change more frequently dependingt upon a number of influences, such as what is perceived to have changed in the market and the rapid improvement in the capability of the organisation.

The process is necessarily iterative, so for continual improvement, the Success Factors will be looked at again in perhaps six to eighteen months time and the process assessment activity starts again.

5.7 PROPOSED INTERNATIONAL ASSESSMENT METHOD

From studies of the many assessment methods and models in current use it has become clear that there is not one current model or set of standards that can be generally applied. There is concern that diversification is occurring rather that the drawing together to a consensus. This is one driving force at international level for a common approach to assessing the software engineering process, [3].

The expectation of the standard is that beyond perhaps specific definitions of key processes and well-accepted best practices, such as those defined in the ISO life cycle model, it will be allowable for national, IT sector, organisation and procurement agencies to use models developed to meet their particular needs within the ISO framework.

This will provide more focused guidance than at present but intentionally not provide one 'off the shelf' assessment model to compare across the whole software engineering industry. Industry involvement at national and business level in support of the development of this standard will contribute to its ultimate value. The target for the draft issue is 1994. Figure 5.3 is adapted from the current plan for the process assessment method and illustrates the steps we have seen in the above 'process benchmarking' method.

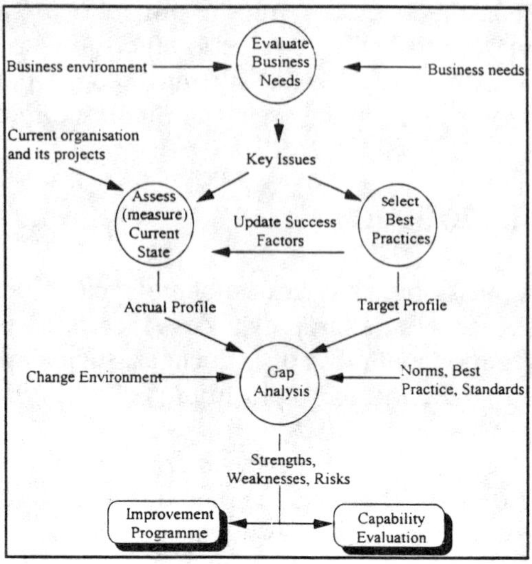

Figure 5.3 Proposed ISO assessment process model

5.8 SUMMARY

Software engineering improvement can only be addressed by consistently using best practice engineering processes where they are selected to meet the particular demands of a business.

Process benchmarking is directed at the project level. Studies across projects provide for the evaluation of an organisation. Project evaluation roll-up to organisation level needs very careful analysis.

It takes some time to make many process improvements effective; early visibility of progress is therefore needed to underpin the acceptance of continual assessment.

Improvements are found to be most effective where staff used in process benchmarking include those who will be involved in implementing changes and be affected by change.

The international standards study effort [3] supports the development of a consistent method of process benchmarking. Process assessment complements BS5950 (ISO 9001) auditing. However a clear distinction must be established during the initial stages to prevent the 'quality audit pass/fail' concept from emerging. Using process benchmarking as an integral management activity, as another engineering process, will assist in maintaining its separate function.

REFERENCES

[1] *Industrial Needs and Practices.* SEMA Scientific, Final Report of Task 1.1, ESPRIT Project METKIT. METKIT/sq/wp1.1/fr 1, March 1990.

[2] *Managing The Software Process.* W.S. Humphrey. Software Engineering Institute, Carnegie Mellon University. Addison Wesley, October 1989. Includes 1987 description of the 'SEI maturity model'. The 1989 and the pending 1991/2 changes do not alter the model concepts.

[3] 'The Need and Requirements for a Software Process Assessment Standard' Issue 1.0 and March 1992. 'ImproveIT' Technical Expert Group sponsored by JTSC1/SC7/WG7/SG1. A study report, proposed standard requirement and justification for a New Work Item Proposal. Input to the ISO/TEC JTSC1/SC7. National Standards Organisations (UK: BSI) are requested to respond.

[4] Best Practice Benchmarking. DTI Publication DTI/PUB 175/5K/1/91, Department of Trade and Industry, Room 320, Kingsgate House, 66-74 Victoria Street, London SW1E 6SW. Tel: 071-215 8142. Forum Productions Ltd, 1991. A wide view of the benchmarking process.

[5] *Improving Perfromance by Using Best Demonstrated Practices.* The Fellowship of Engineering, 2 Little Smith Street, Westminster, London SW1P 3DL. The Wren Press, August 1989. Another view of the benchmarking concepts.

[6] *Systems Thinking, Systems Practice.* P.E. Checkland, Wiley 1981. Includes detailed descriptions of 'soft' system modelling.

[BOL91] 'A Critical Look at Software Capability Evaluations' T.B. Bollinger, C McGowan, IEEE SOFTWARE July 1991.

[HUM91] 'Comments on A Critical Look' Watts S. Humphries, Bill Curtis IEEE SOFTWARE July 1991. This is a reply to [BOL91].

[BAS84] V.Basili, D.Weiss - A Methodology for collecting valid software engineering data - IEEE Trans. on software engineering, vol. SE-10, no 3,Nov 1984 pp 728-738. This paper introduces the GQM - Goals/Question/Metrics data collection and performance improvement approach.

6 Quality Management and Metrics

Ernest Wallmüller
ATAG Informatik AG

6.1 WHY IS MEASUREMENT SO IMPORTANT?

The use of quantitative approaches to management within business and industry is the rule rather the exception. Measurements are integrated into many performance evaluations, estimations, and quality improvement techniques. These techniques are characterised by their emphasis on objectivity and understanding. Problems and results become more apparent to managers and objectives are clearer to engineers.

The effectiveness of these techniques is well documented. They have given proven benefits to a large number of organisations in the US, in Europe, and especially in Japan where they have been used by software engineers and project managers to produce software of the required quality on time, within budget, and with minimum rework.

The application of quantitative process management and quality improvement techniques to software projects addresses the continuing symptoms of the software crisis: budget and schedule overruns, reliability and quality problems, and the high cost of quality itself. This cost, the proportion of effort allocated to reviews, corrections, testing, and maintenance, is significant and often underestimated. Symptoms of this software crisis are now regularly reported in the press. A recent article in *Businessweek* gives some well-known examples which are summarised below:

> The director of Ashton Tate pushed for the release of a new version of their main database product not realising that it was full of errors. The product was subsequently recalled. The consequent financial difficulties resulted in the director resigning and the takeover of Ashton Tate by Borland.
>
> Microsoft have had a similar problem with version 4 of their MS-DOS product. So for version 5, they used 7500 test sites, increasing the cost of quality.
>
> During the Gulf War, a Scud missile landed on an American army barrack, killing several soldiers. A software error in the Patriot missile system had let the Scud pass undetected.

If you are working in the area of software development you will almost certainly know of other examples. They are not new, and the software crisis was identified over 20 years ago. Even though the situation has improved, problems remain and, meanwhile, customers are becoming more technology-literate, sophisticated, and ready to shop around.

As the above examples show, it is necessary to ensure visibility and to think quantitatively. In other words, everyone must know what's going on in objective terms. How much longer will it take? How many errors are being detected? How much testing has been done? How much did it cost?

Once you know where you are starting from, it is possible to improve estimates and performance. If you are using or choosing methods and tools, investment costs, benefits, and problem areas also need to be explicitly stated. Software projects are as much a management and quality management problem as a technical problem.

6.2 THREE EXAMPLES OF QUALITY MEASUREMENT

By showing three empirical examples we will discuss critical and necessary steps and factors for an effective measurement approach.

6.2.1 A measurement process in a research and education environment

In 1986 the author worked at the Swiss Federal Institute of Technology. In the department of informatics a lot of Modula-2 software has been produced for operating systems, database systems, compilers etc. We were interested in a tool for measuring the quality of our programming deliverables by using state of the art software metrics. We implemented this measurement tool in Modula-2.

The following metrics were implemented:

- control flow complexity by McCabe [1]
- nesting complexity by Schmidt
- Halstead metrics [2]
- density metrics such as decisions, functions and comments.

The selected measurement method was very simple. We tried to figure out limits for all these metrics. Arthur [3] and Jones [4] suggest limiting the metric values used as quality indicators. If these limits are exceeded project and quality managers should look at these programs in more detail (requests for code reviews). The programmer gets a hint for complex parts of his program.

The limits are:

- excutable lines of code (eloc) of an procedure $\leq$ 100
- cyclomatic complexity between 10 and 20

- effort < 100 000
- difficulty < 50
- decision density ≤ 20 % eloc
- function density ≤ 10 % eloc
- comment density between 10 and 20 % eloc

The tool run was in a Sun-based programming environment and the training effort for using it was minimal. Running the measurement process for a half year we found the following result:

pros:
+ a better understanding of differing kind of complexities
+ tool support for operative measurements
+ first measurement steps in an environment where the programming language played a very important role

cons:
- a huge amount of data
- a poorly validated measurement approach
- unclear interpretation of measured values.

At that time the paradigm that quality within the process is as important as the deliverables was not understood.

6.2.2 Quality measurement programme at UBS

From 1987 to 1989 the author was involved in establishing and managing a group called Software Engineering and Quality Assurance at the Union Bank of Switzerland (UBS).

UBS is the largest bank in Switzerland with more than 20,000 employees and a revenue of 166 B. sFr. The data processing section employs 1,800 people, 850 of which as project leaders, analysts and programmers.

Quality assurance at UBS has a long tradition. There is an independent system test group and a special group for integration testing at the application level. Furthermore, there exists a central planning group for the architecture of the information systems.

For UBS this measurement programme was new. A leading manager introduced a special measurement programme for the year 1988 at a seminar for internal management. Activities for the middle and lower-level managers were defined. One of these activities was to define two metrics. These metrics were measured periodically for a year. At the end of each quarter a report was published and discussed by the managers.

The Software Engineering and Quality Assurance group had to support this programme. We supported the definitions of the metrics, suggested possible measurement approaches, and analysed and evaluated the results. We used a special form for defining and using the quality metrics.

The most important items on this form were:

- organisational unit (who measures?)
- identification of the metrics
- attribute name (which attribute is to be measured?)
- metric definition (what is the exact definition of the metric?)
- quality goal value (which quality goal should we reach?)
- actual measured quality values (which actual values were measured?)
- source of the measurement data.

The result of this first stage was a list of 45 metrics. Each 'definer' of metrics had a special view of his own quality situation in his organizational unit. Therefore, the definition of his metrics was dependent on this situation and varied strongly from the others.

One of our most important findings was that 40% of these metrics were process oriented and 60% product oriented.

A process-oriented metric is one which characterises activities performed during the process. Examples of this kind of metrics are number of emergency programme transfers to production per quarter, or number of delayed milestones/total number of milestones per quarter.

Product-oriented metrics are those which characterise the results of a phase or the final product. Examples of these are number of errors/1000 lines of code (LOC) or number of failures of an application per quarter.

The results of this first step in our programme were presented in a management course. The best definers of these metrics received a special reward. We also discussed the benefits and costs of the work.

At the end of 1988 we reduced the initial list of 45 metrics to five metrics. The main reason was to unify our approach; another was that measurement without tools is not feasible and does not support the acceptance of metrics.

The remaining five metrics were:

- attribute 'Stable milestones' (see Figure 6.1)

$$\frac{\text{number of delayed milestones}}{\text{total number of milestones}} \text{ per year and per project}$$

- attribute 'Quality of an application in system test' (see Figure 6.2)

$$\frac{\text{number of incidents}}{\text{1000 NLOC}} \text{ per month and per application in system test}$$

- attribute 'Transfer of an application to operation'

$$\frac{\text{number of incidents}}{\text{1000 NLOC}} \text{ within 3 months after start of an application}$$

- attribute 'Stability of an application in operation'

$$\frac{\text{number of incidents}}{\text{1000 NLOC}} \text{ per month and per application}$$

- attribute 'SOS deliveries for an application'

NLOC ...

$$\frac{\text{number of incidents of type 3 \& 4}}{\text{1000 NLOC}} \text{ per month and per application}$$

Noncommentary Lines Of Code

These five metrics were measured monthly. Most of them were calculated by the EIR (Electronic Incident Report) system. This system enables graphics easily. The EIR system is an on-line entry and retrieval system for hardware and software incidents. It is used from the intregration phase to the operation and maintenance phase of an application.

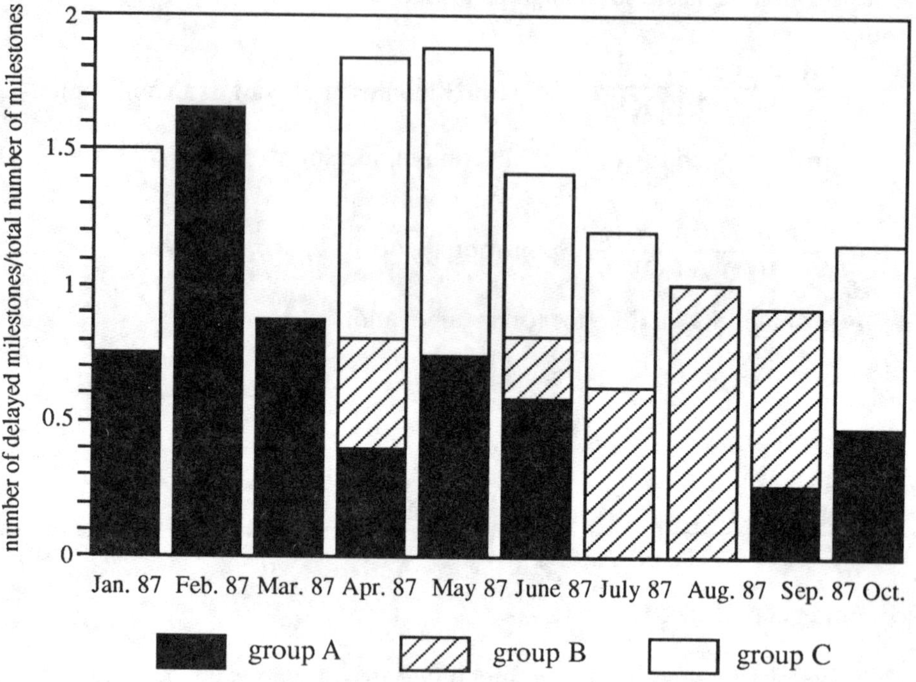

Figure 6.1 Attribute 'stable milestones' for department X

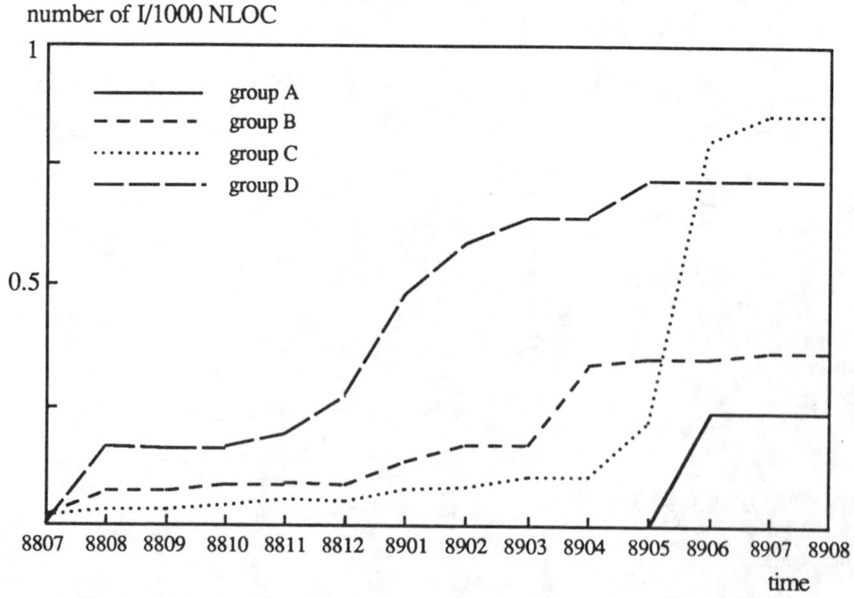

Figure 6.2 Attribute 'quality of an application in system test'

With these five metrics we drew two kinds of measured curves:

- monthly metric curves
- cumulative metric curves

The cumulative metric curves were better accepted than the monthly metric curves. Top management was interested in the aggregation of the cumulative metric curves according to the structure of the organisational units such as group, section, department and main department level.

We found out that the comparison of metrics normalised to NLOC is very difficult. The spectrum of measured values found after a year was very broad for the normalised defect rate. On one side we were not sure whether the validity of measured results was correct. On the other side, in a large enterprise with more than 40 projects running parallel there are always some projects with a lot of problems (such as changing project leaders, transition to products without serious testing and so on).

A relevant influence on our measured results was the change of the database release happening twice a year. Those changes caused obvious 'steps' in our curves.

In our opinion, these metrics should very be very carefully handled. Some managers are convinced that normalisation to NLOC is not correct and falsifies the true measurements. The reasons for not normalising the metric values are twofold:

- incorrect counting of the number of lines of code at a special point of time and
- a good design can have a smaller amount of code than a bad design.

These managers prefer using absolute metric values such as number of incidents with a special priority over a period of three months.

6.2.3 Quality measurement within a programme of quality process assessment

In the north west of England a big system builder invested more than 200 million pounds in new information systems and 400 people in six different software houses and consultancy companies helped to implement the new vision. Ernst and Young were given the job, as quality partner, of assisting the big effort with a quality programme.

A main part of the quality programme was the establisment of a quality process assessment, a kind of audit of the different programmes to implement the vision. These assessments concentrated on identifying problems, deficiences, and symptoms of quality failures in both work products and the methods and approaches to the work. These were analysed and, where appropriate, potential corrective actions have been identified and initiated.

The primary symptoms have been distilled as being:

- rework of products (software and specification)
- time management difficulties
- cost higher than budget
- inefficiency in the form of redundancy and duplication of effort
- communication and co-ordination issues
- products and processes falling short of good practice
- areas of high risk not being effectively managed.

The key causes are:

- programme and project management
- longer term supportability, maintainability and enhanceability
- quality management system
- system performance
- vision and business benefits.

The different development processes can be viewed as transformations from inputs to outputs. There is a need to measure in order to manage these processes.

The metrics proposed will allow for the analysis and comparison of factors significant to managing inputs, development processes, and outputs, both within and across programmes.

For developing metrics we used the goal-question-metric (GQM) paradigm [5]. This paradigm says that goals lead to questions that lead to metrics that supply the answer to the questions. An example illustrates this paradigm:

goal: corrective actions and quality improvements are effectively implemented
question: what is the defect/error rate?
metric: number of errors identified by software incident reports and inspections

This GQM-paradigm was used over all programmes. The resulting metrics are:

- issues raised and resolved
  (+ time taken to resolve issues)
- function points for assessing the volume of work
  - •• cost per function point
  - •• man days per function point
  - •• function points delivered per month
  - •• defects per function point

- skill assessment
- programme satisfaction surveys (both for users and for developers)
- inspection defects
- software incident reports (SIR)
- actuals vs. estimates for cost, effort and milestones
- vision and benefits mapping
- activity analysis.

The first measurements are now available and show interesting details. The goal of measuring over all programmes§ is to make transparent whether value for money is delivered.

6.3 CONCLUSIONS FROM THESE THREE EXPERIENCES

There are five important prerequisites for successful use of a measurement approach:

a Managers must be involved. Control and improvement programmes (and goal-oriented measurements) cannot be brought in as if it were simply a tool. Management must take the lead in initiating measurement, defining goals and asking for feedback.

b Measurement tasks must be clearly allocated and budgeted for so that those concerned will be able to put in the required effort.

c There must be a metrics promoter to write and implement the measurement plan and to organise the presentation and distribution of the information. His or her main role is to keep everyone involved in the metrication process. The analysis of measurement data should relate to the needs of the participants affected by the goals (project managers, designers, etc.).

d There must be a work environment in which goal-oriented measurement programmes are feasible. The essential criteria is not project size or maturity level but continuity of management strategy. There is little point in investing in an improvement programme if there is no element of continuity between projects.

e Don't forget training. Measurement in the workplace is an emotive issue for all members of staff. Typically, the initial reaction is, 'You can't measure software production'. Another common reaction is fear – fear of having your customary working practices subjected to scrutiny and laid bare to criticism. In extreme cases, although these are few, there are experiences of intense hostility.

One of the most used objections to measurement is the cost of a measurement

§ A programme consists of 4 till 6 projects.

programme. Therefore it is important to know all relevant factors influencing the cost of a measurement programme. Five factors can cause variations in these costs:

1 Metrics data already present

Before embarking on a metrication programme, it is worth looking at existing data collections. Most companies collect measurement data without realising it. One example is project management data such as effort spent on different project modules and effort spent correcting and maintaining software. Another source is quality control data relating to the number of modifications requested or to the quality level achieved.

2 Organisations with visible and controlled development processes have reduced costs

If they are certified for ISO 9001, or have a well-defined process, organisations will normally have procedures in place that can be used in measurement data analysis. Examples include project reviews, change control procedures and quality control activities.

3 The more metrics for which data is collected, the greater the cost

The more metrics are used, the more issues are covered, with a corresponding increase in implementation and analysis costs. However, it is possible to build up over time a useful set of metrics without excessively increasing costs. This is achieved by automating key data collection and analysis activities. Goal-oriented measurements are used to target key metrics and avoid excessive data collections.

4 There is a 'trial and error' learning curve to introducing a measurement strategy into the software development process

These 'trial and error' costs can be minimised by using a measurement method, if the method is described in a structured sequence which has been designed and thoroughly proven to contain the essential but necessary actions required for a successful measurement programme.

5 Efficiency and motivation lead to reduced measurement costs

The objectives, results and costs of measurement should be monitored. Reviews help to improve the measurement plan and increase efficiency.

Although there is a clear investment in quantifying software projects, two points should be noted in conclusion: use of a goal-oriented measurement programme leads to predictable and controlled metrication costs; and part of the cost is transferred from existing sources and does not represent additional costs.

A goal-oriented measurement is seen as the most appropriate strategy with which to undertake measurement in software engineering. This is reflected in its favourable cost/benefit ratio.

Costs are kept to a minimum. With a goal-oriented measurement programme, the number of metrics that have to be collected is generally limited to those that correspond to significant goals, thus limiting data collection and analysis costs. Moreover, since the goal is defined and the metrics are derived, there is a certain latitude to choose metrics that are easy to collect. Finally, there is no high entry cost. When getting started the number of goals chosen is best restricted to a small initial set.

On the benefits side, the emphasis on goals, including business objectives, implies that the link with decision making is clearly established. There is a reduced risk of unprofitable measurement and of excessive data overloading the decision-making process. The clear definition of goals increases acceptance of measurement by team leaders and engineers. They are naturally suspicious of measurement programmes collecting data for unspecified reasons and are demotivated by a measurement programme that is not clearly put to good use.

6.4 AN EUROPEAN MEASUREMENT APPROACH – THE ami METHOD

A number of leading practitioners in the software industry have developed practical and effective approaches to measurement. Based on this experience a consortium of European organisations have developed the ami (application of metrics in industry) method [6], a sequence of working steps supported by guidelines and templates. The ami project is sponsored by DGXIII of the Commisssion of the European Communities, through the ESPRIT programme which is promoting the use of measurement programmes in software development.

The application of a goal-oriented measurement programme in a software organisation requires a structured method. Each organisation, while being unique, must construct its own measurement framework. Which organisation, after all, would borrow the mission statement of another?

Without a method it is not possible to build a coherent framework, and the result does not reflect real needs. The organisation wastes a lot of time discovering and trying out more or less successful methods on its own, but out of frustration the measurement programme is usually abandoned before a method is allowed to take root.

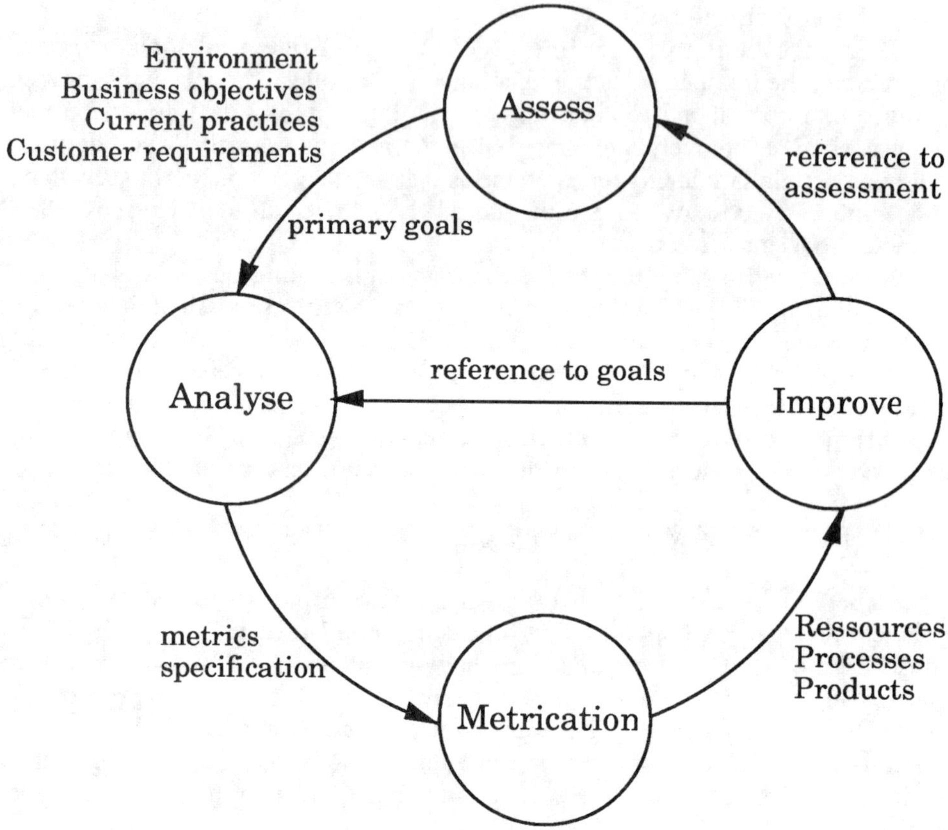

Figure 6.3 application of metrics in industry (ami approach)

The ami method implements four distinct activities – Assess, Analyse, Metricate, Improve:

Assess your project environment (with its objectives and problems) to define primary goals for measurement. Managers who initiate measurement must be involved in this activity.

Analyse the primary goals to derive sub-goals and the relevant metrics. This analysis is formalised as a goals tree with a corresponding set of questions to which these metrics are linked. The participants affected by the metrication goals (metrics promoter, project managers, quality engineers, etc.) will generally carry out this activity.

Metricate by implementing a measurement plan and process the collected primitive data into measurement data. The metrics promoter will write the measurement plan and co-ordinate its implementation.

Improve as the participants affected by the goals start to use the measurement data and implement actions. Comparison of the measurement data with the goals and questions in the measurement plan will guide you towards achievement of your immediate project goals. When your measurements show that you have achieved a goal, you have improved enough to reassess your primary goals.

The final validation stages of the ami method are completed successfully and the approach is endorsed by 19 industrial validation projects which continue to use the ami method as a basis for their measurement programmes.

6.5 PREVIEW

In future we see the following trends concerning software engineering and measurement:

- Software development is changing from an art to a software factory by using mechanisms such as standardisation and automation.
- Assessment of software processes are supported more and more by using quality measurements. They are starting points for software process improvements and enhancements of the maturity levels.
- quality systems and certifications of such systems, based on ISO 9001 also used for software organisations, can be increased in their efficency by more quantification. This means using a measurement programme instead of assessment based only on questionnaires.

We are convinced that measurement of the software processes and its deliverables is an mandatory quality management task for software engineers and their managers.

REFERENCES

[1] T. McCabe, 'A Complexity Measure', *IEEE Trans. on SWE* (December 1976), 308 – 20.

[2] M. Halstead, *Elements of Software Science*, (Elsevier, 1977).

[3] J. Arthur, *Measuring programmer productivity and software quality* (Wiley, 1985).

[4] C. Jones, *Programming Productivity* (McGraw-Hill, 1986).

[5] V. Basili and H. Rombach, 'A Quantitative Approach to Quality Assurance', *Informatik Spektrum* (June 1987), 145 – 58.

[6] ami consortium, 'ami handbook', CSSE (1992).

LITERATURE

Boehm, B. 1981. *Software Engineering Economics*. Prentice-Hall.

Card, D. and R. Glass 1990. *Measuring Software Design Quality*. Prentice-Hall.

Fenton, N. 1991. *Software Metrics: a rigorous approach*. Chapman & Hall.

Grady, R. and D. Caswell 1987. *Software Metrics Establishing a Company-wide Program*. Prentice-Hall.

Hetzel, W. 1984. *The Complete Guide to Software Testing*. QED.

Humphreys, W. 1989. *Managing the Software Process*. Addison-Wesley.

Wallmüller, E. 1992, 2nd Ed. *Software-Qualitätssicherung in der Praxis*. Hanser.

7 Planning for Quality: Assessing, Achieving and Preserving Quality

Dorothy R. Graham
Grove Consultants, Cheshire

7.1 INTRODUCTION

The word quality has had many meanings attached to it through the ages and the proliferation of meanings has possibly never been as great as now. But what exactly is the meaning of 'meeting the customers' requirements'; 'exceeding the customers' requirements' (!); 'conforming with the standard'; 'meeting the specification'; etc.? All these have been quoted (many times) by developers, users, quality assurers, certification agencies, all with a confidence mostly unmatched by experience!

Essentially any definition of quality will suffice a particular situation provided the definition is stated in terms that are verifiable, that is, in measurable terms. It seems to me somewhat clichéd to restate (inaccurately) the, by now well over-used, Lord Kelvin saying 'What you cannot measure, you cannot control' (subsequently rephrased by every 'expert' in the field!). The fundamental truth of the statement (however phrased) is inescapable. In which case, given the frequency with which it is stated and the frequency with which everyone in the audience mutters their agreement, is it not time we **all** started to try to comply with the principle of measurement.

Developers are often (interminably?) blamed for the poor 'quality' of software systems, but who buys these systems? The answer is we all do (of one sort or another – be it an office spreadsheet or a command and control system for a nuclear submarine). Who is responsible therefore for the quality of a system? The developer, the user, the purchaser/buyer, the QA staff (in-house or independent), the Standards makers? Who? Perhaps all? Obviously everyone has a vested interest in 'quality' and their own concept of quality, in which case everyone is responsible for the quality (or lack of) of every system.

The purchaser of shoes which fall apart in a week, or a new dishwasher that breaks all the china has every right to, and always (well nearly always) does complain vociferously to the manufacturer, and expects full refund or free replacement. So why is this still a rarity for poor quality software systems? Why does the developer still, in general, expect the user to pay for debugging (euphemistically called maintenance), and why does the user still do so? Apart from the obvious answer of complacency ('it has always been thus') the reasons are many, but essentially: lack of proper controls by all parties concerned in development; lack of understanding by many involved in what is going on; lack of agreement of fully understood specifications (resulting from poorly stated and continuously changing requirements); lack of properly implemented measurement procedures, etc.; or no management, poor process, misunderstood and unmeasured product.

What is said here represents not the definitive statement on the management and measurement of software system production but a selection of current thought in the area, based on the best practice in Europe and state-of-the-art research in the domain.

The book was originally to be a purely testing oriented work, a field which should in fact deserve its own work. However testing, albeit important, is but an aspect of quality assurance and the ensuring of good quality systems development. It is also imperative that testing techniques and philosophy incorporate proper quantifiable processes (i.e. testing in measurement!).

7.2 QUALITY: A GOOD THING?

7.2.1 Who's in favour of quality?

If you ask whether people are in favour of quality for software, generally everyone is. However, just having the intention to achieve quality is not enough; not everyone does achieve the levels of quality which they would like. Quality does not happen by accident; it must be planned.

7.2.2 The balance of quality, cost, and time

A software development project can be considered from three different points of view: cost, time, and quality. Getting the balance right between these three areas is a real challenge for any manager. In the past, software development projects have been known to fail not just in one area, but in all three. Projects which were over budget, late, and unsatisfactory to the customers have led to what has been called the 'Software Crisis', which was the basic rationale for software engineering. Software engineering methods and techniques have helped to gain control over software development in all three areas, but particularly in cost and time.

If you talk to users or customers of software projects which were developed say two years ago, which is the most important of these three to them now? Will they remember that it cost slightly more than they had planned, or that it was delivered a few weeks late? Unless the project was very late, or very much over budget, it is unlikely that these aspects will be important to the users to day. The quality of the system will be the most important thing to them now; the way in which they use the system on a daily basis to accomplish their work is continually being affected by the quality of that system. If we are developing software to meet the needs of our users, quality must be considered as at least as important as budgets and time-scales and, the more customer-oriented we are, the more important this becomes.

Most organisations have careful plans for time-scales and schedules, and for budgets and costs. But the plans for quality may not be nearly as well spelled out, partly because quality is more difficult to 'tie down'. Yet, if the quality plans are not as specific as time-scales and budgets, they are even less likely to be achieved in the area which is even more important.

7.2.3 Quality: assessing, achieving and preserving

Quality is vital for competitiveness in today's world. How can we know if we have achieved quality?

We want to build quality in from the beginning – how can we ensure that this is done?

We want to ensure that the quality levels achieved and seen to be achieved through assessment, are preserved over the operational life of the software systems we develop – how can we do this?

We will concentrate on one aspect of quality planning which is a vital component but is currently often under-emphasised, i.e. software testing. Testing is certainly not the only aspect of quality and not the only quality aspect which needs to be planned. For further information on the management of quality and details of quality planning, see Ould [1].

Testing is chosen as the area to concentrate for two reasons: most software developers actually spend around 40% of their effort in testing, although this is seldom adequately planned for. Consequently, testing offers a major development opportunity for time and cost savings if it can be improved.

Although 'front-end' software development activities have been significantly refined over the past decade, the 'other half' has been neglected. In particular, the recent ways of integrating test design with software design are not yet well practised or even well known. Those organisations which do practice more modern testing techniques have achieved significant benefits.

7.3 SOFTWARE TESTING IS A QUALITY ASSESSMENT ACTIVITY

7.3.1 What is a test?

The dictionary definition of a test is 'to ascertain the worth of a thing by subjection to certain examinations, etc.' [2]. The purpose of testing software systems is to ascertain their worth, i.e. to investigate certain properties of the system. If a new software system is not tested then the level of confidence that the system would actually work as intended would (and should) be low. If a system is tested and does work as intended then confidence in the system tends to be high. However, this high confidence may or may not be justified. Paradoxically, the best way to justify confidence is to try to destroy confidence; trying to find errors is a far better testing strategy than trying to show that the software works, as Myers so vividly described [3].

The main purpose of testing is, therefore, to assess the software; testing is firstly a quality assessment process.

7.3.2 The quality of the testing

In order to assess software quality effectively, it is essential that the quality of the testing itself is taken into consideration. The reason for this is that the same result, that of 'No errors found', can be achieved in a number of different ways:

1 the software is good and the testing is also good
2 the software is good and the testing is bad
3 the software is bad and the testing is also bad.

All three of these routes give us no (or few) errors, but without knowing whether the testing was good or bad we cannot draw any conclusions about the quality of the software. Actually, we normally assume the software is good but, unless you can show that the testing is good, this is an unjustified conclusion. If the testing is good, then good software is the only way to get the desired result – with good testing and bad software you get lots of errors.

For example, suppose a system has 100 inputs to process, there are 100 tests and no errors are found. What can you say about the quality of the software? Absolutely nothing! The 100 tests may have exercised one input 100 times, leaving the other 99 totally untested.

7.3.3 Testing and quality activities

Testing is very closely associated with many quality activities, in quality control, quality assurance, and quality management.

The quality plan addresses testing issues such as the testing strategy, test tools needed, acceptance criteria, what reviews are to be performed (of test documentation as well as other project documentation), risk management (e.g. what tests not to do, when to stop testing), user involvement, what training is needed in test techniques, and what test metrics will be used. In addition to the quality plan, the project should also have detailed test documentation, such as test plans, test designs, test cases, test logs, test procedures, etc. [4].

Quality control testing activities, included in the quality plan, assess the software products after they have been built.

Quality assurance ensures that the tests are developed according to the prevailing standards and at the right times, and performs checks on test quality.

QA ensures that the quality management sSystem is working in the testing activities, and may provide training in test methods, standards, and tools. Some QA departments act as independent test teams, or they may monitor the activities of the test team. Quality assurance also checks that the testing which is planned or being performed is effective in achieving the test objectives as set out in the test strategy.

The quality management system also addresses testing issues, and ensures that the right balance is struck between testing and other V and V activities. The QMS ensures that quality control and quality assurance are effective in testing, and uses the test metrics collected to improve the entire software development and testing processes.

7.3.4 What type of quality activity is testing?

What type of quality activity is software testing in your organisation?

Quality control activities are applied to finished products after they have been manufactured. They detect faulty parts and throw them away.

Quality assurance activities concentrate on the product development process. They seek to prevent errors from being engineered into the product.

Quality management activities are people-oriented, ensuring that everyone is aware of their own responsibility for quality. They seek continual process improvement.

If testing is applied only as a 'necessary evil' after coding, it is equivalent to manufacturing processes of 100 years ago. The way in which quality is planned for in other industries, and in other areas of software development, can and should also be applied to software testing.

7.3.5 Certification does not guarantee quality

There is currently a high level of interest in quality certification schemes, such as BS 5750 (equivalent to the European EN 29000 and the international ISO 9000), which require a formal organisational approach to quality. This is certainly a step in the right direction but is not enough in itself. To be certified, you need do two things: 'Say what you do' – record your working procedures in a quality manual; and 'Do what you say' – ensure that those procedures are followed.

A certification is therefore in two parts; firstly, assessing the quality manual, and secondly an audit of actual practice. This audit is continued at regular intervals throughout the duration of the certification, to ensure that the procedures are still being followed.

The assessment of the quality manual does ensure certain basic standards for testing. However, you do not necessarily have to do the 'right' or best thing in order to achieve certification. As long as what you write down conforms to the procedural requirements of ISO 9001, you will pass. This will involve things like having a basic organisation and approach to testing, and ensuring that faults found are followed up.

However, it does not specify the detail about what type of testing should be done, when it is done, or by whom. It will bring a level of testing discipline to an undisciplined organisation, but it will not give all of the benefits which are easily achievable through following the current best practice in software testing. It may improve quality-control-type testing, but may not move testing practices forward into their full potential.

For example, it would be generally agreed that a good quality system would be 'usable', but exactly what does this mean, and how can you tell a usable system from an unusable or less usable one? Measuring attributes or qualities, such as usability, portability, reliability, maintainability, and so on, is often a very fuzzy area, not only for testing but also for specification. There is a technique for making such 'ilities' testable [5], but this level of detail is not within the scope of a certification scheme.

7.3.6 Quality versus testing

It should be obvious that testing and quality activities are very closely linked and should work hand in hand. Yet a quote which I often hear is 'We want to build quality in, not test the bugs out'. This is a very laudable sentiment; of course we should build quality into our software systems – we can't bolt it on afterwards. But there are a few important points to qualify this seemingly innocuous statement.

7.3.6.1 Quality instead of testing?

The last three words of the quote above tend to be written in disappearing ink. It becomes 'We want to build quality in, not test'.

If it were strictly a choice between quality and testing then of course quality is preferable to testing. But quality and testing are not diametrically opposed – they are not alternatives. Testing is the only way to assess whether a software system actually does what it should do in its final operational environment. It is not a choice: testing assesses quality; quality needs to be assessed.

7.3.6.2 Test the bugs out?

There is a significant misconception that one of the phases of the life cycle is the single activity called 'Test-and-debug' (which takes far too long and consumes too much resource). However, there are actually four things concerned here.

- bugs are inserted (during development)
- testing reveals bugs
- debugging removes bugs
- retesting reveals incorrect fixes. (3 and 4 are a loop).

Testing should not be confused with either of the other activities. If there were no inserted bugs, tests would only have to run once, and no debugging or retesting would be needed at all. It is important to keep track of time spent on initial testing (i.e. assessment) activities separately from the other activities, to know what savings could be achieved by putting fewer bugs in during development.

Testing often seems to get the blame for creating the bugs, which is somewhat unfair (like shooting the messenger who brings bad news). If the bugs are there, the only way to improve the quality of the software is to remove them, so testing is essential to identify them.

7.3.6.3 Testing activities help to build quality in

Building quality into software systems is the right approach. However, one of the secrets of successful software developers is that testing activities, performed early in the development life cycle, are among the most effective ways of achieving quality. This leads to the second purpose of testing: to help achieve quality.

7.4 SOFTWARE TESTING IS A QUALITY ACHIEVEMENT ACTIVITY

7.4.1 Testing is more than testing

A common misconception is to confuse testing with running tests. Testing involves much more than running test cases with executable code. Testing activities include test design, test estimation, test planning, monitoring and controlling test progress, the evaluation of the effectiveness and efficiency of the testing process, the integration of testing activities with other quality activities (e.g. review of test designs), non-execution quality evaluation (e.g. static analysis), as well as test execution.

7.4.2 Testing starts before the test phase

Testing activities should be planned and managed from the beginning of development, and tests should be designed at every stage in the development life cycle. The test activities are shown in the life cycle model in Figure 7.1 below; on the left-hand side is where tests should be written; on the right-hand side is where those tests are run. If tests are designed and written alongside the associated life-cycle phase, e.g. system and acceptance tests with requirements analysis, sub-system or link tests with architectural system design, etc., then the very act of writing the tests acts as a verification activity which improves software quality. By asking ‘How will I test this?’ of every requirement, the untestable, overly complex, and infeasible requirements are highlighted well before they are designed and coded. When the code is written, all the quality that the system will have has already been built. We want to build quality in – this is achieved through testing activities as well as other quality activities.

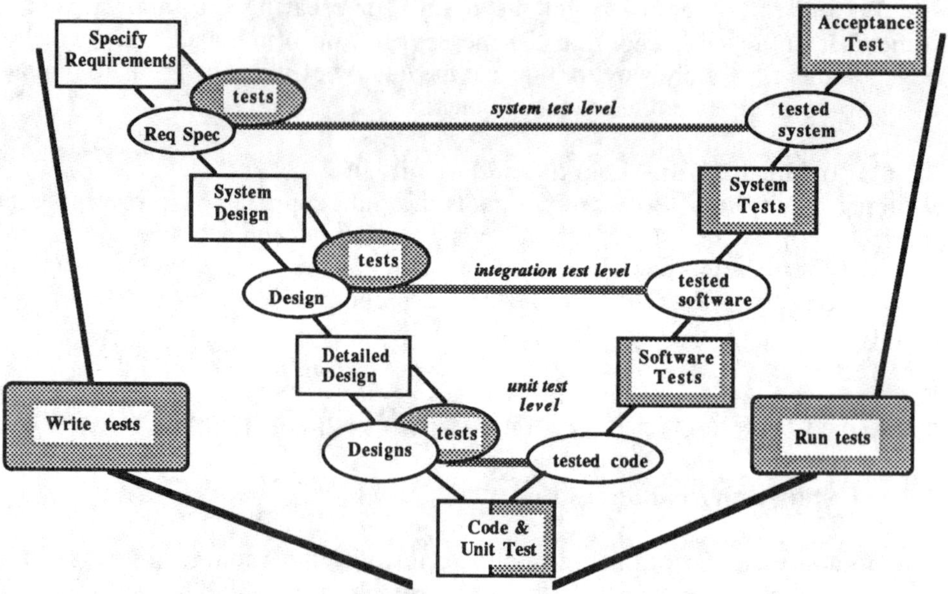

Figure 7.1 Testing activities throughout the life cycle

7.4.3 When are tests designed?

7.4.3.1 As late as possible

Tests are needed for assessing software, but when should they be designed? A common belief is that they should be designed as late as possible in the life cycle, i.e. only just before they are needed. The reason for this is supposedly to save time and effort, and to make progress as quickly as possible. What effect does this really have?

Whenever a test for anything is designed, whether for code, a part of the system, the system as a whole, or the user's view of the system, there is one inevitable guaranteed effect: **designing tests finds errors in the specification.** This happens no matter when the tests are designed. Of course, no test can be designed without a specification, since the specification is the source of what the correct results of the test should be, even if that specification is not formally written down.

If we leave test design until the last possible moment then the errors are found late when they are most expensive to fix. In addition, the errors in the highest levels, the requirements specification, are found last – these are the most critical and most important errors, and are the most expensive to fix. The actual effect of this approach is the most costly and time-consuming approach to testing and software development.

7.4.3.2 As early as possible

If tests are going to be designed anyway, why leave it until the last moment? There is no additional effort required to move a scheduled task to a different place in the schedule (provided it was going to be done anyway).

If tests are designed as early as possible, the inevitable effect of finding errors in the specification comes early, when those errors are cheapest to fix. In addition, the most significant errors are found first. This means that those errors are not built in to the next stage, e.g. major requirements errors are not designed in, so errors are prevented.

7.4.3.3 Changing requirements

One aspect which may be a problem is that of changing requirements. If requirements are changed then the tests will also have to be changed – will this lead to additional effort? Although there are some cases where this will be true, there is a major flaw in this argument as a reason for postponing test design activities.

One of the major causes of requirement changes, especially late in development, is because the tests are being defined at that stage. When the users only begin to think about their tests just before the acceptance tests are about to start, they realise the errors in the requirements specification, and request changes to it. If they had designed their tests at the same time as they were specifying those requirements, the very mental activity of test design would have identified those errors before the system had built them.

The way in which the system will be tested also serves to provide another dimension to the development; the tests form part of the specification. If you know how it will be tested, you are much more likely to build something which will pass those tests. Thus the acceptance criteria becomes the completion criteria for what is built at every stage of development [6].

The end result of designing tests as early as possible is that quality is built in, costs are reduced, and time is saved in test running because fewer errors are found, giving an overall reduction in cost and effort.

7.5 SOFTWARE TESTING IS A QUALITY PRESERVATION ACTIVITY

7.5.1 What happens to tests?

Once a system has been developed and put into operation, it is important to ensure that the quality levels achieved are not allowed to slip back over time.

What happens to tests after they have been designed and run for the first time? A significant investment of time and effort has often gone into test design, even if it is done informally. The usual receptacle for test plans is the bin. Then when changes are made to that software in maintenance, new tests are informally designed and again thrown away. If tests are planned from the beginning as an investment in preserving quality, those tests are likely to be of much higher quality and can be used over and over again.

7.5.2 Testing for expected and unexpected change

When a change is made, most people do check that what was expected to change has indeed changed, but often the worst effects come from unexpected changes. Testing for things which are not expected to change is called 'regression' testing, although it should probably be called 'anti-regression' testing, because we are testing to ensure that the software has not regressed to an erroneous state. Full regression testing involves rerunning every test which has ever been run on a system. Full regression testing is very rarely done if testing is performed manually. Partial regression testing, where an impact analysis identifies those areas which are more likely to be inadvertently changed, or where the risk of unexpected change is highest, is often done to some degree.

7.5.3 Manual regression testing is not possible

The only way to preserve quality with complete confidence is to perform full regression testing for every change. This is simply not practicable to do manually for any reasonable sized system. If tests are fully automated using test execution tools, this is now possible for the first time. By rerunning all existing tests at the push of a button, although this does not increase quality, it does ensure that the quality of the system has not slipped back, so it preserves quality.

7.6 CURRENT STATUS OF TESTING IN QUALITY PLANNING

7.6.1 Imbalance of attention

The amount of attention paid to some areas of software engineering is quite out of proportion to the amount of time which most practising software engineers spend in those activities. For example, it is widely accepted that 70% of total system life costs are in maintenance, and only 30% in development. Yet from the emphasis of the literature, conferences, tool support, etc., one could be forgiven for thinking it was the reverse. The establishment of the Centre for Software Maintenance at Durham [7] is a welcome step towards redressing the balance.

Even within software development and maintenance activities, the balance is out of proportion. Analysis and design seem to be the 'hottest' topics around (e.g. anything object-oriented, CASE tools). Even coding activities seem to be well-served (C, C++, 4GL's code generators). Yet testing, which typically consumes 40–50% of the effort of software development, has received very little attention up to now. For example, how many developers in most organisations have been on a course for an analysis or design methodology? How many programmers have been on a language course? Probably more than half at least. And how many have been on a testing course? In my experience, fewer than 10% of all software developers have ever been trained in even the most rudimentary software testing techniques, either on academic courses or industrial courses. The situation is even worse at the management level, where there are few courses on test management available and testing is now dealt with in general software management courses.

Perhaps this is why testing consumes so much effort.

7.6.2 Evidence of change in testing

The attitude to testing is about to change dramatically. There is currently an upsurge of interest in software testing both in the UK, Europe, and elsewhere. In the US, Boris Beizer [8] has detected a dramatic increase in the sales of testing books over the past four years. Other indicators include the number of articles, conference, standards, technical terms, university courses, etc. He predicts that the 1990s will be 'The Testability Decade'. There are now three major testing conferences in the US every year; the first UK testing conference will be held in 1993, organised by the BCS Specialist Interest Group on Software Testing [9].

Another indication is that software tools are now becoming available to support software testing, and this has also shown a recent dramatic increase. A leaflet describing commercial tools available in the UK in 1989 contained 25 tools [10]. The CAST Report [11] published in 1991 contains 82 tools, 74 from the UK. The testing tools catalogue in the US contains over 150 tools, with over 800 on the database [12]. At the Software Tools Conference and Exhibition in June 1991, I found another 39 tools among the exhibitors alone. Another interesting phenomenon at that exhibition was that the testing tool vendors all reported being busy, while the CASE tool vendors found the level of interest to be disappointing [13].

CASE tools have not lived up to the high expectations in improving productivity and quality [14] One reason for this is that they address only the first half of the life cycle at best, and even in the first half they do not support all of the activities which they should (e.g. testing activities). The very term 'CASE', Computer-Aided Software Engineering, is misleading in its accepted use, since it generally applies only to analysis and design activities and not the other half of the life cycle activities. The ultimate aim must be to have tools which integrate both CASE and Computer-Aided Software Testing (CAST). Currently few CASE tools provide support for testing activities, there is a growing awareness from CASE tool vendors of the need for testing and test support [15].

7.7 TESTING AND QUALITY IN THE FUTURE

The future of testing and quality in the 1990s will be in three major areas: implementation of testing within a quality framework, the use of test metrics in assessing the quality of the testing, and the increasing automation of testing.

7.7.1 Implementation in a quality framework

The momentum which has already built up towards certification in quality standards will continue. It will become the accepted norm that software developers, to be considered worth buying from, will need to confirm to ISO 9001 because all of their competitors already do.

Testing will become a recognised specialisation within software engineering, distinct from, but closely associated with, quality-related specialisations.

Training in testing techniques will be provided on academic courses for software engineers, and industrial courses in testing will be widely available. Managers will be given training in the techniques of test management. Senior executives will be aware of the need for testing and how to assess and achieve quality through testing.

In short, the methods and techniques which are known today but not generally practised, will be put in place in industry in the context of Quality Management Systems.

7.7.2 Quality of testing through test metrics

The issue of quality will apply not only to the development of software but also to the assessment of that software, i.e. the quality of testing will become far more important because it will be increasingly relied upon to demonstrate the quality of software products.

An example of a metric-driven approach is outlined below. This procedure is included as an experimental attempt to define levels of testedness in the draft Standard for Software Component Testing [16], prepared by a working party subgroup of the British Computer Society Specialist Interest Group in Software Testing.

The procedure for using the testing standard is as follows:

- set structural test coverage objectives
- choose functional test techniques to be used to derive test case suites, from the collection detailed in the standard
- run functional tests and assess the structural coverage achieved (this is easiest done using a coverage measurement tool)
- extend the test suites until the desired coverage has been achieved (note that this step and the assessment of structural coverage may be omitted if tool support is not available)
- compute the testedness scores
- validate testedness by recording errors not found by testing, i.e. found after testing was stopped (in operation or in later stages of testing).

The future of testing will involve planning for levels of testedness for different types of systems to control the quality of the testing. The testing can then be used with confidence to assess software quality.

7.7.3 Computer-aided software testing

The most significant change in software testing in the next decade will be the take-up of software testing tools. Some of the organisations which have already implemented tool support for testing have been able to achieve dramatic improvements in productivity and quality, not only of the testing but also for overall software development. For example, improvements of 30% software development productivity [17] and testing costs reduced by 75% [18]. The best success stories have one factor in common: they have already instituted good testing practices.

The tool functionality areas which are available today include: capture playback, comparators, input generation, static analysis, simulators, test harness, test coverage measurement, debug, test database, and test management tools. See The CASE Report [11] for details of current testing and verification tools.

Future directions for tool support in testing include the following areas:

- Test management tools will support project management activities unique to testing, configuration management of test documents and objects, test metrics collection and analysis, and test control reporting.
- Individual test running tools will include many already available such as test harness, capture playback, comparator, input generation, debug, test database, simulator. Test execution tools will become more sophisticated in integrating results comparison with test running, through the use of

powerful scripting languages. Future tools may also include requirements capture and traceability tools (what tests need to be rerun when something is changed), selective regression test selection, knowledge-based or Artificial Intelligence debug tools or test harnesses, debug tools for special environments such as real-time, 4GL, object-oriented, WIMP interface, statistical test generation tools, and tools for graphics applications (e.g. graphic object comparators).

- Test quality evaluation tools already include structural coverage measurement tools, and will also include more functional coverage measurement data coverage and system-level coverage tools. Mutation testing may eventually become economic.
- CAST tools and CASE tools will be integrated through common repositories, so that tests can be designed at analysis and design level, linked to all related documents and provide input to test case generators. There are currently only a few CASE tools which are integrated to testing tools.

7.8 SUMMARY

The purpose of testing is to assess software quality, but confidence in the assessment cannot be justified without considering the quality of the testing process itself. Testing and quality activities are closely linked, but it is not a choice between them. Testing is not only a quality assessment activity, but also a quality achievement activity and a quality preservation activity.

Currently little attention is paid to testing activities within software development and maintenance, but this is now beginning to change. The future of quality and testing will see progress in three areas: the implementation of good testing practices within a quality framework, assessments of test quality through test metrics, and, most significantly, the increasing automation of software testing.

REFERENCES

[1] Martyn A. Ould 1990. *Strategies for Software Engineering: The Management of Risk and Quality.* John Wiley & Sons.

[2] The New Collins Concise Dictionary of the English Language, 1985.

[3] Glenford J. Myers 1979. *The Art of Software Testing*. John Wiley & Sons.

[4] IEEE Standard for Software Test Documentation, ANSI/IEEE Std 829-1983, Institute of Electrical and Electronics Engineers Inc., 1983.

[5] Tom Gilb 1988. *Principles of Software Engineering Management.* Addison-Wesley.

[6] Geoff Quentin, QCC training material.

[7] Centre for Software Maintenance Ltd., Mountjoy Research Centre, Stockton Road, Durham, DH1 3SW. Tel: 091 386 0420.

[8] Boris Beizer. On becoming the mainstream *American Programmer*, April 1991.

[9] British Computer Society Specialist Interest Group in Software Testing, administration from QCC, 73 West Road, Shoeburyness, Essex, SS3 9DT. Tel: 0702 298290.

[10] Software Tools for Verification Validation and Testing 1989. The National Computing Centre.

[11] Dorothy R. Graham 1991. Computer Aided Software Testing: The CAST Report. Unicom Seminars.

[12] Testing Tools Reference Guide 1991. Software Quality Engineering.

[13] Kevan R. Jones 1990. *Measured benefits of using established CASE tools.* Software Tools Conference. Blenheim Online Ltd.

[14] Personal observation.

[15] Author's informal survey of CASE tool vendors at Software Tools, 1991.

[16] A Standard for Software Component Testing. Dorothy R. Graham and Martyn Ould (eds), for the British Computer Society Specialist Interest Group in Software Testing, November 1990.

[17] Renault Truck Stays Ahead with Compuware, press release, March 1991.

[18] Mark Fewster 1991. *The MD wants 100% automated testing: a case history.* Software Tools Management Conference. Blenheim Online Ltd.

8 Realistic and Cost-effective Software Testing

Brian Hambling
MEG Associates

Consideration of software testing is always associated with some key questions. Why do it at all? How much testing should we do? When should we begin testing? Who should do it? Which testing techniques should we use? All of these are relevant and serious concerns and we must be sure to address them through an appropriate strategy which is both realistic and cost-effective.

A cost-effective strategy is one which addresses how we can achieve an acceptable level of quality for our customers with the minimum of effort and cost, or how much we should spend now to avoid excessive costs later from rework or 'unplanned maintenance'. The aim is minimum total cost over the period for which we have some responsibility for the software. Realistic software testing is testing we can practically expect to be able to do in a real software development project. Having determined what is a cost-effective level of testing, our next concern must be with practicality in terms of schedules and available resources. In other words, how do we construct a realistic test plan and a realistic project plan with an appropriate level of testing integrated into it?

8.1 WHAT IS SOFTWARE TESTING?

If our aim is the achievement of software products of assured quality, three criteria emerge: the ability to define the required level of quality; the ability to construct products of that quality; the ability to assure ourselves and our customers that the required level of quality has been achieved. The first of these is mainly about requirements analysis and expression, but testing for the existence of an adequate quality definition is also required if we are to have control over the achievement of quality. Similarly, the ability to construct quality products is about selection of appropriate development methods and techniques (among other things), but we can only be assured of the effectiveness of those methods and techniques by testing the quality of intermediate 'products' of the process (specifications, designs etc). Finally, we come to the issue of assuring the quality of the completed software product – the 'usual' form of software testing. We conclude that, to be an effective part of developing quality assured software, testing must extend across the entire development process and be integrated with other development activities.

8.1.1 Testing in a software development life cycle

We need some model of the development life cycle as a framework for a discussion of software testing. Any model would do, but we will here use the fairly well known V life cycle shown below:

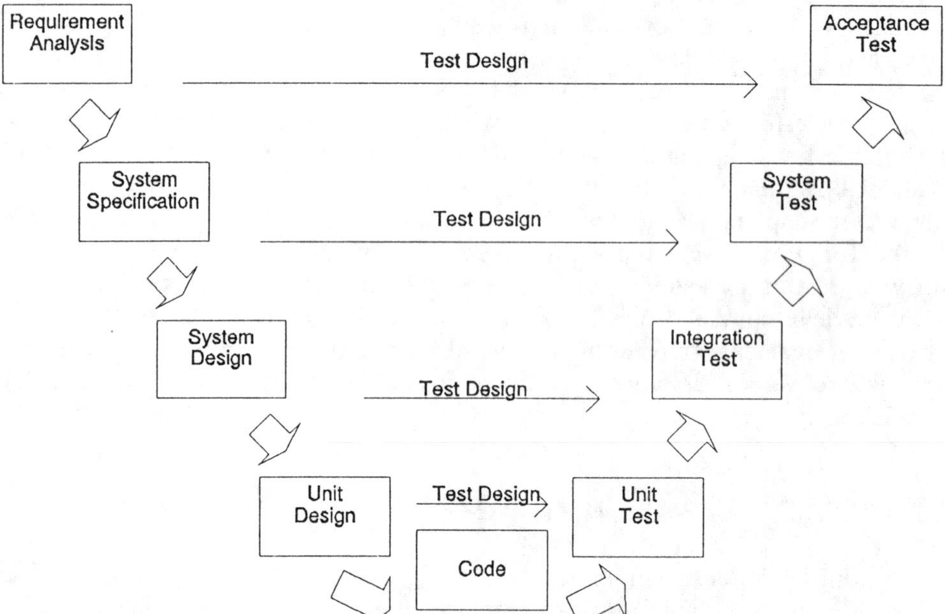

Figure 8.1 The V life cycle model

A cursory examination of the diagram reveals that the V is actually a sequence of phases beginning with requirements analysis and ending with acceptance testing. The apex of the V is the coding phase where a design is set down in some programming language and the program modules compiled. This is an important stage because it is the first time that a previously 'fluid' design concept has become hard reality. Once the code is compiled and run, some machine or system will acquire behaviour which previously did not exist. This is the stage at which the system really 'comes to life'. From this moment on we can add nothing new, nor can we remove errors, without going back into design and producing new or modified code. This is an important watershed because, once code exists, the process of change becomes more difficult and more complex. While the design existed only on paper it was relatively easy to change or correct as necessary, but now life is more difficult. Two important factors are in play. The 'cost to fix' curve, below, shows how the cost to correct an error grows very rapidly so that faults corrected late in the development process cost much more than those found early.

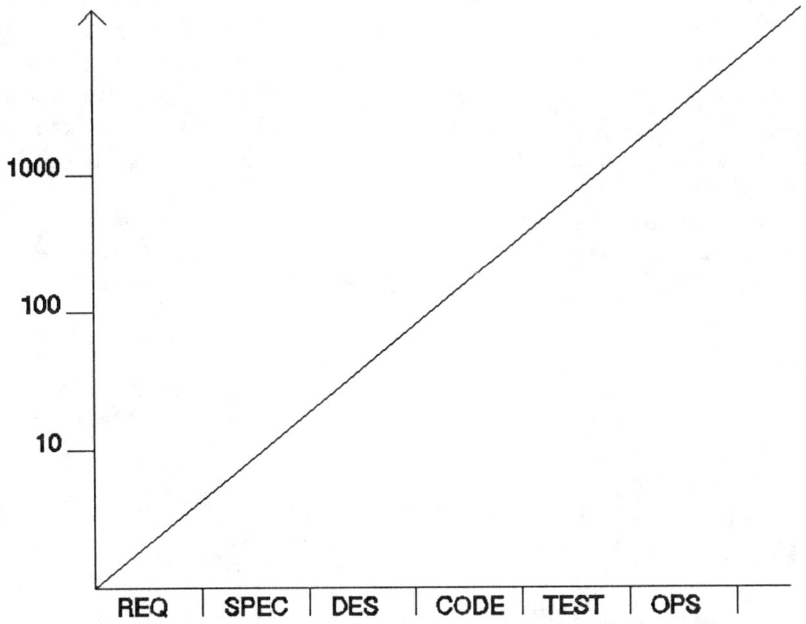

Figure 8.2 The cost of correcting errors

This, combined with the relative fluidity of design early on, is a strong argument for testing early – even before code exists. The most important and cost-effective testing we will ever do will be applied to documents rather than programs. By the time we have built the code we have determined the quality of the product, so we had better be sure the analysis and design were good!

8.1.2 Verification and validation

At this stage, it is important to be clear about the meaning of the terms 'verification' and 'validation', and the relationship between them.

Verification is the term usually applied to tests of a deliverable with respect to its specification, that is, with respect to the deliverable produced at the previous stage. It is essentially a check of correctness rather than value and provides us with confidence in the development process and, in consequence, confidence that the products will be of suitable quality, provided always that we started with a complete and correct specification of what was required. Some people think of this as addressing the question 'Are we building the product correctly?' Validation is the natural partner to verification, in that it is concerned principally with the quality of the eventual product to the customer. It is an activity which attempts to look forward to assess the validity of the design as a solution to the customer's expressed requirements. It is product-oriented where verification is process-oriented, and could be thought of as addressing the question 'Are we building the right product?' There is a third testing component which could also usefully be applied here, and that is a simple internal consistency check. This asks straightforward questions about the state of the deliverables: does it contain the right information; is the quality of the English acceptable; are there any obvious gaps or discrepancies?

We can capture these ideas in a diagram:

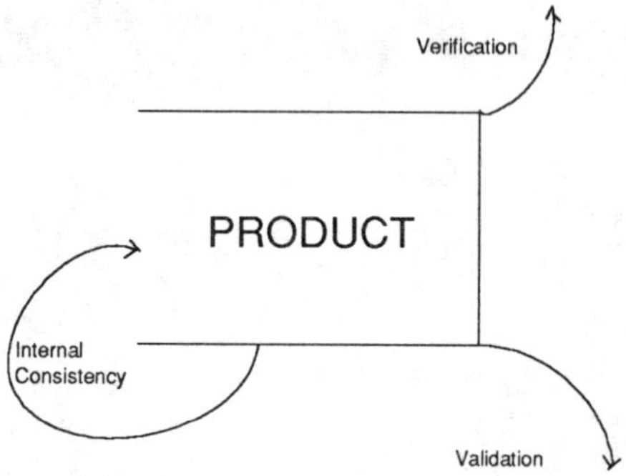

Figure 8.3 Three types of test

This model can now be used as a component in our V life cycle, where we interpret verification, validation and internal consistency in particular ways.

Verification and internal consistency will be in the domain of design reviews, as will some of the validation concerns – those concerned with our ability to tackle the next development step. The last and critical element, though, is the creation of test cases for later execution when the code – and ultimately the system – is built. These serve two vital purposes: first to ensure that test cases are objective, based on the requirement, rather than subjective, based on the products we have constructed; and secondly to test the design itself by our ability to construct real test cases. An inability to create test cases would reflect a fatal flaw, since the information we would have needed to construct test cases is precisely that which we would need to progress successfully the next design step.

8.2 WHEN SHOULD TESTING BEGIN?

The V life cycle exemplifies the primary issues clearly, and illustrates the increasingly well-known phenomenon that 50% of the effort in a typical software development project is committed to testing. Coupled with the 'cost to fix' curve, this phenomenon demands that we test early – as early as possible – and during the requirements analysis phase is not too early! Another interesting feature of the V life cycle is the natural separation of pre-coding activities (which I shall call analysis) and post-coding activities (which I shall call synthesis). Analysis consists of describing a requirement in an increasingly detailed and formal way, transforming an imperfectly understood and informally expressed requirement into a formal (or at least semi-formal) description of the requirement, together with a proposed implementation of it. The synthesis phase then constructs the components of the proposed implementation and synthesises a system from them by a process of structured integration and test. It is important to realise that, in such a process, quality can be added only during the analysis phase; the synthesis phase detects the level of quality but cannot contribute any increase in quality except by a return to the analysis phase. This is, of course, why so much effort is (apparently) devoted to testing; most of it is actually concerned with rework forced by discovering significant errors during testing. The V life cycle actually represents a situation where this problem has been addressed and testing has started early, the result of which is that more effort is devoted to testing but less rework results at the later stages.

8.3 TESTING TECHNIQUES

8.3.1 The psychology of testing

Any discussion of techniques should begin by establishing a need. There must be some motivation for investing time, energy and money in techniques which will require more attention to design and documentation. In the case of testing, the motivation arises from a recognition of the cost of current unstructured approaches as a result of errors remaining undetected. An investigation into causes will readily reveal that programmers are consistently bad at uncovering errors in their own work. This is a natural consequence of their role as constructors of system components. Having constructed a software component to achieve some specified function, the programmer will be testing a product in which he or she believes; if it were otherwise, the component would not have been released for testing. With this 'mind set', the programmer is ill-equipped to uncover errors of his or her own making. As well as labouring under this psychological handicap, the programmer will be constructing test cases from the same understanding of the specification as that which led to the implementation under test; any errors arising from misunderstanding will also be present in the test cases, creating a 'blind spot'. Effective testing requires that the tester (or at least the test designer) is independent of development to avoid the 'blind spots' and to enable a positive testing psychology to be developed.

8.3.2 What is a positive testing psychology?

The idea of a positive psychology arises naturally from our desire for cost-effective testing. If we apply resources to a testing activity, run tests and find no errors, what are we to conclude? There are no errors? Unlikely – our experience argues against this possibility, since customers have an unhappy knack of exposing errors within minutes of taking delivery of software. We can only conclude, therefore, that errors are present but unaccounted for. The same point can be made in another way. Once we begin testing, our product's quality will be enhanced only by discovering errors and correcting them. Any errors which remain undetected cannot be corrected, and a test run which yields no errors has therefore contributed nothing to the quality of the product; hardly a cost-effective performance! What constitutes a positive psychology for testing is an attitude which highly values the discovery of errors, cost-effective testing is testing which reveals errors. Test teams need a psychology which not only believes in the existence of errors but is highly motivated towards uncovering them at the earliest possible opportunity. A team motivated in this way needs a testing 'toolkit', providing techniques which enhance their ability to track down errors in a systematic way.

8.3.3 Structured testing

The idea of structured testing is to provide a systematic approach to tracking errors and to assessing the effectiveness of the testing activity. Structured testing techniques exploit our understanding of the structure of software systems, the nature of software errors, and the observed patterns of error occurrence. The techniques can be split both 'horizontally' and 'vertically': horizontally they can be split into functional and structural categories; vertically they can be differentiated by the stage at which they are applied, as depicted in the V life cycle diagram.

The benefits of structured testing are best understood by reference to Figure 8.4, which represents the idea of an input domain.

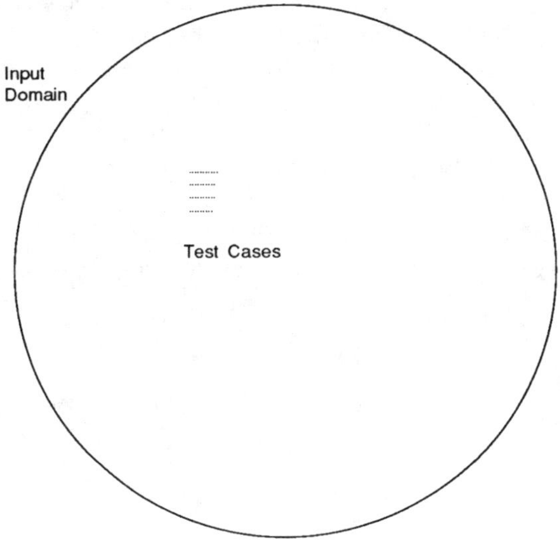

Figure 8.4 Program input domain

The boundary in Figure 8.4 represents the boundary of a set of possible inputs to a program – the input domain. The domain can be assumed to consist of a finite but very large number of individual points, each of which represents some combination of feasible inputs. Any test case applied to this program can be represented by a point in the input domain. An *ad hoc* approach to testing will generate an arbitrary number of points in the input domain, but the cases chosen may cause these points to cluster as shown in Figure 8.4. Although Figure 8.4 depicts a large number of test cases, the value of the tests is very limited because there are large areas of the input domain which remain untested. A structured technique is designed to ensure that test cases are more evenly distributed and that any clustering coincides with areas of the input domain where errors are also believed to cluster. By measuring the total number of points in the input domain and the number of points included in some set of test cases, we can also gain some measure of the 'coverage' of the test cases as a crude but useful estimate of the effectiveness of the testing.

8.4 FUNCTIONAL TESTING TECHNIQUES

Functional testing techniques are often referred to as 'black box testing', based on the analogy of the electronic black box which is assumed to provide a set of functions in a manner which is completely opaque to the average user. Functional testing is based on a simple comparison of input with expected output, based on predictions made from inspection of the program specification. The program is thus tested for correctness with respect to its specification. Easily the most popular of the functional testing techniques is that known as equivalence partitioning.

8.4.1 Equivalence partitioning and boundary value analysis

The basic approach of equivalence partitioning is to split the input domain into a collection of mutually exclusive subdomains, as depicted in Figure 8.5.

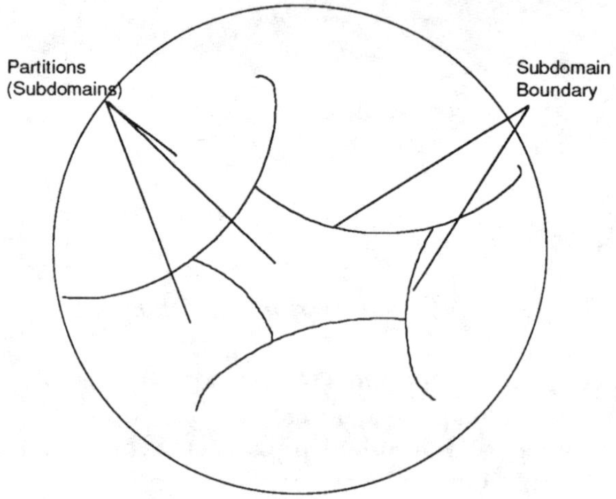

Figure 8.5 Equivalence partitioning

Each of the subdomains represents some collection of points in the input domain which will be handled similarly by the program and will therefore be indistinguishable in terms of the output they produce. Any member of one of these subdomains is therefore representative of the whole subdomain and so one test case can be used to test the program's behaviour with respect to that subdomain. A relatively small collection of test cases can be constructed which will provide complete functional coverage by distributing the points around the key areas of the input domain. Equivalence partitioning is often combined with a technique called Boundary Value Analysis to add even greater value to test cases. The observation of program behaviour reveals that errors tend to cluster near boundaries (loop termination, for example), and tests which create clusters of test cases at boundaries will therefore have a higher than average probability of revealing errors. Fortunately, the equivalence partitioning technique has identified partitions and, in so doing, has highlighted the boundaries between them. It is, therefore, a simple task to add further test cases at and around the boundaries. Figure 8.4 demonstrates how the test cases might be distributed.

A simple example should help to clarify the approach. Imagine a program fragment which converts a positive decimal integer less than 16384 into its binary equivalent; the program is designed to offer helpful error messages for any other input value. We can immediately define three equivalence partitions: less than zero; 1 to 16383; 16384 and greater. For each we can identify correct output by checking the specification. Representative values could be -10, 178, 20345. Boundary values can also be easily identified: -1, 0, 1 will exercise the lower boundary; 16383, 16384, 16385 will exercise the upper boundary. For both boundaries, additional values have been added to explore possible misunderstandings about where the boundary should lie. Figure 8.6 illustrates this example.

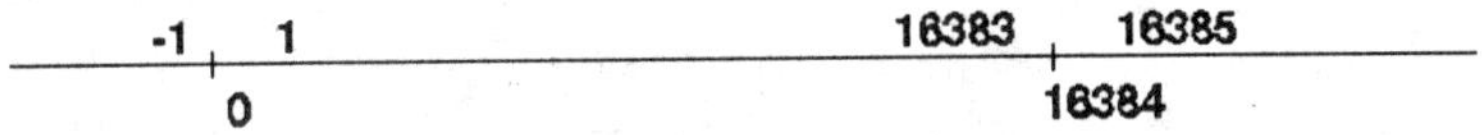

Figure 8.6 Equivalence partitioning and boundary value analysis example

8.4.2 Other functional testing techniques

Other functional techniques include cause-effect graphing, which simplifies analysis of complex decision logic in the specification (e.g. social security benefit payment rules) and enables decision tables to be constructed from which test cases can be easily derived; syntax-directed testing, which creates a structure for testing programs designed to handle input conforming to arbitrarily complex rules (e.g. telephone exchanges); and state-transition testing, which simplifies testing of programs designed to work by switching between well-defined states according to inputs received.

8.5 STRUCTURAL TESTING TECHNIQUES

Structural testing techniques are sometimes called 'white box testing' as a natural contrast to 'black box testing'. The nature of structural testing is clearly complementary to that of functional testing, in that structural testing concerns itself with internal structure rather than function. There are two related purposes in applying structural testing: the first is to construct additional test cases to supplement functional testing; the second to measure the effectiveness of testing. The use of tools is almost an essential component of a structural testing approach, principally because the sheer volume of data to be handled would otherwise be beyond our ability, but manual techniques do exist for relatively simple programs.

8.5.1 Static and dynamic analysis

We can consider structural testing for test effectiveness measurement to comprise two phases: static analysis and dynamic analysis. Static analysis is concerned with discovering the structural components of a program and recording the information for later use in dynamic analysis. Much can be learned directly from static analysis, such as the number of paths through a program, the number and type of variables declared and used and the relationships between them, the calling structure of subprograms, and many other characteristics which may point to particular dynamic behaviour. Dynamic analysis relates to structural measurements made while the program is running, using the static analysis outputs to identify the structural elements which are of interest. Dynamic analysis necessarily involves modification of programs to incorporate code which detects entry to and exit from particular structural components, a technique known as instrumentation. Measurement of test effectiveness is currently limited to three standard test effectiveness ratios (TERs), known as TER1, TER2 and TER3. TER1 is defined as statement coverage – it measures the number of statements covered by a particular test case (or suite of test cases) and reports the simple ratio of statements covered to total statements. Branch coverage is measured by TER2 – a similar measure but related to program branches (decisions). TER3 refers to LCSAJ coverage, where LCSAJ abbreviates Linear Code Sequence and Jump – best thought of as a path fragment. An LCSAJ is not a complete path through a program, but is a particular kind of subpath comprising a linear sequence (no jumps) followed by a jump. LCSAJs have the merit of being relatively easy to define, detect and measure but they do not constitute a true measure of path coverage. Indeed, test effectiveness does not yet extend to decision condition coverage (taking account of possible conditions at a branch controlled by more than one logical expression) and therefore also not to decision condition combination coverage (taking account of the possible condition combinations at a branch controlled by more than one logical expression). Test Effectiveness Testing is a technique still in its infancy but of immense importance for the future.

In all of these cases, the data on which the measures are based is extracted during static analysis and measured during dynamic analysis. Using test effectiveness ratios is one way of determining the 'quality' of functional tests, using dynamic analysis during the test runs to measure achieved coverage. Typically, well-structured functional tests will achieve 100% coverage against TER1 and TER2 but will fall to perhaps 40% for TER3 – a stark reminder that even 'well-tested' software may go to its intended users with over half of its code unexplored! We may choose to extend coverage by adding a selection of structurally defined tests to cover areas of the program shown by dynamic analysis not to have been exercised adequately or at all.

One further advantage of test effectiveness testing lies in the measurability of effectiveness via the TERs. What can be reliably measured can also be specified and predicted, and so specification of a required level of test effectiveness can form part of the overall specification of the required quality characteristics of a system. As well as requiring satisfactory testing against an agreed acceptance test schedule, we could define a minimum acceptable level for each of the three TERs so that we achieve a product with known functional characteristics and which has been tested to an agreed level of both functional and structural coverage. A similar advantage can be gained in the management of testing. Determination of the time, cost and resource requirements of testing is made easier by quantitatively defining the test regime. Equally important, when delays or overspends force hard decisions about the extent of testing still achievable, some understanding of the value of testing so far completed and the risks of terminating testing before the test plan has been fully accomplished is essential to making rational and economically justifiable decisions.

8.5.2 Basis test set

The construction of structural test cases is, in effect, a subset of test effectiveness testing and uses the output of static analysis to identify structural elements on which to base test cases. A simple technique suitable for manual construction of test cases in relatively small programs will also serve to outline the basic technique for constructing test cases.

The technique, known as the basis test set method, relies on the construction of a program control flowgraph which embodies all the control information but excludes all other detail; an example is shown in Figure 8.7.

```
Min := 9999;
Max := 0;
Read(Item);
N := 1;
while Item < > eof and N < = 100 do
        if Item > = 0 and Item < = 9999 then
                if Item < = Min then
                        Min : = Item
                endif;
                if Item > Max then
                        Max := Item
                endif;
        endif;
                Read(Item);
        N : = N + 1;
enddo;
Print("Min is ",Min,', and Max is ',Max);
```

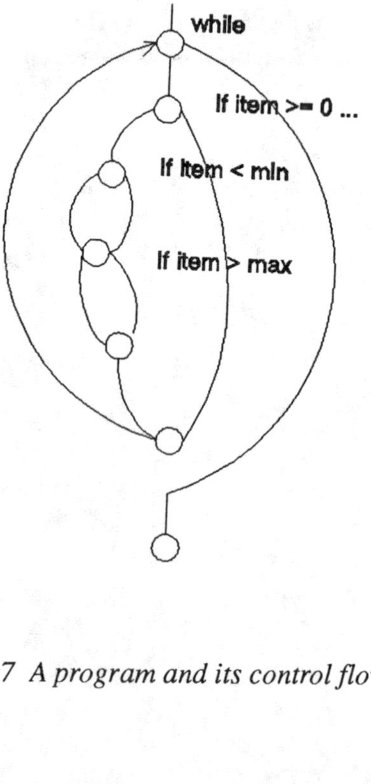

Figure 8.7 A program and its control flowgraph

Having constructed the flowgraph, we can calculate the McCabe complexity metric – a measure of the number of decisions in a program. The complexity metric can be determined easily by counting the number of enclosed regions in the flowgraph and adding one. This simple metric has enormous value because it identifies the **maximum** number of independent test paths in a program and thus provides an upper bound on the number of test cases required for basis path coverage. The actual number of test paths could be smaller than the complexity metric if the structure of the program causes some paths to be dependent on others so that data which forces control down one path will also cause another path to be traversed; under these conditions, where dependent paths exist, the maximum number of test cases will be smaller than the theoretical limit. The maximum in any specific case is easily determined because dependence is revealed when an attempt is made to construct actual test cases. The next step is to identify each individual path on the flowgraph (it is actually easier to produce a set of flowgraphs and mark one path on each copy) and then to calculate from the specification the test data required to force the program down each of the paths.

8.6 WHAT RESOURCES ARE NEEDED?

Early testing means early resources, and acceptance testing will require resources right up to the end of the project. In the early phases, effort is needed to conduct reviews and inspections and to prepare test definitions; later, effort will be needed for unit testing, integration testing, system testing and acceptance tests. Where do all these resources come from? Unquestionably, some resource will need to be dedicated to testing throughout the project as the core of the testing team and the chief source of testing knowledge and skill. This core team can then be supplemented by adding different skills at different times. In the early stages, when reviews predominate, the constituency of review teams will change as the development proceeds. At the very early stages, users may be able to make the most important contribution, then business and systems analysts will come to the fore, followed in turn by operations staff and designers. Throughout, the dedicated testing resource will be 'conducting', ensuring that review panels are properly constituted, that reviews happen on schedule, and that rework is followed up. In parallel, test definitions will be drafted, reviewed, and approved in preparation for code testing. Once code is written and code testing begins, it should be possible to release design and implementation resources to supplement the test team and, in so doing, provide invaluable design background during code testing.

8.6.1 The independent test team

Overall, the need is for a small dedicated test team to be in place throughout the project with a responsibility for defining a test strategy, identifying phased resource requirements, defining test cases, scheduling test activities and maintaining complete records. While this will undoubtedly increase the resource requirement for testing in most companies, the increased resource will be met partially by resource savings elsewhere (by reducing late rework, for example) and partially by a reduction in the number of errors which reach the customer (and are therefore the most expensive to correct). As well as being dedicated to testing, the test team should remain independent the development activity and the development team.

8.7 TESTING STRATEGY AND QUALITY ASSURANCE

Having a set of techniques is essential as a starting point, but some consideration must also be given to where they can be employed. The V life cycle identifies four stages of testing: unit testing, where individual programs are tested; integration testing, where individual programs are integrated into larger components and tested at that level; system testing, where the entire system is tested; acceptance testing, where conformance to the requirements is confirmed. In unit testing, function may be partial and possibly not visible in terms of easily measured inputs and outputs, in which case structural testing is required; otherwise functional testing is to be preferred. At the integration stage, functional testing of components will be the predominant method, though some structural testing at the component level (testing system structure rather than program structure) will also be required. At the system test level, functional testing will ensure that the system performs to its functional specification, but other tests may be required to determine non-functional features such as performance, reliability, and ease of use – these should be based on criteria agreed at the requirements stage. The overall strategy should be embodied in a test plan supported by suitable test procedures and test case designs.

What has all this testing effort contributed to quality? A great deal. As well as providing confidence in the quality of the finished product, the creation of an environment in which testing is integrated with development will also enhance the development activity by unearthing errors earlier, improving visibility of the process and providing measurable testing criteria. At the management level, the testing disciplines have made decisions on testing resources, time-scales and effectiveness more quantifiable and created an economic basis for discussion of the value of alternative testing approaches. While testing cannot be the whole of quality assurance, it is an indispensable component. Correctly used, it makes software development more visible, more manageable and less prone to technical risks.

8.8 PRACTICAL TEST PLANNING AND DESIGN

All the components are now available; all that remains is to use them to construct a practical test strategy.

The testing process starts at requirements analysis, where a table of test scenarios is constructed to reflect a user-centred view of the requirement. A scenario represents a user task which the computer system is designed to assist. The scenario may include clerical activities, human decisions, and one or more computer system requirements. If this set of scenarios is prioritised, we obtain a prioritised table of requirements and combinations of requirements as a basis for test planning. At this stage it is also essential to identify acceptance criteria and to make individual requirements measurable. As the development proceeds to logical design we define the functions associated with each requirement, and the scenario table is expanded accordingly. At physical design we add the actual program and data elements associated with each function, which helps with implementation planning and is the basis of integration planning. When individual programs are specified, the scenario table is complete and we have a list of the most important candidates for structural testing. Now economics take over and help to define the extent and level of structural testing, the nature of integration testing and the scope of system testing.

We can visualise this as a process of building test cases from a strategy defined at requirements so that, at every level of design and test, the testing exercise is directly related to the emerging design.

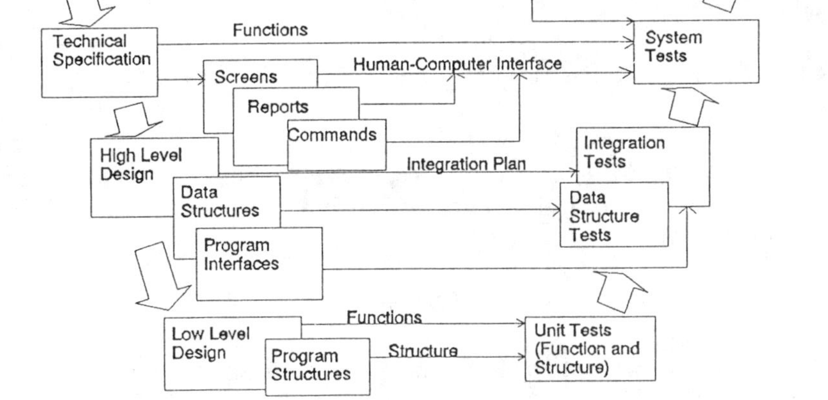

Figure 8.8 Tests built with the design

At the requirements phase, the scenario table is built to provide an overall structure for tests based on the users' perception of the most important and most urgent functions and attributes, and representing a systemic view of the system in its operational environment. As the design proceeds, progressively more detailed information becomes available to fill in the detail of each test. Eventually, the scenarios will generate 'routes' through the program and data structures and suggest the prime candidates for detailed structural testing. In the words of the old saying, 'well begun is half done'; all the difficult decisions about what and how to test at the detailed level are resolved by referring everything to the users' own criteria.

BIBLIOGRAPHY

The bibliography which follows includes all those publications which could form references, but the ideas are so widely accepted that it would be impossible to positively assert the origin of any particular idea. I am indebted to all of the authors below and acknowledge that any insights I may have had stem from their initial guidance.

Beizer, B. 1983. *Software Testing Techniques*. Van Nostrand Reinhold.

Beizer, B. 1984. *Software System Testing and Quality Assurance*. Van Nostrand Reinhold.

Graham, D. A Standard for Software Component Testing, for the British Computer Society Specialist Group in Software Testing. Available from Quentin Computer Consultants, 73 West Road, Shoeburyness, Essex SS3 9DT.

Hetzel, W. *1988. The Complete Guide to Software Testing*, 2nd edn. QED Information Sciences Inc.

Howden, W.E. 1987. *Functional Program Testing and Analysis*. McGraw-Hill.

Kaner, Cem *Testing Computer Software.* TAB Professional and Reference Books.9 Roper, M. and N Parrington 1989, *Understanding Software Testing*. Ellis Horwood.

Myers, G.J. 1979. *The Art of Software Testing* . Wiley.

Perry, W.E. 1988. *A Structured Approach to Systems Testing*, 2nd edn. QED Information Sciences Inc.

Roper, M., and N Parrington 1989. *Understanding Software Testing* Ellis Horwood.

9 Effective Test Planning: Knowing When to Stop

Elliott Manley
Elliott Manley Associates

The first step in fulfilling system objectives is to understand exactly what those objectives are. The purpose of requirements analysis is to understand the business that the system will have to support. This is done by identifying and recording the objectives of the business and by formulating parallel objectives for the system.

The purpose of acceptance testing is to measure the system's success in meeting those objectives.

In order for that measurement to be meaningful, it is necessary for the system objectives to be defined in very precise detail and for decisions to have been taken about what constitutes success or failure in each case. In order to build the tests, examples of every case must be constructed.

All these activities are usually carried out during the phase of development known as acceptance test planning – one of the last activities in the typical development cycle. Yet if the system objectives have been properly understood, as is the declared intent of requirements analysis, then all these activities can be performed as part of that early process.

Test planning, then, is merely the detailing, metrication and instantiation of system objectives. Acceptance test plans are a natural product of requirements analysis. In the same way, system test plans are a natural product of system design; and unit tests of programme design.

Adopting this approach has four important consequences:

- The act of documenting a test plan as part of the design process tests the analyst's understanding of the objectives. It is clear that if an acceptance test plan cannot be developed during or immediately after requirements analysis, then the objectives have not been understood.
- It has been well documented (e.g. in Myers) that effective testers set out to add value to a system by finding and eliminating errors. These people are distinguished from ineffective testers who regard the exercise as 'proving the correctness of the software' and are often psychologically incapable of discovering errors. The former attitude is clearly the one to be encouraged, and if it is adopted by analysts early in development then

many potential errors are eliminated before they have a chance to occur.

- The material product of any stage of analysis is a document which will form the working basis for the next stage. If this document contains precisely defined success criteria then misunderstandings and wasted effort can be avoided and the product can be built to meet those criteria.
- All too often, in the author's experience, testers who plan their tests after the system has been built are greatly influenced by what they know the system to do, rather than what it is supposed to do. This is a subtler form of 'proving the correctness of the software'. Clearly, this pitfall is avoided by planning tests in the light of objectives and not in the light of the system.

With regard to the third point above, it can be argued that telling the designers how a system will be tested will create the risk that they will build a system 'just to pass the tests' but which may not work in general. If the specification includes test data (i.e. the product of instantiation) then this argument would indeed hold. This is one of the reasons why the author does not in fact advocate developing **test data** (as distinct from test conditions) at an early stage. Another is that the inevitably iterative nature of software development could necessitate huge amounts of rework on the data. A third reason is that until the system design has been specified in detail it is often impractical to document the data. However, building a system which meets specified **test conditions** in specified **test paths** will give exactly the desired result – a system that meets its success criteria, i.e. a system that works. This is in keeping with the basic philosophy of quality management: 'Do it right first time'.

The challenge of functional testing is the challenge of enumerating possibilities. At the level of, say, a hardware logic gate, it is a simple matter to list all the possible inputs and outputs. As one moves up through machine instructions to program statements to transaction designs to business function descriptions, such enumeration becomes increasingly difficult and increasingly reliant on business knowledge, common-sense, experience, intuition, and creativity.

The first problem is to decide where the boundaries of the function lie – in other words, to get the 'chunking' right. This same problem is addressed by many top-down structured analysis techniques, e.g. data flow diagrams (DFDs) and functional hierarchies. A solution is to use the products of such analysis techniques directly. This means defining a 'function' as whatever is an elementary process *at the current stage of design*. For example, acceptance tests might be based on logical processes described in a level 3 DFD.

The next problem is to produce a complete set of valid, invalid, and boundary conditions for each function. While the objective many be to list everything the system should do and everything it should not do, it is as well to acknowledge that it is impossible ever to complete the list. This is where the subjective qualities listed above must be used to the full, together with checklists of common errors relevant to the type of function being considered. Common sense and experience are particularly important in developing invalid or error conditions where the invalidities should be restricted to what the system 'just might do'.

By this stage the analyst has described success/failure criteria for numerous system components. It still remains to consider the interaction of those components. This requires structural analysis.

Historically, structural testing has been restricted to flow-of-control graphs, and hence to unit testing. Many modern development techniques result in digraphs of various forms. These allow the possibility of structural testing at system test and even acceptance test because structural analysis can be performed on any digraph.

All analytical techniques known to the author model one or more of the following to different degrees: function, data, and sequence. DFDs, for example, focus on function, although they also model data to a certain extent. In theory they do not model sequence, but in practice it is often implied in the progress of information through the processes. Entity/Relationship Diagrams (ERDs), on the other hand, focus exclusively on data while Flow Charts and Functional Dependency Diagrams deal principally with sequence. Logical Access Maps (LAMs) and Entity Life Histories (ELHs) both bring all three aspects together. LAMs do so from the point of view of a transaction which requires data in a particular sequence. ELHs consider how data is transformed by a sequence of functions.

This model for categorising analysis techniques is presented as a tool to help identify the kinds of tests that can be generated from each technique. In passing it is worth noting that the model can also be used to evaluate the completeness of structured development methods.

Techniques that focus on function can clearly be used to generate functional tests. Techniques which focus on data are a less rich source for the test planner but, to the extent that they encapsulate rules about data relationships and integrity, they can also be used to generate 'functional' tests. Any technique which models any element of sequence, logical dependency, or time dependency is capable of being transformed into a digraph. It is necessarily true that such techniques model interaction among system components and hence it is valid, possible, and wise to use structural analysis techniques to generate sequences of functional tests.

The problem of structural testing is that of controlling the combinatoric explosion. How do we go about testing all the paths through a digraph? It is immediately obvious that any digraph which contains a loop also contains an infinite number of distinct paths. What is meant by 'completeness' in this context?

There have been a number of attempts to redefine the problem so that it becomes a finite one. The most popular of these is a restriction to 0, 1 or 2 on the number of permitted iterations of a loop (Howden, 1986). This approach has always struck the present author as arbitrary and unrealistic.

'Structured Basis Testing' (SBT), a technique due to McCabe (1976), is another approach. Despite enthusiastic support from Perry (1988) among others, SBT has never really gained popularity. This is surprising on two counts: firstly, the technique is first described in McCabe's paper on cyclomatic complexity which has had so much influence in the fifteen years since its publication and continues to do so despite Sheppard's highly effective critique in 1988, and secondly because remarkable power has been claimed for the technique. It is claimed that the cyclomatic complexity of a graph is the same as the number of paths through that graph which are both necessary and sufficient to test it completely. Perry says 'the theorem ellipsis establishes that for a programme of complexity 5, a sixth, seventh, eighth ellipsis path in a fundamental sense is redundant. ...Testing beyond v independent paths is redundantly exercising linear combinations of basis paths.' (Perry 1988). (Where v is the cyclomatic complexity.)

Sadly, the 'theorem' establishes no such thing. The technique relies on numbering the arcs of a graph and describing any path through the graph as a vector where the nth component is the number of times the path passes through arc n. From this model a set of basis vectors can be derived which can be linearly combined to form any valid vector. The number of such basis vectors is equal to the valency or cyclomatic complexity of the graph. The basis vectors are then translated back into 'basis paths', which in some sense are supposed to encapsulate all possible paths. The drawback is that method of producing vectors from paths models only the number of times each is traversed. It does not model the sequence of execution, surely the most vital characteristic of a path!

Also the mathematics requires the existence of negative test paths!

Anyone using SBT and believing they have tested the essence of every possibility in their program is dangerously deceived. In fact, SBT does genuinely offer one guarantee: testing will be 'branch complete', i.e. every arc in the graph will be covered. But as a means of achieving this, SBT is cumbersome and inefficient.

The author's preferred approach to controlling the combinatoric explosion is to acknowledge that structural tests can never be complete in an absolute sense but to use a scale of increasing 'levels of completeness' which an be tuned as appropriate. (Remember also that it is functional test conditions which are being combined to create 'structural' paths, and it was shown above that functional tests are themselves inherently incomplete.)

A set of test paths is said to be complete to S_n if it is possible to select any n successive nodes at random and be sure that that sequence of nodes is included in at least one of the test paths.

The S_n notation is used to indicate 'sequence-bounded' paths. The approach of limiting the number of iterations of a loop described (and criticised) above also fits into the general schema of 'levels of completeness'. Such 'iteration-bounded' paths are indicated by I_n where n is the maximum number of times any one 'backward-facing' arc is traversed.

Applying the sequence-bounded approach to a flow chart in order to generate a program test, it can be seen that

$S_1 \equiv$ 'statement complete'.
$S_2 \equiv$ 'branch complete'.

If the flow chart contains at least one loop then

$S_\infty \equiv$ 'path complete'.

Clearly, any integer value of n can be selected. For values of n up to about 3, the paths can readily be derived by hand. For higher values of n, automated assistance is required.

It is also clear that for all k: $S_k \leq S_{k+1}$ and $I_k \leq I_{k+1}$ and that $S_2 \leq I_1$.

To apply this or any other structural approach to system or acceptance testing generated from structured analysis, it is first necessary to decide what the nodes of the digraph are going to mean. This should be carefully considered in each case, but the author has successfully followed this general guideline: each elementary system function is represented by two nodes, one for valid conditions relating to that function, the other for invalid and error conditions. Especially in system test planning it is sometimes necessary to distinguish further between logical and physical invalidities. Next, any node with exactly one entry and one exit arc is merged with the node sequentially following it. In this way, each node represents not one test condition but a class of test conditions which are structurally equivalent.

The arcs of the digraph which sequence the condition classes are of course determined by the sequence, flow of control, or dependency inherent in the original model.

The process of generating the test paths from the digraph can be carried out independently from the process of devising functional test conditions. Once the functional conditions are sorted into their condition classes it is simple to correlate the two lists. It is likely to be necessary both to generate extra functional tests to fill all the 'slots' in the test paths and to create one or two extra test paths to accommodate 'stray' test conditions.

If test paths are constructed by hand it is fairly easy to keep the total number of conditions low. The problem of finding the minimum possible total number of test conditions is an example of the unsolved 'travelling salesman' problem. While it is advisable to keep the number low, the inherent mismatch between the two lists and the consequent adjustments means that there is little practical value in trying to minimise the number. If optimisation does prove to be a problem in incorporating the process into a CASE tool, it is likely that simulated annealing would be a fruitful approach to take.

The remaining question is which 'level of completeness' to select in a given circumstance? Because there is such wide variation in the potential uses for this technique, it is really only useful to point out that calibration is required in each case. As a rule-of-thumb, on a medium risk commercial project the author suggests carrying out system and acceptance tests at S_2 and unit tests at S_3. Modules which will be reused, for example library sub-routines, should be tested to S_4. Critical components should be system tested at S_3 and unit tested at S_4.

As a final note, one of the benefits claimed for cyclomatic complexity (and other complexity metrics) is that they yield estimates of the testing effort which the system will require. Using the 'levels of completeness' process during analysis gives an exact count of the number of tests to be run and thus a very sound basis for estimating required effort while avoiding controversial measurements of 'complexity'.

REFERENCES

Howden, W. 1986. *Functional Program Testing and Analysis*. McGraw-Hill.

McCabe, T.J. 1976. A Complexity Measure, *IEEE Transactions on Software Engineering*, **2** (4), pp. 308–20.

Myers, G.J. 1979. *The Art of Software Testing* Wiley.

Perry, W.E. 19888. *A Structured Approach to Systems Testing* 2nd edn. QED Information Sciences.

Shepperd, M. 1988. A Critique of Cyclomatic Complexity as a Software Metric. *Software Engineering Journal*, March, pp. 30–6.

10 A Structural Approach to Improving the Testing Process

Hélène Lassalle
Verilog

10.1 INTRODUCTION

The consequences of software failures can be of varying severity. Incorrect management of the traffic lights of a city can produce enormous traffic jams, which generates annoyance and loss of time for all the drivers. Bad management of the trajectory of a satellite can cause it to explode, destroying expensive equipment. An unreliable encryption program for magnetic credit cards can generate problems of integrity. An unsafe braking system in a train or in the underground can be disastrous and result in loss of lives. Any complex system presents a risk of failure. The question is: could the risks be mastered and limited?

The quality of software (for the same reason as hardware) is no longer considered as a luxury but as a necessity. The objectives for software development are now also defined in terms of correctness, reliability, integrity, efficiency and maintainability.

A strategy must be defined in order to reach these objectives. The right choice of rules, methods, techniques will limit the risk of failure.

The first steps of the software life cycle are the construction of the software and of its quality. The next steps are testing and validation. One of their goals is the prevention of non-quality.

A lack of quality can have unacceptable consequences. But the cost of a high-level quality is important.

That means that as soon as the project begins it is necessary to define the level of quality required. And then the adequate means can be determined and expressed for the various steps of the life cycle.

10.2 TESTING ACTIVITY THROUGHOUT THE LIFE CYCLE

The construction of the software includes the construction of its quality. This corresponds to the first phases of the software life cycle: specification, general design, detailed design, and coding.

The testing activity is also prepared during these phases through documents which will be used as reference for the verification of the software.

Validation is the determination of the correctness of the final software with respect to the user needs and requirements.

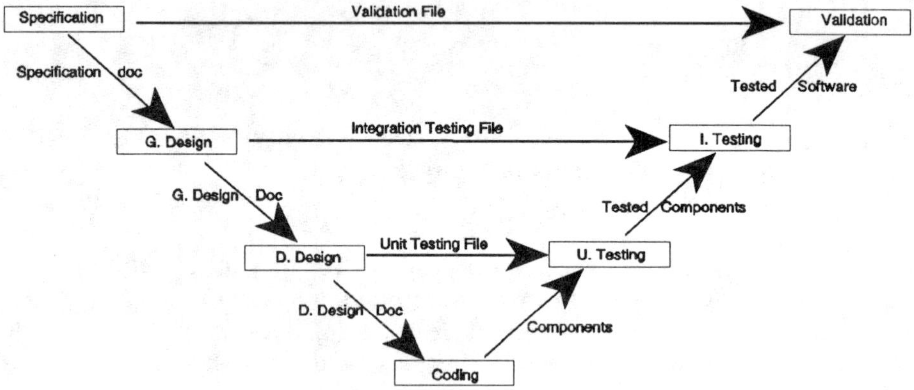

Figure 10.1 Testing activity throughout the life cycle

During the **specification phase** a validation file is produced. It contains a description of the test objectives in terms of functions, conformity, robustness, performance, and integrity.

Testing is the examination of the behaviour of the software by executing it on sample data sets. It consists in the execution of the software, or part of it, in order to identify the differences between expected results and achieved results.

During the **general design phase** an integration testing file is produced. It describes the method chosen for the integration of the various components of the software. Several methods exist. The 'big-bang' is the integration of all the components at once. The 'bottom-up' is a progressive integration of the components into aggregates up to the complete software. Test harnesses are needed at each step. The 'top-down' is realised through top-level skeleton tests with dummy stubs, and then lower-level tests down to complete integration. Finally, there is a 'mixed' method between 'bottom-up' and 'top-down'.

The test objectives are defined as functions of each integration aggregate and as relationships between components. The test techniques are also chosen in order to reach these objectives.

During the **detailed design phase** a unit testing file is defined. It is achieved during the **coding phase.** Its purpose is to specify how each component has to be tested. It details the drivers and stubs necessary for each component.

The test objectives are to check the functions of the component and its algorithm to ensure completeness and no extra code.

The inputs of the **unit testing phase** are the software components and the unit testing file. For each component the appropriate test environment is built and the input data are chosen in order to achieve the objectives defined in the unit testing file.

After execution, the results are evaluated (functional and structural verification).

The inputs of the **integration testing phase** are the individually tested software components and the integration testing file. The integration plan is applied according to the recommended integration method. For each integration aggregate the test environment is built and tests are executed.

The evaluation of the results is also a functional and structural verification.

The need appears clearly for two testing strategies: functional testing and structural testing.

10.3 TESTING METHODS AND TECHNIQUES

Functional testing aims at checking that the tested element conforms to the behaviour described in the testing file. Nominal input values must yield nominal output values under normal conditions.

Robustness testing has an equivalent purpose for abnormal conditions.

Both are executed through a 'black box' strategy. The difficulty is to choose the right input data sets in order to guarantee the best coverage of the functional test. Several techniques have been developed to help this selection, including:

- equivalence partitioning: division of the input data space into classes so that all the elements of a class generate equivalent software behaviour;
- boundary values analysis: similar approach but with an analysis oriented towards the class bounds. This analysis can also concern the output data;
- syntactic derivation: approach applicable if the input data can be described through a syntactic form. Then input data can be derived from this syntax;
- finite state machine: system description into states that can be observed and transitions between states;
- cause-effect graphing: definition of a graph showing the relationships between an input condition (cause) and the corresponding output condition or system transformation (effect).

Functional testing contributes to improving the quality of the service.

Structural testing aims at proving that the internal structure of the tested element conforms to its requirements. Each code sequence has to be executed through a test case.

This is a 'white box' strategy. The internal structure of a software is composed of several aspects, including:

– control-flow analysis: study of the execution sequence inside a component
– data-flow analysis: study of data modification during execution
– call-graph analysis: study of the execution of calls between components.

Structural testing contributes to improving the quality of the software product.

10.4 INDUSTRIAL MASTERY OF THE TESTING ACTIVITY

The first important step is to define adequate test objectives.

Exhaustive testing is almost always impossible. The combination of input data values is usually infinite. And even when exhaustive testing can be performed it is often economically prohibitive.

Analysis of the consequences of software failure allows the definition of required reliability. This required reliability can be translated into qualitative and quantitative objectives, taking into account the available means and deadlines.

The satisfaction of qualitative objectives can only be appreciated by an expert and this appreciation is inevitably subjective. Obviously, to master the testing activity it is necessary to define quantitative objectives as soon as possible.

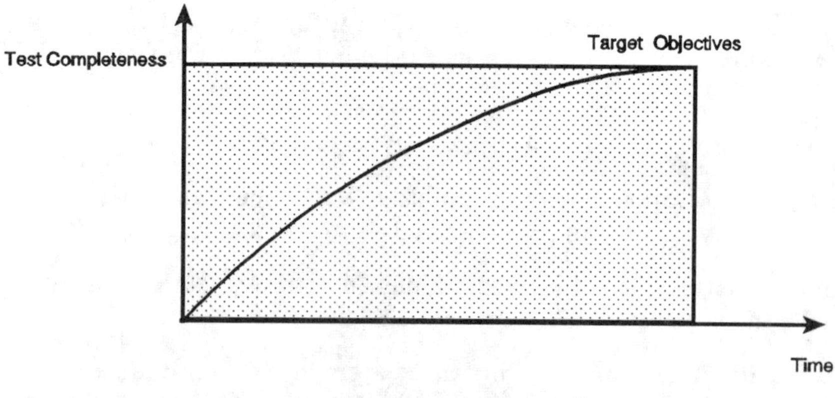

Figure 10.2

In order to control the progress of the test we need to be able to measure time and test completeness. Coverage measurement is a way of verifying that we are continually moving towards the objectives.

The decision to stop the testing activity will be motivated by the time available, the appreciation of qualitative objectives, but also by the guarantee through measurements of acceptable coverage levels.

The coverage measurement is expressed by a ratio.

$$\text{ratio} = \frac{\text{number of tested objects}}{\text{number of objects to be tested}}$$

Figure 10.3

The **structural testing** approach allows the definition of realistic objects for measurement.

At the component level, logical structure is tested through a control-flow analysis. The objects used for coverage measurement are:

– the block of instructions (IB), which is a sequence of statements (execution of the first statement leads to execution of the last one)

– the decision to decision path (DDP), which is a sequence of nodes in the control graph:

- starting at the component entry point or at a decision node
- terminating by the component exit point or by a decision node
- with no decision node in between

– the linear code sequence and jump (LCSAJ), which is a sequence of nodes in the control graph:

- starting at the component entry point or at the target of a jump
- terminating by the component exit point or by the target of a jump
- with no jump in between.

(A jump is a control of transfer causing a break in the read sequence.)

Example: Let's take a simple component with the following pseudo-code.

```
1     begin
2       if (N>=1) then
3           for I = 1 to N
         .
         .
4          ----
         .
         .
5           end for
6       end if
7     end
```

The associated control graph is:

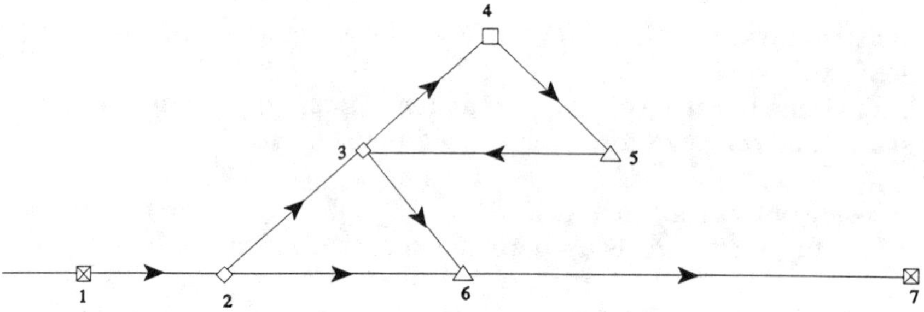

A functional approach could lead us to the following tests: test 1 (N=1), test 2 (N=0), test 3 (N=2).

Let's identify the block of instructions (IB) and their coverage ratio.

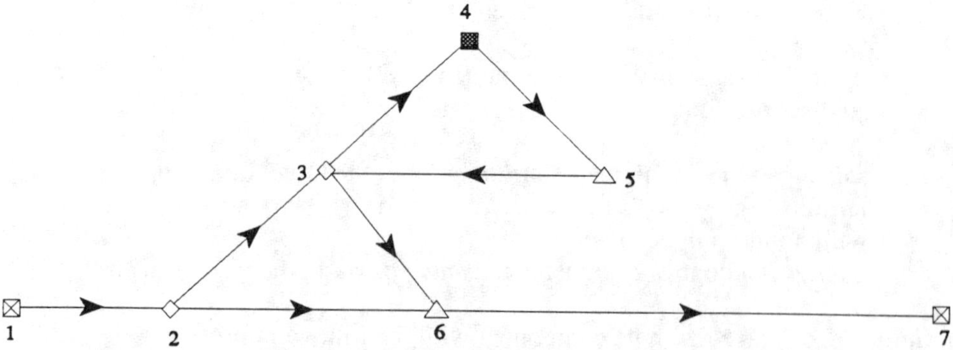

There is only one IB (the fourth node). It is executed during test 1 and test 3, not during test 2.

The IB coverage rate is then:

for test 1 100%
for test 2 0%
for test 3 100%

One test leads to 100%.
Let's consider now the decision to decision paths (DDP).

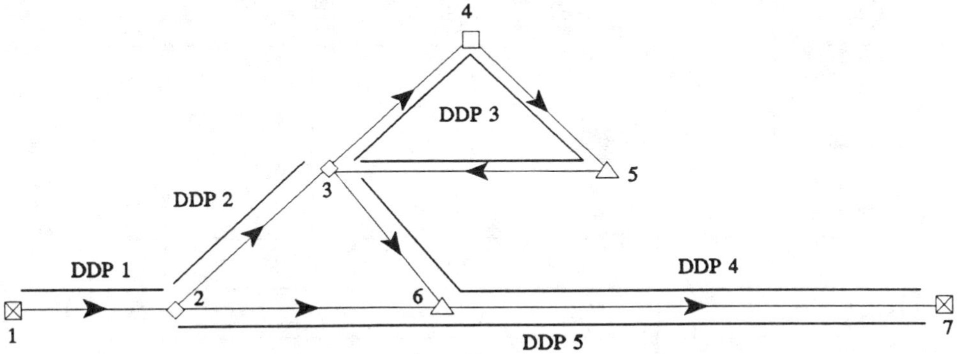

We identify 5 DDP. Their coverage during the test execution is:

test	executed DPP	coverage rate
1:N=1	1, 2, 3, 4	80%
2:N=0	1, 5	40%
3:N=2	1, 2, 3, 4	80%

The cumulative ratio of two tests (test 1 and test 2) leads to 100%. The DDP measurement allows us to verify in this example the execution of the empty ELSE part of the IF statement.

The identification of the linear code sequence and jump (LCSAJ) leads to 6 objects:

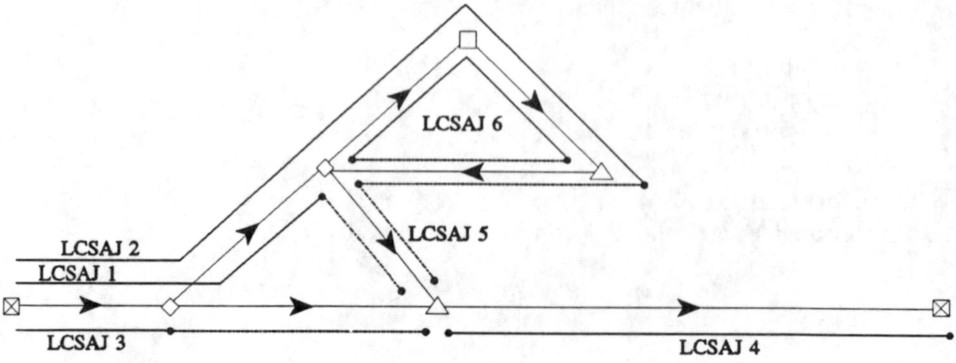

Test coverage during test executions is:

test	executed DPP	coverage rate
1:N=1	2, 5, 4	50%
2:N=0	3, 4	33.33%
3:N=2	2, 5, 6, 4	66.66%

The cumulative ratio after 3 test cases is 83.33%. We did not succeed in the execution of LCSAJ 1. The reason is that it is impossible due to the conditions applied to value of N. The IF statement is unnecessary.

As shown in this example, these three objects lead to three levels of severity. This allows us to balance the test effort according to the required reliability.

At the architectural level, the call structure is tested through the following object:

– the procedure to procedure path (PPP), which is a path joining two nodes of the call graph; it represents a call between two components.

The coverage measurement of PPP allows us to verify the completeness of structural testing during the test integration phase.

We are now able to measure the efficiency of the executed tests. We can then recommend a natural and pragmatic strategy for the testing:

– begin by defining functional tests based on the specification
– measure their coverage rate with the appropriate objects

– as soon as the coverage rate levels out, define complementary structural tests.

The functional and structural approaches are complementary. Their combination allows more completeness in an optimised time.

Examples: Testing a FORTRAN 77 compiler (= 65,000 lines of code).

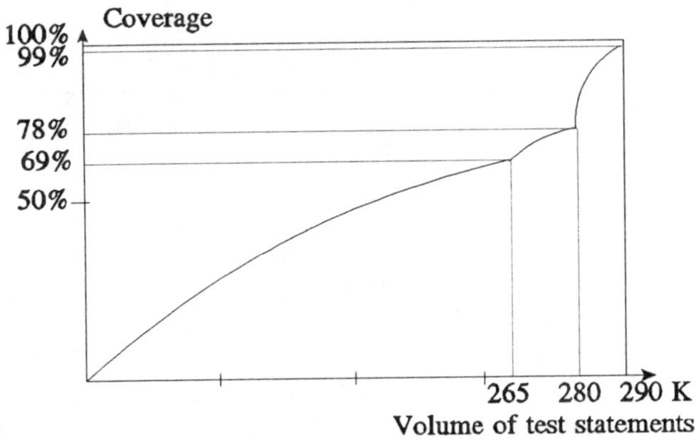

– 265,000 lines of miscellaneous code written without structural approach generated a coverage ratio of 69%;
– 15,000 lines, written using a structural approach but without any tool, generated an increased ratio of 78%;
– 9,677 lines written using a structural approach and a tool allowed 99%.

The VERILOG strategy for mastering the quality of a software is to use an industrial approach following two axes. On the one hand, a static analysis technique ensures a better construction of the software. On the other hand, a dynamic analysis technique helps to guarantee greater software reliability.

This approach enables the mastering of software development issues by answering some critical questions such as: How can we be sure that the required quality is achieved? Is the software well built? May we stop the test and deliver the software?

The VERILOG solution is LOGISCOPE: a CASE tool which is the leader in its field.

11 Formal Methods and Testing

Patrick Hall, Department of Computing, Open University
Robert Hierons, Department of Computer Science, Brunel University

11.1 INTRODUCTION

Formal methods are software development methods in which the development processes are grounded in mathematics. Much of the focus of formal methods is in formal specifications, but all other parts of the software development process should be informed and influenced by formality and mathematics for the software development method to truly count as a formal method. Testing is an important component of the development process, and in section 2 we look at the total development process from a testing point of view, identifying where formal techniques can fit in and enhance the process.

Specifications are of great importance in testing for they determine what the software ought to do, and they must necessarily form the basis for the verification testing of the functionality of the software. Yet most work on the testing of software addresses the implementation rather than the specification. This has been observed by Richardson, O'Malley and Tittle (1989):

> Current software testing practices focus, almost exclusively, on the implementation, despite widely acknowledged benefits of testing based on software specifications.

Construction of test cases for functional testing is taken up in section 2.

Testing requires more than test cases. During integration missing components have to be simulated by 'stubs'. Batteries of test cases have to be sequenced, and test failure has to be handled with tests continuing where they can return useful results. This is taken up in section 4.

If we are looking at the use of mathematics to understand and enhance the process of software development, we should also apply our mathematics to the understanding of testing itself. In section 5 testing theory is examined. What does the successful execution of a piece of software on a set of tests really tell us about the software? Many theoreticians and philosophers would claim that from the result of a set of test cases we can deduce nothing, but nevertheless we continue to test. What do we gain? In section 6 we look forward to developments that will further enhance the process of testing in the context of formal methods.

11.2 TESTING IN THE FORMAL DEVELOPMENT PROCESS

Specifications are the basis for black-box testing and random testing. A formal specification is given in a language with a precisely defined syntax and semantics. Such specification languages are based upon mathematics and fall into three main groups, these being model based, algebraic, and process algebras (e.g. Jones 1980, Spivey 1989, Ehrig and Mahr 1985, Bergstra et al. 1989, Milner 1989). This use of a precise mathematically defined syntax and semantics leads to unambiguous specifications that can be analysed mathematically, and in particular it is possible to prove properties of the specification and to prove the conformance of an implementation to such a specification. Analysis of such a specification can also be used to enhance the testing process, and the mathematical nature of the specification gives us the possibility of automating much of this analysis. This can save much time and effort and so make testing from the specification more attractive. Thus formal specifications give us the opportunity to automate black-box testing and random testing.

Formal development methods typically take the view that following a specification the software is developed through processes of refinement leading to an implementation that provably conforms with the specification (e.g. Jones 1980, Diller 1990), though few accounts take any regard for the total development process. These accounts disregard the role of testing, but others do recognise the need for verification and validation where

verification means proving formally the conformance of the implementation with the specification, and

validation means checking back with respect to users' real needs, which should ultimately involve execution and testing.

But testing is required for deeper reasons than that.

If we develop software formally, and in the process prove conformance between specification and implementation (verification), do we still need to test? While the proof of the conformance is undoubtedly very useful, proofs themselves are fallible and could contain errors in the steps of deduction in the proof, or errors in the assumptions used in the proof. Tests could provide an extra cross-check, though the tests must be designed to detect this kind of failure. Further software is built upon hardware for which precise formal models may not exist, and for which the only method of 'proof' is by experiment, by test, as has been pointed out forcibly by Fetzer (1988).

The place of testing within the software development process has been widely described (e.g. Myers 1979, Hetzel 1984, and Ould and Unwin 1986) and is illustrated in Figure 11.1

We have a formal specification and a path of normal development shown on the left. The *specification* is used to derive an *implementation* (with proofs possibly being used in this development process), and later put into *operation* when it is subject to *maintenance*. Testing is shown on the right: the specification is used as the basis for test planning and test case generation, which drive the running of the implementation during cycles of *test execution*. Any faults found lead to feedback up the development, and rework at the appropriate level, and further test execution.

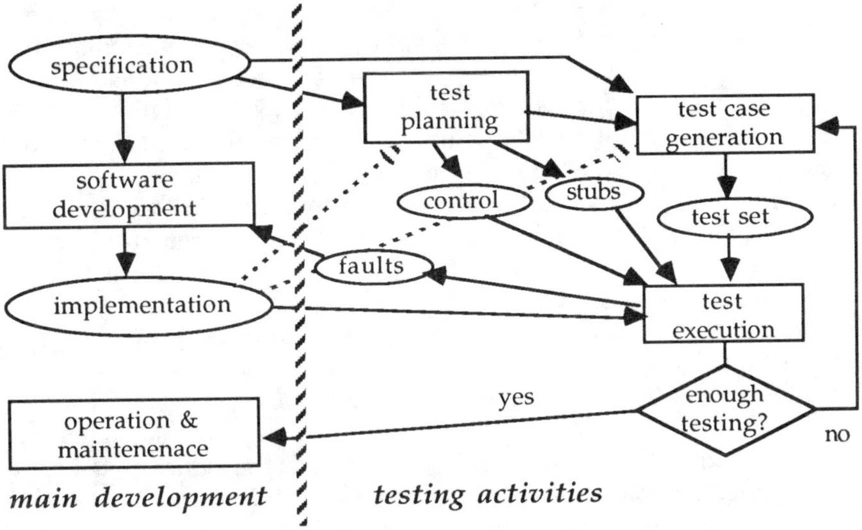

Figure 11.1 Testing in the software development process

Test case generation, which could be manual or automatic (e.g. Tsai et al 1990), gives us a number of test sets for use in test case execution, with the use of a formal specification making the automatic or semi-automatic generation of test cases from the specification feasible. Test planning determines a sequence for execution of the test sets and what to do when particular test cases fail, what to do about missing modules (e.g. where and how to build test stubs), and possibly also a system to control the test case execution and automatically check the output. We stop executing our tests when software quality is sufficiently high, and thus we have some termination criteria for the test execution loop.

11.2.1 The ORACLE problem

A key issue in much testing is deciding whether the output observed at the end of a test run is what should (or, at least, could) have been expected. Being able to answer this is known in testing as the Oracle problem. For complex software it appears that divine intervention is necessary to know whether the software is behaving correctly; we need an all-knowing all-seeing god.

With formal specifications we have precisely that. We can use formal specifications in one of two ways

- to check the result
- to predict the result.

Checking the result seems in principle easier. Typically, in Z say, the function will be specified by a predicate which the input and output must satisfy - it would seem that all that is necessary is to insert the values and evaluate the predicate. For example, for SORT, given an input set the specification will not tell us how to sort the elements, but given a set claimed as output, it can be checked whether the elements are in ascending order and are a permutation. But it may not be that easy, for the predicate may also depend on stored state, and the stored state will then depend upon the history of all previous states.

The alternative would seem to be to use the specification to calculate or predict the output that should be expected, but that requires an executable specification, and many specifications will be essentially non-executable (such as the specification of SORT). However, if it is executable, then the specification and actual system are run on the same sequence of inputs, and the outputs compared. This is a variation of parallel running or back-to-back testing that are well established methods among test practitioners.

So, while in some cases these two approaches might be satisfactory, in general they are not. As we shall see in the next section, typically the Oracle problem is tackled as part of the test case generation activity, and it is only in random testing that the problem remains. Here, if neither of the above two approaches work, we could go for something weaker, and simply attempt to prove that the observed output is reasonable – that it satisfies some weaker predicate than the actual post-condition (for example, with universal quantification over the input state and existential quantification over the output state).

11.3 TEST CASE GENERATION

11.3.1 Black box testing

Black box testing works from the specification, and the specification alone. It treats the software as a box whose internal structure is unknown, but for which the required or intended behaviour is known through the specification. Testing from the specification thus tests that its behaviour is what is specified and only what is specified.

By contrast, white box testing (also called structural, or code-based testing) can only discover behaviour that is manifestly incorrrect, such as catastrophic failure, and can discover whether the test cases do exercise ('cover') all the code. The two methods complement each other, with the methods having different strengths and weaknesses. Code-based testing is unlikely to detect special cases that are in the specification but not the code, even if it is using a specification-based oracle; while specification-based testing is unlikely to detect special cases that are in the code but not the specification. This is made explicit in Hennesey (19xx) for testing from process algebra specifications, where they show that it is possible to generate a finite test set from the specification that will guarantee that any implementation that behaves correctly upon the test set will contain a copy of the specification, i.e. the implementation is guaranteed to have all of the behaviour specified but may exhibit behaviour that is not specified.

Many systems have some sort of stored state and this causes problems in testing these systems. For such systems a test case involves an initial state as well as parameters for an operation, and the output is the final state as well as values explicitly output to the user by the system. Thus to test such a system we must be able to both set up and interrogate the system state. In order to do this we have to use operations upon the system, but in order to test these operations we must be able to set up and interrogate the system. We thus appear to have a paradox, in order to test the correctness of the operations upon the system we have to assume the correctness of a subset of these operations. In such situations we have to test sequences of operations. This need to test sequences of operations is made explicit for process algebra specifications and algebraic specifications but is certainly still there for model-based specifications – see the later sections on these specification methods.

Another problem comes with real-time systems, where we can produce asynchronous events such as the break-in to an interactive system. These could happen at any time. Such actions are impossible to repeat precisely, and when we do them we are unable to predict what the state of the system ought to be. Nevertheless we must test these asynchronous interrupts, and what we need to do is, after the event, determine whether what happened was to be expected – we have already seen some flavour of this in discussing the oracle problem. The difficulty comes in that repeatability is not possible, and thus simple regression testing is not possible. Much more theoretical work is required in the area of real-time systems, not only in the testing of such systems but also in their specification.

11.3.1.1 Testing from a model-based specification

The basic idea is the partitioning of the input-output behaviour space into subdomains in which the behaviour of the software is in some sense equivalent (we call this Partition Analysis). If the software behaves correctly for one test case within a subdomain, then we believe that we can reasonably assume that the behaviour of the software is correct for all possible test cases within that subdomain. We may wish, however, to take more than one test case within each subdomain in order to increase our confidence in the conformance of the implementation upon this subdomain.

(a) Informal specification

DISCOUNT INVOICING

A company produces two goods, X and Y, with prices 5 ECU for each X purchased and 10 ECU for each Y purchased. An order consists of a request for a certain number of Xs and a certain number of Ys. The cost of the purchase is the sum of the costs of the individual demands for the two products discounted as explained below. If the total is greater than 200 ECU a discount of 5% is given; if the total is greater than 1000 ECU a discount of 20% is given. Also the company wish to encourage sales of X and give a further discount of 10% if more than thirty Xs are ordered. Non-integer final costs are rounded down to give an integer value.

(b) Formal specification in Z.

```
round : N × N → N
─────────────────────────────────────────────
round(a, b) * b ≤ a < (round(a, b) + 1) * b
```

```
── DISCOUNTINVOICE ──────────────────────────
x?, y?: N
c!: N
─────────────────────────────────────────────
∃ sum, discount1, discount2 : N •
(sum = 5 * x? + 10 * y?) ∧
(sum ≤ 200 ⇒ discount1 = 100) ∧
(sum > 200 ∧ sum ≤ 1000 ⇒ discount1 = 95) ∧
(sum > 1000 ⇒ discount1 = 80) ∧
(x? ≤ 30 ⇒ discount2 = 100) ∧
(x? > 30 ⇒ discount2 = 90) ∧
c! = round(sum * discount1 * discount2, 10000))
─────────────────────────────────────────────
```

(c) Input space for DISCOUNT INVOICING module

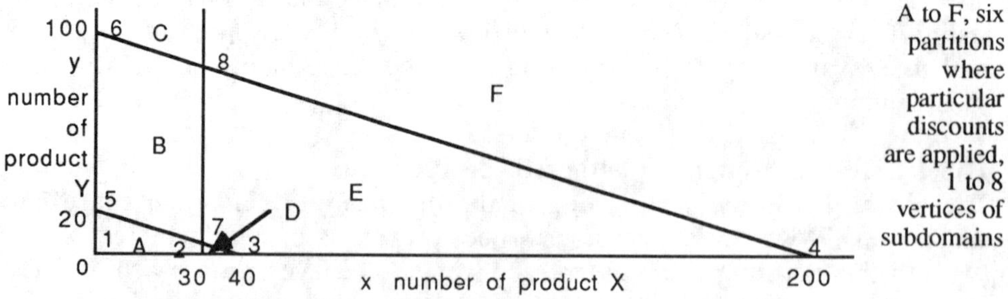

Figure 11.2 Example of partition analysis, using geometrical arguments to locate boundary test cases at vertices

(d) Typical test cases within subdomains

Region A	(10,3) => 80
Region B	(20,48) => 551
Region C	(7,105) => 868
Region D	(34,2) => 171
Region E	(53,18) => 380
Region F	(84,157) => 1432

(e) boundary values – could find test cases on and near the boundaries, like (100,50) and (101,51), but with straight line boundaries here we can take a test case at the vertex and a test case near to the vertex for each of the other subdomains.

Vertex 1	(0,0) => 0
Vertex 2	(30,0) => 135
Vertex 3	(40,0) => 180
Vertex 4	(200,0) => 855
Vertex 5	(0,20) => 200
Vertex 6	(0,100) => 950
Vertex 7	(30,5) => 200
Vertex 8	(30,85) => 950

(f) Test cases just off the vertices in each of the adjacent subdomains:

Just off vertex 1	(1,1) => 15
Just off vertex 2	(31,0) => 139
	(29,1) => 155
Just off vertex 3	(40,1) => 179
	(39,0) => 175
Just off vertex 4	(200,1) => 727
	(199,0) => 850
Just off vertex 5	(1,20) => 194
	(0,19) => 190
Just off vertex 6	(1,100) => 804
	(0,99) => 940
Just off vertex 7	(31,5) => 175
	(29,5) => 195
	(31,4) => 175
	(29,6) => 194
Just off vertex 8	(31,84) => 850
	(31,85) => 723
	(29,86) => 804
	(29,85) => 945

(g) Comment. The specification does not tell us what happens for negative input and thus we cannot test with test cases that involve negative input as we would have no way of determining whether the outcome of the test run was valid. In fact, with such a specification any result would be valid for input involving either x or y being negative as, for model-based specifications, if the specification does not give the behaviour for a particular input then anything can happen for that input. In practice we would have this specification combined with a specification giving the outcome for negative input, and we could then test the behaviour for negative input.

Figure 11.2 (cont'd) Example of partition analysis using geometrical arguments to locate boundary test cases at vertices

Next, having checked the behaviour of the implementation within the subdomains, we have to check that the subdomains are correct, which involves making sure that the boundaries are positioned correctly. This is thought to be particularly useful as it has been noted that people make mistakes most frequently at the boundaries between partitions. In order to check that the boundaries are correctly positioned, extra test cases must be produced on the boundary and very close to the boundary.

This basic approach goes back to an important paper by Goodenough and Gerhart (1975), and is discussed at length by Myers (1979). This method can be seen as testing that the specified behaviours are present and correct, with the behaviours on each subdomain representing the separate behaviours that have been specified. Both Scullard (1988) and North (1990) produce a partition by hand from a model-based specification in VDM, with test cases then being generated from this partition. It has also been discussed as a basis for the automatic generation of test cases from Z (Hall 1988), analysing a formal specification automatically to produce the partition and thence the test cases. White and Cohen (1980) give an approach for checking that the boundaries between the subdomains are correct that is based upon a geometrical argument for linear boundaries, and this is further extended by Clarke et al. (1982). In particular they note that test cases around the vertices of the subdomains are particularly effective at detecting any shift in the boundaries. Figure 11.2 shows an example of how this works.

The boundaries and subdomains given in Figure 11.2 can be derived automatically from the Z specification and, while this is not required for a small specification such as this one, it is important for large or complex specifications. The boundaries come from predicates in the specification that involve only input variables, intermediate variables, and global variables, and these can be found automatically. For cases that involve linear boundaries, such as that in the figure, we can also have a system that will automatically generate test cases such as those given. For a Z specification with linear boundaries it is thus possible to fully automate the process of generating test cases from the specification. For Z specifications whose boundaries are not linear, we can still generate the partition automatically but the generation of the test cases may require some human assistance.

The specification used in the example above simply involves the input of a set of parameters and the output of a result and thus there is no stored state involved. We expect that in practice many systems, especially the larger systems, will involve a stored state and in such cases we must use test sequences to test the system. The testing of such systems is further discussed below and in the section on test case sequencing and checking.

11.3.1.2 Testing from process algebra specifications

Process algebras (e.g. Milner 1989) have states and transitions between these states, thus making the problems of the stored state explicit, and have proved to be particularly useful in specifying communication protocol software. Brinksma (1988) discusses the generation of a canonical tester from a process algebra specification, with the property that an implementation conforming on the test set guarantees that it has exhibited the specified behaviour, though it may still have behaviour that is not specified. While this is weaker than full conformance, it is not in general possible to guarantee full conformance with a finite test set; the most that we can hope for is to show that the specified behaviour is present.

Finite state automata are simple process algebras, and their frequent use for specification has led to much research in testing from such specifications. Again the most that can be done is to demonstrate that the implementation exhibits all of the specified behaviour or, equivalently, that the implementation contains a copy of the specification. In order to do this it is necessary to execute a sequence of tests that 'cover' the specification. However, in order to guarantee that the implementation contains a copy of the specification, the sequence of tests must contain executions that check that the final state after testing is correct. There are three different methods discussed by Sidhu and Leung (1989) for checking the final state, these being:

a) using distinguishing sequences
b) using unique input/output sequences (UIOs)
c) using a set of sequences of executions that characterise the state.

A *distinguishing sequence* for a finite state automation (FSA) is a sequence of executions that produces different output for each different state. A unique input/output sequence (UIO) for a particular state in a FSA is a sequence of executions that produces an output for that state different from that for any other state – it distinguishes that particular state from all other states but need not distinguish between the other states. Each state may have the same UIO, in which case this is a distinguishing sequence. Unfortunately it is not guaranteed that either a distinguishing sequence or UIOs for every state will exist. In the case that neither exist, then for those states that do not have a UIO we have to execute the test a number of times, each time followed by a different sequence of executions. For a minimised finite state automaton it is guaranteed that for each state there is a set of such sequences of executions that distinguish that state from all other states. Thus for a specification that does not have a distinguishing sequence we use UIOs where they exist and predefined sets of test sequences elsewhere.

With the use of distinguishing sequences, test sequences can be generated that can demonstrate that the implementation contains a copy of the specification. Chen et al. (1989) prove that by using UIOs plus the verification that the UIOs and the sets of test sequences also characterise the state in the implementation, test sequences can also be generated that can demonstrate that the implementation contains a copy of the specification.

(a) the state diagram

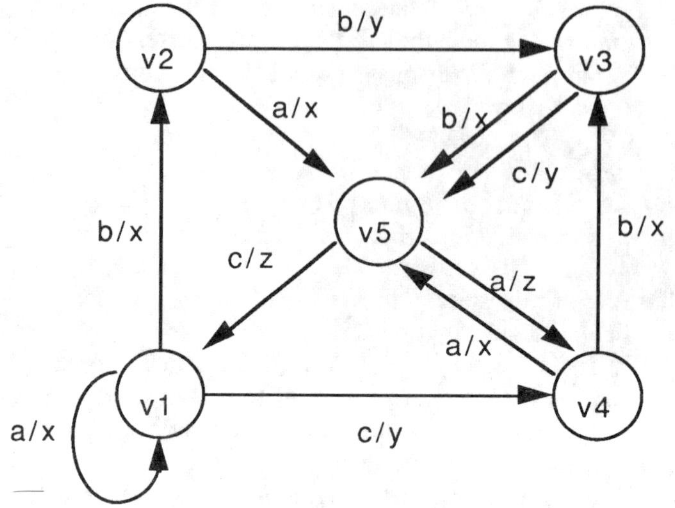

(b) Unique Input/Output sequences used by Aho et al [1988]

state	UIO
v1	(b/x)(a/x)
v2	(b/y)
v3	(b/x)(c/z)
v4	(b/x)(c/y)
v5	(c/z)

(c) Test sequence generated by Aho et al [1988]

(reset/null)(b/x)(b/y)(c/y)(c/z)(a/x)(b/x)(a/x)(a/z)(b/x)(c/y)(c/z)(b/x)(a/x)
(reset/null)(b/x)(a/x)(a/z)(a/x)(c/z)(c/y)(b/x)(c/y)(a/z)(b/x)(b/x)(c/z)(b/x)
(b/y)(b/x)(c/z)(b/x)(a/x)(c/z)(b/x)(reset/null)(b/x)(a/x)(a/z)(b/x)(reset/null)
(b/x)(a/x)(a/z)(b/x)(b/x)(c/z)(reset/null)(b/x)(a/x)(a/z)(reset/null)(b/x)(a/x)(c/z)

Figure 11.3 Example finite state machine and its test sequences

An important issue is the question of how we can produce routes that have this power and are as short as possible. Aho et al [1988] showed that this problem can be solved using UIOs and rephrasing the problem as a Rural Chinese Postman Tour (RCPT) problem, for which there are standard algorithms. The RCPT problem is to find a minimal tour of a directed graph, with the tour having to include each edge that is marked necessary. Though it is, in general, NP-complete there are low order polynomial algorithms that solve some cases. For each transition an edge that represents the transition followed by an UIO for the final state is added to the graph, and these added edges are those that are marked necessary.

Aho et al [1988] use a low order polynomial method to solve the RCPT problem that involves generating a minimal strongly connected symmetric subgraph that contains the set of necessary edges and then finding an Euler Tour of this subgraph. Aho et al [1988] showed that a sufficient condition for the method they use to work is that the set of necessary edges is weakly connected, and that this condition is satisfied if the FSA has a reset capacity or if each state has a self loop. A FSA has reset capacity if there is a transition that takes each state to the initial state, and a state has a self loop if there is a transition that takes this state to itself. Figure 3 gives the FSA that, once a reset transition was added, was studied by Aho et al [1988], with a test sequence of length 55 being generated.

Shen et al [1990] demonstrated that the use of multiple UIO's for each state can lead to a more efficient solution, again rephrasing the problem as a RCPT problem. Their method involves choosing the UIO to be used for each transition so that the set of necessary edges is as close to symmetric as possible, and when they applied this method to the FSA in Figure 3 they generated a test sequence of length 44. This method need not, however, generate the set of necessary edges that leads to the shortest test sequence, as the length of the test sequence is not only dependent upon how close the set of necessary edges is to being symmetric. This can be seen by looking at the case where the set of edges gives only two vertices that are not symmetric, one with one more edge leaving it than entering it, and the other having one more edge entering it than leaving it. In order to make this set of edges symmetric a path has to be added that connects these two vertices and thus the number of edges that must be added is the length of the shortest path between these two vertices. The method of Aho et al [1988] can be generalized to deal with multiple UIO's, producing shorter test sequences than those generated by the method advocated by Shen et al [1990].

Yang et al [1990] show that this can be further improved by choosing the UIO for each transition in order to maximise the amount of overlap between the test sequences for each transition and then taking advantage of this overlap to reduce the length of the test sequence. Using their method they generated a test sequences of length 29 for the FSA in Figure 3, with this representing a sizable improvement on the previous methods. Unfortunately their method relies upon heuristics and it is not clear that it is practical for large FSAs.

For particularly large finite state automata models it may not be practical to generate test sequences as described above. An alternative method is to execute a random walk of the model. Although a random walk cannot provide the same degree of confidence as the test sequences generated as above, a study by West [1989] suggests that they can be remarkably successful at detecting any errors that are present.

The use of process algebra specifications makes explicit the problem of the stored state and the use of test sequences in order both to set up the test case and to check that the state after the test execution is correct. They also make explicit the fact that the most we can guarantee when testing from the specification is that the specified behaviour is present.

11.3.1.3 Testing from algebraic specifications

An algebraic specification (Ehrig and Mahr 1985, Bergstra et al 1989) consists of a signature which declares the sorts, constants, and operations, and of a set of equations which define the semantics. For an implementation to conform to a given algebraic specification it certainly must contain elements which can be identified with the sorts, constants, and operations, and these elements must satisfy the equations. Typically algebraic specifications include an implicit internal state, that may appear in some of the equations, while others would not, as seen in Figure 4.

To test that an implementation satisfies an algebraic specification we must test that the equations are satisfied. We could, in principle, instantiate the equations (implicitly universally quantified over the variables in them) with all of the elements of the sorts, but this would to lead to vast numbers of test cases, and as always exhaustive testing is impractical. Some method is therefore required to find test sets of practical size. Bouge et al [1985] and Gaudel and Marre [1988] discuss a number of such methods, with these methods being based upon complexity measures for the algebra. The basic idea is that given a suitable complexity measure, such as the length of the term, for any integer a set of terms of complexity at most this integer can be developed for each sort of interest and these terms can then be used to instantiate the equations. This leads to a sequence of test sets for each complexity measure, with Gaudel and Marre [1988] demonstrating that the limit of these test sets is program proof (just as Goodebough and Gerhart [1975] did for black box testing from decision tables). The test sets generated in the above fashion are often very large and it may be necessary to add hypotheses in order to reduce the test set size. The test sets will have the same power as before if these hypotheses are correct, but otherwise will be weaker, with the use of such hypotheses being very much dependent upon human judgement. An example of such a hypothesis is that for a particular variable in a particular equation, this variable need only be instantiated with one term of each level of complexity.

Algebraic specification provide a good representation of the problem of the stored state, where the equations of the specification determine the sequences of operations to be tested. A simple example is that academic favourite, the stack, shown in Figure 4. PUSH(item,stack) pushes the value on the top of the stack, and TOP reads this value, with the equation TOP(PUSH(item,stack))=item determining one test sequence for particular values of item and arbitrary values of stack. We could, however, have been very unlucky and had compensating errors in the two operations leading to an incorrect test execution looking correct, we get the correct answer for the wrong reasons.

(a) the specification of a stack

STACK + ITEM

sort stack
operations
NEW: → stack
PUSH: item*stack → stack
TOP: stack → item
POP: stack → stack

preconditions
TOP(s) is defined when not s = NEW
POP(s) is defined when not s = NEW

equations
TOP (PUSH (k,s)) = k
POP (PUSH (k, s)) = s

where
k:item
s:stack

(b) test cases for a stack of integers

TOP(PUSH(1,NEW)) = 1
POP(TOP(PUSH(1,NEW))) = NEW
TOP(PUSH(0,PUSH(1,NEW))) = 0
TOP(POP(PUSH(0,PUSH(1,NEW))) = TOP(PUSH(1,NEW))
POP(POP(PUSH(0,PUSH(1,NEW))) = NEW

Figure 11.4 Algebraic specification example and associated test cases

11.3.2 Random testing

An alternative method for testing with respect to specifications arises with 'random' testing. The idea here is to describe precisely the set of possible inputs, and then arrange to generate all possible inputs and input combinations. This would usually be done using a tool which runs without stopping, such that in the long run it would generate all possible inputs.

There are two ways we could go about generating random tests. The most thorough would be to get a precise description of possible inputs, for example using a syntax notation, and from this generate the input sequences at random. We would then arrange for the distributions of test cases produced by our test case generator either to reflect the distributions of input that can be expected when the software is used or, as is suggested by Maurer [1990], to reflect the expected distribution of errors. The former approach has been taken in the testing of compilers [eg. Burgess 1986, Homer and Schoder 1989], where the input to a compiler is the programme, and the structure of programmes is precisely and fully defined by the syntax of a programming language.

Syntax notations are themselves a form of formal specification, and specifications in Z such as that given above can also form the basis for random test pattern generation. Given a Z specification of an operation we can derive the input syntax and preconditions and use these to generate test cases randomly. A compromise on the preceding very thorough method of random testing would be to produce a number test cases or sequences of test cases, and then to fragment these and generate input at random from these fragments, varying the sequences of them. This is the approach taken in the clean room of Harlan Mills [Mills, Dyer, and Linger 1987], and by Bird and Munoz [1983].

With random generation of test cases, we obtain test inputs, but may not know whether the output obtained is correct. What we need is a 'test oracle' - and as discussed in subsection 2.1, a formal specification may find yet another application here.

There has been considerable debate about whether random testing makes sense. Surely, it is thought, the construction of a few well chosen test cases would be more effective than random testing. Two experimental verifications have been reported by Duran and Ntafos [1984] and Hamlet and Taylor [1988]. Both these experiments give the surprising results that there is not much to chose between the two approaches. By contrast a theoretical argument by Jeng and Weyuker [1989] has argued that the partitioning method can be better.

11.4 TEST MANAGEMENT AND CONTROL

11.4.1 Integration and stubs

During the integration of software the generally adopted method used to build the system is one unit at a time. With only a part of the system available for integration at any time, the missing parts have to be replaced by test stubs or test harnesses. If we have formal specifications of the missing parts, we could hope to use this to provide a temporary substitute. If the specification is executable, such as for the algebraic specifications language OBJ3 [Goguen and Winkler, 1988], we could use the specification as a stub. However the degraded performance may not be acceptable, and we could instead derive from the specification some approximate executable which does something sufficiently reasonable for integration test purposes, with in the limit just returning a single fixed value for any input, as is frequently done in test stubs

Test harnesses are already commonly generated from code interfaces, and would not benefit from formal specifications, other than through the generation of the test cases that the test-harness needs to drive the software-under-test (see section 3 above).

11.4.2 Test case sequencing and checking

System testing requires the execution of many test cases and suites of test cases. When a test shows an error, we shouldn't stop there, but carry on testing to execute as many tests as possible. We do this so that we can characterise the software as fully as possible, reporting as many faults as possible for another cycle of bug-fixing, before the software is returned for retest. Because any significant software has internal states, the decision of what tests to execute when one fails is not trivial. Later tests may rely on some internal state having been established, and a test failure indicates that the state may be unreliable. But to back-off completely and re-initialise the state may be very expensive. We need some means of working out where we are, what we can rely on, and then keep on going.

A system to do this can be based upon the modelling of the high level behaviour of the software as a Finite State Automaton, with this model being used by a system to control the testing process. The system executes test cases and checks the output against this model. If the output conforms to this model then the system executes further test cases, while if an error is detected this fact is recorded and either a homing sequence is executed, returning the system to a known state, or further executions are performed in order to ascertain which state the system is in. This may involve the use of a distinguishing sequence, as discussed in the section on testing from process algebra specifications, or the use of a predefined strategy, or a random walk.

If an error occurs in execution there is also the problem of determining where the error occurred, as the error may have occurred at a much earlier test, but only surfaced now. We are investigating how this can be characterised, looking at provably correct strategies for isolating the error, systematically varying the test sequence and using further sequences to identify the state that results.

In order to develop a finite state automaton model we need to group together system states according to some notion of equivalence and use these equivalence classes as the system states. We have already seen a possible equivalence relation - two system states are equivalent if and only if they are treated in the 'same fashion' according to the specification - as used in Partition Analysis as the basis of black-box test case generation. Such a system can also be used to 'cover' the model - to execute every transformation from every state, as is discussed in the section on testing Process Algebras. If we have developed the finite state automaton model from a specification using the equivalence relation suggested above then covering the model is equivalent to taking a test case from each of the subdomains of the partition analysis.

11.4.3 Test completion

When do we stop testing? What we need are some metrics to assess the quality of our tests, and also the quality of the software. We need to go on testing as long as we are dissatisfied with this quality of the software and have a reasonable chance of finding more errors and more bugs which need repair. However, we need to also consider the quality of our test set, for when we find that a piece of software passes on all the tests, this could just mean our test set is low grade, not that the software is high grade.

Approaches to the assessment of software quality could be to measure the reliability directly in terms of mean-time to failure, using some form of reliability growth model [eg. Littlewood, 1990]. Alternatively it could be some form of error-seeding, to estimate the number of residual errors using a population statistics argument. Both approaches relate to the theoretical underpinnings taken up in the next section.

To measure the quality of tests we could use the specification test coverage metric we considered in 4.2. We could also use code based metrics such as those discussed in the draft BCS Standard for Software Component Testing [BCS 1990]. An alternative method could be mutation analysis [eg. Budd et al 1978, De Millo 1989] where the programme is transformed according to some view of how people make mistakes. In these mutation approaches a good test set would discover the added errors. As yet these methods do not have a solid foundation in theory, though one could project such a basis around the testing of conformance relationships between specification and implementation.

We stop testing when both software quality metrics and test quality metrics are sufficiently good.

11.5 THEORETICAL UNDERPINNINGS

In testing, the difficulty is that we cannot test everything. We have to use a small set of test case, a *sample*. What can we say about the whole software from these test cases? It was claimed by Dijkstra in 1972 that:

> 'Program testing can be used to show the presence of bugs, but never their absence'

This has been quoted by a number of computing theoretician's (eg Hoare [1982] page 9, Jones [1980] page 7, and Backhouse [1986] page 3) to persuade us that a testing approach is not acceptable and that we must follow a deductive approach to the development of software and aim to prove through mathematical logic that software is correct.

However Fetzer [1988] has argued that the deductive approach is also essentially limited, and wherever the software system impinges upon the real world we are necessarily in the region of experimentation and induction and testing - see Figure 5. We have a requirement arising in the real-world which is connected to a specification through some informal process of discussion with the client and possibly the display of samples of the intended behaviour using prototypes or scenarios. From specifications through to programs one is in the closed world of pure mathematics, and the program can be deduced or calculated from the specification through the process of refinement (eg. Jones [1980]). Once again when we come to execute the program we have to connect to the real world of hardware, of physics, and again must face the prospect of experimentation and testing. Clearly the two approaches, of formal verification and experimental testing, are not in competition, but are complimentary.

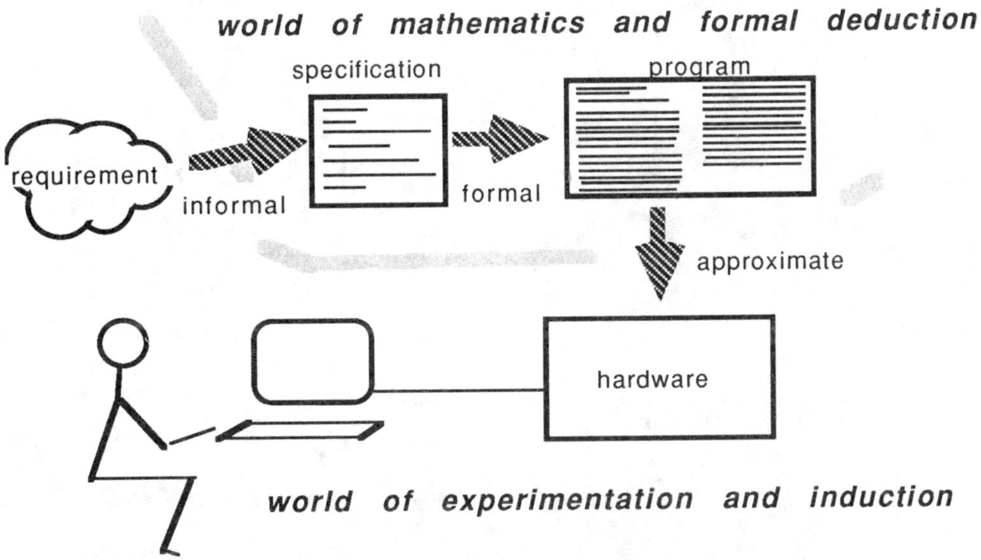

Figure 11.5 Division between verification and proof, and experimentation and testing

The Fetzer paper suggests that we look at induction as the basis for testing. Indeed several papers on testing have taken this approach, looking at induction and machine learning [eg. Cherniavsky and Smith, 1987]. A variation on this is to view testing as approximation, and this has been done by Roe and Rowland [1987] for numerical software. Hall [1991] has taken this further as shown in Figure 6.

In Figure 6 we have drawn an input set 'X' and an output set 'Y' and show two functions 'f' and 'g' where 'f' is the function as specified and 'g' is the function as implemented. At the top of the figure we see a case where 'f' and 'g' coincide, while at the bottom we see a case where they differ. One issue we need to consider is where they differ, how badly do they differ, and to do this we need some way of measuring difference in the output set 'Y'. We need a metric on 'Y'. We also need to consider how important this difference is, how often the particular inputs arise which could make this important. To do this we need some kind of measure on the set 'X'. Measures are generalisations of probabilities. So what we are doing is to measure the difference e(f,g) between the two functions 'f' and 'g' in output set 'Y' and weight it by the probability of the inputs occurring. We get the formula

$$\mathbf{E(f,g)} \quad = \quad \int \mathbf{e\ (f,g)\ d}\ \mu$$

integrating the differences between the two functions over all possible inputs in 'X' with differences in 'Y' to get a measure of the difference between the two functions, E(f,g). [See for example, Achieser 1956, Kingman and Taylor 1966]

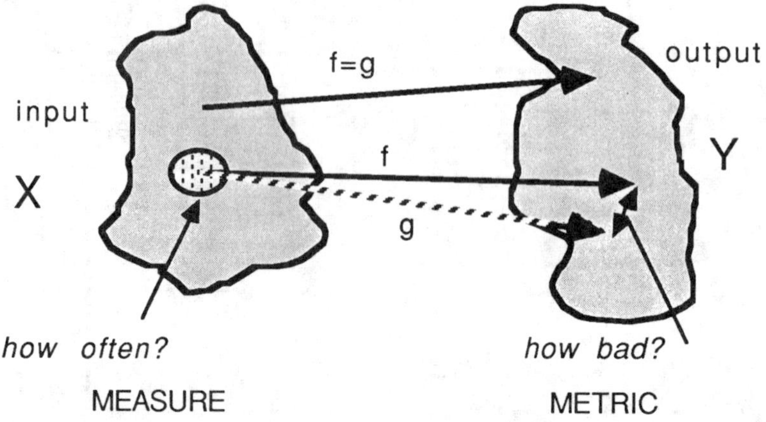

Figure 11.6 General Approximation Theory view of testing

What we are doing in testing, is to estimate this integral,

$$\mathbf{E(f,g)} \quad \cong \quad \Sigma \quad \mathbf{e\ (\ f(x_i\ ),\ g(x_i\ )\ )\ /\ N}$$

if we sample randomly with respect to the underlying input distributions modeled by the probability measure m. We know from ergodicity theory [Kingman and Taylor 1966] that providing we do the sampling of test points randomly, the sum does converge to the integral.

11.6 CONCLUSIONS

We have argued that testing is still necessary when using formal methods and that formal methods help testing. In particular we have seen that formal specifications, essential as a first step in formal refinement and development of software, also provide us with the basis for the automatic generation of test cases, test stubs, and test control software. While some algorithms and methods for doing this are being worked out, there is much more that can be done here.

As well as using the theories underpinning the formal methods developed for the deductive production of software, we must produce theories to underpin the testing itself. We have focussed on a theory derived from approximation theory, but this theory still needs further exploration, and we are working with Hong Zhu and Jin Lingzi on extending their theory (Zhu and Lingzi 1989) of functional programming program induction.

11.7 REFERENCES

Achieser, N.I. 1956 *Theory of Approximation*, Frederick Ungar, New York. 1956. Translated by Charles J. Hyman from Polish.

Aho, A.V., Dahbura, A.T., Lee, D., and Uyar, M.U. 1988 An Optimisation Technique for Protocol Conformance Test Generation Based on UIO Sequences and Rural Chinese Postman Tours, *Proceedings of Protocol Specification, Test, and Verification VIII*.

Backhouse, R. C. 1986 *Program Construction and Verification*, Prentice-Hall, pp. 3.

BCS Specialist Group in Software Testing 1990 *A standard for Software Component Testing*, November.

Bergstra, J.A., Heering, J. and Klint, P. 1989 *Algebraic Specification*, ACM Press and Addison Wesley.

Bird, D.L. and Munoz, C.U. 1983. Automatic generation of random self-checking test cases, *IBM Systems Journal*, **22** (3), pp. 229-245.

Bouge, L., Choquet, N., Fribourg, L. and Gaudel, M.C. 1985 Application of Prolog to Test Set Generation from Algebraic Specifications, *Proceedings of International Joint Conference on the Theory and Practice of Software Development*, Berlin, March.

Brinksma, E. 1988 A Theory For The Derivation Of Tests, *Proceedings of Protocol Specification, Test, and Verification VIII.*

Budd, T.A., Lipton, R.J. and Sayward, F.G. 1978 The design of a prototype mutation system for program testing. *National Computer Conference, IEEE*, pp. 623-627.

Burgess, C.J. 1986 Towards the automatic generation of executable programs to test a Pascal compiler, in Barnes, D. and Brown, P. (eds) *Proceedings of the Software Engineering 86 conference*, published by the Institution of Electrical Engineers, England, pp. 304-316.

Chen, W.Y.L, Vuong, S.T, and Ito, M.R 1989 An Improved Protocol Test Generation Procedure Based On UIO's *ACM SIGCOMM 89*, pp. 283-294.

Cherniavsky, J.C. and Smith, C.H. 1987 A Recursion Theoretic Approach to Program Testing, *IEEE Transactions on Software Engineering*, **SE-13**, (7), July, pp. 777-784.

Clarke, L.A., Hassell, J., Richardson, D.J. 1982 A Close Look at Domain Testing, *IEEE Transactions on Software Engineering*, Vol 8, No 4.

DeMillo, R. 1989 Test Adequacy and Program Mutation, *1989 International Conference on Software Engineering*.

Dijkstra, E.W. 1972 Notes on Structured Programming, in *Structured Programming*, by Dahl, O.-J., Dijkstra, E.W. and Hoare, C.A.R., Academic Press 1972, pp. 6.

Diller, A. Z. 1990 *An Introduction to Formal Methods*, Wiley.

Duran, J. and Ntafos, S. 1984 An evaluation of random testing, *IEEE Trans Software Engineering*, **10**, July, pp. 438-444.

Ehrig, H. and Mahr, B. 1985 *Fundamentals of Algebraic Specification 1. Equations and Initial Semantics*, Springer Verlag.

Fetzer, J.H. 1988 Program Verification: the Very Idea, *CACM* **31** (9), Sept, pp. 1048-1063.

Gaudel, M.C. and Marre, B. 1988 Algebraic Specifications and Software Testing: Theory and Application, *Rapport number 407 LRI*, February.

Goguen, J.A. and Winkler, T. 1988 *Introducing OBJ3*, SRI-CSL-88-9 Computer Science Laboratory, SRI International.

Goodenough, J.B. and Gerhart, S.L. 1975 Towards a Theory of Test Data Selection, *IEEE Trans Software Engineering*, **SE-1** (2), June, pp. 156-173.

Hall, P.A.V. 1988 Towards Testing with respect to Formal Specifications, Second IEE/BCS Conference *Software Engineering 88*, IEE Conference Publication, No 290, pp. 159-163.

Hall, P.A.V. 1990 Defect Detection and Correction, in *Software Reliability Handbook*, Rook P. (ed), Elsevier, pp. 111-136.

Hall, P.A.V. 1991 Relationship between specifications and testing, *Information and Software Technology*, January/February.

Hamlet, R. and Taylor, R. 1988 Partition Testing does not inspire confidence, *Proceedings of the Second Workshop on Software Testing, Verification, and Analysis*, Banff, Canada, July, pp. 206-215.

Hetzel, W. 1984, *The Complete Guide to Software Testing*, Collins.

Hoare, C.A.R. 1982 *Programming is an Engineering Profession*, Oxford University Computing Laboratory, Programming Research Group, Technical Monograph PRG-27, May 1982, pp. 9.

Homer, W., Schoder, R. 1989 Independent Testing of Compiler Phases Using a Test Case Generator, *IEEE Transactions on Software Engineering*, Vol 15 Number 1.

Jeng, B. and Weyuker, E, 1989 Some Observations on Partition Testing, ACM Sigsoft '89: *Third Symposium on Software Testing, Analysis, and Verification (TAV3)*, ACM, pp. 38-47.

Jones, C.B. 1980 *Software Development, A Rigorous Approach*, Prentice Hall, pp. 7.

Kingman, J.F.C. and Taylor, S.J. 1966 *Introduction to Measure and Probability*, Cambridge University Press.

Littlewood, B. 1990 Modelling Growth in Software Reliability, in *Software Reliability Handbook*, Rook, P. (ed.), Elsevier, pp. 137-154

Maurer, P.M. 1990 Generating Test Data with Enhanced Context Free Grammars, *IEEE Software*, July.

Mills, H.D., Dyer, M. and Linger, R.C. 1987 Cleanroom Software Engineering, *IEEE Software*, September, pp. 19-2.

Milner, R. 1989 *Communication and Concurrency*, Prentice Hall.

Myers, G.J. 1979 *The Art of Software Testing*, Wiley Interscience.

North, N.D. 1990 *Automatic Test Generation for The Triangle Problem*, National Physical Laboratory Report DICT 161/90, February.

Ould, M. and Unwin, C. 1986 *Testing in Software Development*, Cambridge University Press.

Richardson, D., O'Malley, O. and Tittle, C. 1989 Approaches to Specification-Based Testing, ACM Sigsoft '89: *Third Symposium on Software Testing, Analysis, and Verification (TAV3)*, ACM, pp. 86-96.

Roe, R.P. and Rowland, J.H. 1987 Some Theory Concerning Certification of Mathematical Subroutines by Black Box Testing, *IEEE Software Engineering*, Vol. 13, no. 6, June, pp. 677-682.

Schmidt, D.A. 1986 *Denotational Semantics, A methodology for language development*, Wm Brown.

Scullard 1988 Test Case Selection Using VDM, *VDM 88*

Shen, Y.N., Lombardi, F., and Dahbura, A.T. 1990 Protocol Conformance Testing Using Multiple UIO Sequences, *Proceedings of Protocol Specification, Testing, and Verification IX*.

Sidhu, D.P., Lenung, T.K. Formal Methods in Protocal Testing: A Detailed Study, *IEEE Transactions on Software Engineering* **15** (4).

Spivey, J.M. 1989 *The Z Notation. A Reference Manual*, Prentice Hall.

Tsai, W.T., Volovik, D. and Keefe, T.F. 1990 Automated Test Case Generation for Programs Specified by Relational Algebra Queries, *IEEE Transactions on Software Engineering*, **16** (3), March, pp. 316-324

West, C.H. 1989 Protocol Validation in Complex Systems, *ACM SIGCOMM 89*

White and Cohen 1980 A Domain Strategy for Computer Program Testing, *IEEE Transactions on Software Engineering*, Vol 6, no3.

Yang, B. and Ural, H. 1990 Protocol Conformance Test Generation Using Multiple UIO Sequences With Overlapping, *ACM SIGCOMM 90*, pp. 118-125.

Zhu, H. and Jui L. 1989 A Knowledge-Based System to Synthesise FP Programs from Examples, *Lecture notes in Artificial Intelligence EPIA 89*, Springer.

12 Formalising Testing Concepts

Monika Müllerburg
National Research Centre for Computer Science

12.1 INTRODUCTION

Software testing based on dynamic execution is the method of software quality examination which is most frequently used in practice. The expenditure on testing is very high. One reason for this is that testing is still more based on the intuition of the tester than on systematic procedures. In spite of many advances made so far, too much still depends on the creativity of the individual tester. Moreover, the quality of the achieved results, in particular with respect to the effectiveness of the test runs, can hardly be proved. Much work has still to be done in order to support effective and efficient testing.

The term 'test' is used in two ways. On the one hand, it refers to a development phase which has to be planned and controlled just like other phases. On the other hand it refers to a class of examination methods, whose strengths and weaknesses must be known in order to use them efficiently (in the development phase 'test'). Testing may be used for checking different dynamic characteristics, such as correctness, run time efficiency or reliability. In this paper we concentrate on testing for correctness, i.e. on testing with the aim of detecting faults. The term 'test concept' here is used to denote a test data selection criterion and respective testability and test coverage measures, i.e. measures that can be derived from the criterion. We do not discuss how to obtain the required test data.

The development phase 'test' is usually divided into test steps. There is a procedure which can lead to a systematic definition of such test steps and a goal-oriented selection of test concepts [11]. The idea is to specify test steps depending on the development process in such a way that a test step is identified for each relevant construction document. In each identified test step those aspects are examined that are described in the corresponding construction document. Thus, for each test step we have to find test concepts suitable for the aspects to be examined.

This paper attempts to answer the question of how to select suitable test concepts; it presents an approach that supports a systematic selection of them. The approach is based on the assumption that different objects must be tested by means of different concepts. Though this seems obvious, the same concepts are often used for many purposes. For example, branch testing is sometimes rejected as useless, only because its use in all test steps (i.e. for testing whole systems) leads to so many test cases that the test becomes unfeasible.

The approach suggested here is based on the idea of defining test concepts not directly on the objects considered in testing, but on formal models which can be interpreted as abstract representations of those objects. This allows an exact definition of test concepts and provides a solid basis for their analysis. On the other hand, the approach helps to find adequate abstract representations, i.e. models, for a given object and via these models to identify applicable test concepts. The METKIT CAI System can support this selection.

The rest of the paper is organised as follows: Section 2 gives a short introduction to the concepts of testing software for correctness. The general idea and the motivation for the approach are presented in Section 3 and demonstrated in Section 4 by means of an example. This example uses a graph of specific characteristics as a model; it discusses the interpretation of the graph as an abstract representation of call relations between procedures and indicates the implications for test concepts. Section 5 shows how to embed this approach in the development process and Section 6 discusses the practical use of the approach using the METKIT CAI System in order to support software developers in the selection of test concepts. Section 7 presents a concluding summary.

12.2 TESTING CONCEPTS

A basic problem of testing results from the fact that, generally a program cannot be tested with all possible input data but only with some few selected data. The principle of testing is that of a sample, and the problem is how to define the sample. The definition of the sample, i.e. the selection of test data, depends on the characteristics to be examined.

In checking for correctness, we try to detect as many faults in the program as possible. The reliability of the statement about the correctness depends on the effectiveness of the tests with regard to fault detection. Fault-oriented testing needs test data that are likely to expose faults. We therefore are interested in the criteria a sample should fulfil in order to expose faults.

Different types of faults need different concepts. An example of a fault type is that of a missing function [5]. In this case a function is specified but not implemented in the program. This type of fault cannot be exposed by using test concepts such as statement or branch testing[1]. We rather have to ensure that there are test data for checking every specified (sub) function.

Another example is an incorrect predicate in a decision statement.

...; IF ($a \leq b$) THEN ... ELSE ... ENDIF; ...

If instead of '$a \leq b$', the condition '$a < b$' was meant, this fault would not be

1. Statement testing means executing every statement, branch testing every outcome of decision statements.

detected with test data for '$a < b$' and '$a > b$' but only with a third one for '$a = b$'. Again, test concepts such as statement and branch testing do not address this type of fault.

As a third example let us look at a swapping of '+' and '–' in a statement $a = b + c$. For exposing this type of fault we would need test data causing $c \neq 0$.

A more detailed discussion of test data selection criteria and their fault revealing capabilities may be found in [10], while general discussions on testing are given in [2, 6, 9, 14].

For a given test data selection criterion, both testability and test coverage measures can be derived. Test coverage measures are used for evaluating the effectiveness of the test and testability measures for estimating the necessary test expenditure. The criteria and their respective measures are referred to here as test concepts.

Test coverage measures are defined as a ratio of used, required elements (e.g. statement, modules or functions) to required elements. A statement coverage of 80%, for example, would mean that 80 from 100 statements available in the program were actually executed during the test. Test coverage measures point to program parts tested inadequately and can also be used as an end criterion for the test.

Testability measures can be defined as the minimum number of test data (test executions) which is necessary to achieve a complete test coverage for a test data selection criterion. This is based on the assumption that all required elements can be used. Testability measures enable us to estimate the test expenditure and thus support the management in the organisation of testing. However, they can also be used to manage construction in order to obtain programs which can be tested. Such measures can be defined and computed for control-flow-oriented test conceptsn [1].

12.3 OBJECTS, MODELS AND TEST CONCEPTS

There are many test concepts, each of which has its strength and weakness with respect to specific types of faults. Furthermore, there are many different types of objects to be handled in software development today, and thus many different types of faults. On the one hand, software is developed step by step resulting in different types of descriptions, such as specifications, designs, and programs. On the other hand, there are several development paradigms resulting in different types of programs, i.e. programs in functional, logical, and object-oriented languages. Different paradigms may emphasise different aspects. Control flow as a sequence of statements, for example, has a central role in algorithmic programs, while it is not as important in object-oriented programs. From the testing point of view, we must therefore be able to handle different types of objects for each of which we need adequate testing concepts.

We suggest here the systematic application of the idea of modelling as a basic framework for defining and analysing testing concepts. The thesis is that we can understand test concepts better if we define and analyse them on the bases of formal models. Modelling is used in science for explaining and investigating real world phenomena. Modelling attempts to present relevant aspects of the real world (objects and relations) in models. This representation of reality is an abstraction neglecting all other aspects. Abstraction, i.e. concentration on the relevant aspects, facilitates understanding. Using formal models we can make use of the findings and results of the theory behind that model.

When considering an object, we can find different representations. The same formal model can be an abstract representation of different objects, and the findings with respect to that model can be used for conclusions about all of these objects.

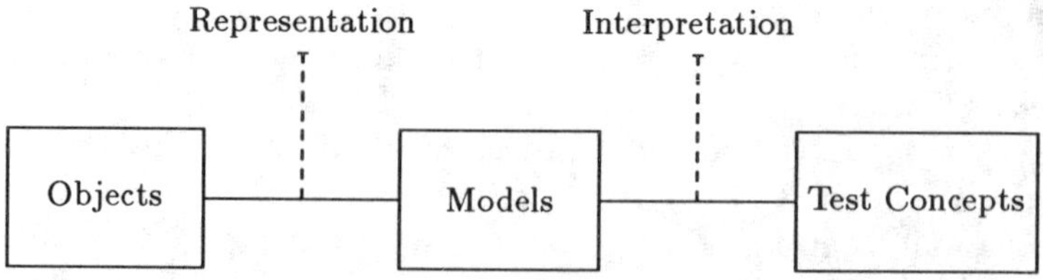

Figure 12.1 Objects, models, and test concepts

The best known example of a formal model in the testing area is that of a directed graph; this can be used for representing the control flow in programs. Many test concepts, such as statement and branch testing (see Section 2) have been formally defined on such graphs. These definitions include test data selection criteria, testability measures and test coverage measures. Using directed graphs we have a model which is formally defined by means of graph theory, and we can use findings and results of that theory for investigations and conclusions about program control flow. These findings and statements are language-independent and apply to all objects for which the model is accepted as an abstract representation.

When considering a program, we can identify other aspects than control flow: we may look at data flow, values of variables at specific positions, values of expressions, call relations between procedures, or data flow between procedures. Such aspects may be formally represented in models to be interpreted as abstract representations.

Thus, we suggest systematically defining testing concepts not directly on the objects themselves but on formal models that can be interpreted as abstract representations of those objects. Figure 12.1 shows the relations between objects, models, and test concepts; Figure 12.2 shows some concrete examples.

This route via formal models makes clear what we can and cannot achieve by means of a test concept. Defining test concepts (i.e. test data selection criteria as well as testability and test coverage measures) on formal models allows an exact definition which is independent of particular languages. In addition, formal models provide a solid basis for analysing and comparing test concepts. Furthermore, formal models make clear which types of faults can be handled by means of a test concept and thus point to the individual advantages and disadvantages of the test concept.

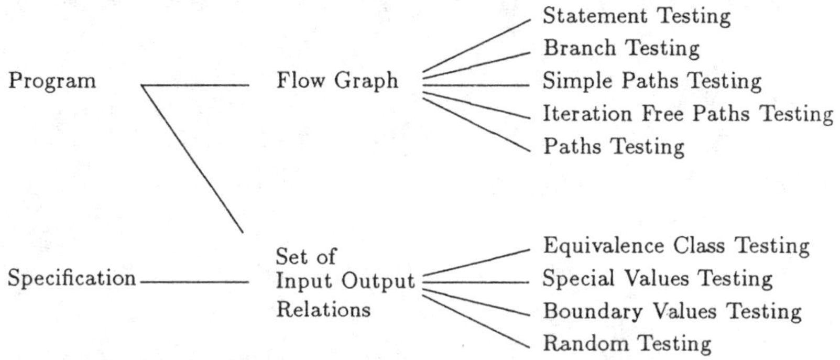

Figure 12.2 Some examples of objects, models, and test concepts

Interpreting a model as an abstract representation of some object makes clear what can be addressed by a test concept defined on that model, i.e. what can be tested and what cannot. Test concepts which are defined on a flow graph, for instance, only cover control flow aspects, not other aspects such as complex data structures or computations.

Using this route via formal models we get a systematic access to test concepts. The understanding of test concepts is facilitated and the specific selection of test concepts is supported. The model world, i.e. the relevant theory, defines what can be addressed by a test concept.

12.4 AN EXAMPLE

This section shows how to use our idea of testing via models. As an example of a model we use a specific form of a finite directed graph for representing call relations between procedures of a program or software system. We discuss concepts of graph theory relevant for that specific model, show how these can be used for defining test concepts on this model and discuss the consequences for testing.

12.4.1 The model world

First, we define a finite directed graph and specialise this to obtain an appropriate representation of call relations.

> **Definition 1** *A finite directed graph G is a tuple G = (N,E), where N is a finite non-empty set of nodes and* $E \supseteq N \times N$ *a set of edges.*

On the basis of this definition, we can define some terms unambiguously. These terms do not only apply to this general graph, but also for all its specialisations (see below).

- A sequence of nodes is called *path* if there is an edge between all adjacent nodes: $(n_1,\ldots, n_k)$ with $(n_i\ n_{i+1}) \in E$ for all $1 \leq i \leq k-1$.
- We refer to a path as a *simple path* [15] if each edge occurs only once: $(n_1,\ldots, n_k)$ with $(n_i, n_{i+1}) \neq (n_j, n_{j+1})$ for all $i \neq j$.
- We refer to a path as a *loop* if the first node and the last node are identical: $(n_1,\ldots,n_k)$ with $n_1 = n_k$.
- We refer to a path as an *iteration* if it is a loop and if the first node occurs once more on the way to the last node: $(n_1, n_2,\ldots,n_{k-1}, n_k)$ with $n_1 = n_k = n_i$ for one $2 \leq i \leq k-1$.

These definitions indicate the essential structure of a graph. We can distinguish nodes, edges as sequence of two linked nodes, paths and specific types of paths, for example, simple paths and loops.

We now define a specific form of graph, called a P graph, which we want to use for representing call relations.

> **Definition 2** *A P graph* $PG = (N,E,n_s)$ *is a finite directed graph with exactly one start node* n_s ($n_s \in N$ *and indegree* $(n_s) = 0$)[2] *and the following additional characteristics:*
>
> - *PG is a connected graph, i.e. all nodes are connected (at least indirectly).*
> - *PG is a multigraph, i.e. two nodes may be connected by more than one edge.*

Since a P graph is a connected graph with exactly one start node, each node is reachable on a path from the start node.

As in the general graph, nodes, edges and paths can be considered. In

2. *indegree* $(n_s) = 0$ means that there are no incoming edges; *outdegree* $(n_i) = 0$ means that there are no outgoing ones.

addition, we can define a complete path:

- A path from the start node n_s to an end node (node without leaving edge) is referred to as a *complete path.*

It is still a graph theoretic question to find a set of complete paths that is as small as possible whilst fulfilling specific requirements, for example, one of the following.

- the set of (complete) paths covers all nodes
- the set of (complete) paths covers all multiple edges, i.e. at least one of several edges between two nodes
- the set of (complete) paths covers all edges, i.e. if there are several edges between two nodes, each of them
- the set of (complete) paths covers all simple paths
- the set of (complete) paths covers all iteration-free paths
- the set of (complete) paths covers all paths.

The requirements become stricter from top to bottom. For example, the coverage of all nodes in general a smaller number of complete paths than that for the coverage of all simple paths. Concerning the last criterion, i.e. to find a set of complete paths that covers all paths, there is a problem for graphs with loops, since in this case there are in principle infinitely many paths.

12.4.2 Interpretation and importance for test concepts

The model of the P graph can be interpreted as an abstract representation of the call relations in a program. We assume that we have a program or system consisting of procedures (or modules). We represent each procedure (or module) as a node and each call of a procedure in another procedure as an edge between the corresponding nodes. It should be noted that if a procedure is called repeatedly in another procedure, the number of edges between the nodes is increased accordingly. The fact of several call statements could not be modelled if we had not used a multigraph.

Example:

> Let a program consist of the main program A and the procedures B, C, D, E, F and G. A calls B and C, B calls D and E, C calls E twice, D calls E and E calls F and G.

It is important to note that a path in the P graph represents a sequence of descending calls and that this descending sequence is independent of the call sequence within a procedure. The P graph in Figure 12.3 shows, for example, that the main program A calls the procedures B and C. However, It contains no information about whether this is done in a specific order or independently of each other since using that graph model as an abstract representation of the system all aspects except call relations are ignored.

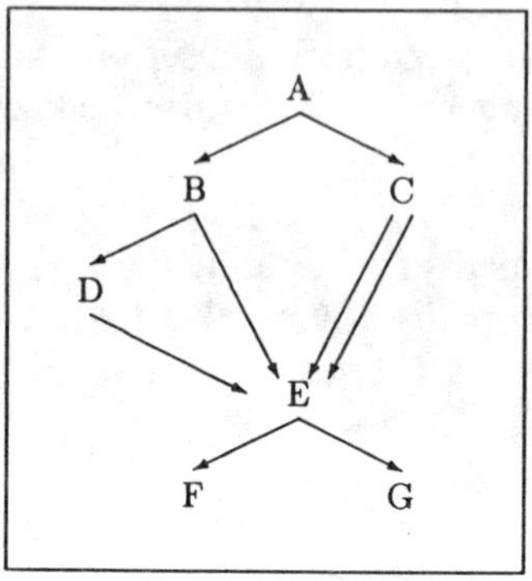

Figure 12.3 An example

The graph theoretic concept of a set of complete paths that fulfils a specific requirement can be used for defining test concepts with the aid of this interpretation.

1. The set of complete paths covers all nodes: each procedure must be executed at least once.
2. The set of complete paths covers all multiple edges: each call relation must be executed at least once.
3. The set of complete paths covers all edges: each call must be executed at least once.
4. The set of complete paths covers all simple paths: each sequence of descending calls must be executed at least once and each call must occur only once in the descent.
5. The set of complete paths covers all iteration-free paths: each sequence of descending calls without loops must be executed at least once.
6. The set of complete paths covers all paths: each sequence of descending calls must be executed at least once.

Defining test concepts on the graph model, we import the problems of the model world, i.e. the problem of the 'in principle infinitely many paths' in the case of loops. In addition, there is another problem resulting from the abstraction. Not all descending sequences represented in the graph need necessarily be executable in the program. In Figure 12.3, for example, there is a path from E to F and one from E to G. It may well be, however, that depending on conditions in the program F is called only if B was called previously, and G only if C was called previously. In such cases, test data selection criteria which consider paths cannot be satisfied.

The test concepts defined on the P graph consider only the execution of call statements. This is necessary for fault detection, but not sufficient. Relevant aspects, such as call sequences within a procedure and data flow between procedures (via parameters) are neglected by the abstraction. Considering such aspects, we also find need for control flow and data flow graphs respectively [7, 4, 3]. An example of a type of fault which is covered is the call of a wrong procedure (e.g. if in procedure B, G was called instead of E). Examples of fault types not covered are the call of procedures in an incorrect sequence or with incorrect parameter values.

12.5 EMBEDDING IN THE DEVELOPMENT PROCESS

The approach we have described can be embedded in the development process and thus used for a concrete selection of suitable test concepts. Within the test process we distinguish test steps, for example, module test, integration test and system test. Müllerburgh [11] presents the method of stepwise testing (MOST) for decomposing the test process into test steps. This method is based on the assumption that there is no generally applicable decomposition into test steps, but that both the decomposition into test steps and the selection of test concepts, depends on the specific development process. Since organisations and even projects in an organisation use, in general, different processes and methods for their software development, the test process has to be adapted appropriately.

The idea underlying the method of stepwise testing is to decompose the test process in such a way that a test step which examines just the aspects emphasised in the construction is identified for each important construction document. The test concepts which are suitable for examining these aspects must be selected and used accordingly for each test step. The basis of a test concept (i.e. for the test data selection) is a document, for example the source code, an informal description of requirements, or a formal specification of system functions. If we are defining test steps by means of this method, we get two documents for each test step, i.e. the source text and the corresponding construction document. For examining the consistency of these documents, we must systematically derive test data from the two documents. Glass- (or white-) box and black-box test methods are distinguished accordingly: in the case of the glass-box test, the test data are derived from the source code, in the case of the black-box test, from the construction document. However, there is in principle no difference between the test concepts. By means of the construction document, the abstract representations relevant to this testing step can be determined. Corresponding representations can then be selected from those for the source test.

The embedding of the approach presented in this paper in the method of stepwise testing leads to a systematic definition of test steps and a goal-oriented selection of test concepts. In this way, the test expenditure can be used more effectively.

12.6 SUPPORT BY THE METKIT CAI SYSTEM

The approach suggested here leads to a plethora of information which cannot be handled manually. Many objects need to be distinguished and accordingly we have many models and test concepts.

The systematic examination of test concepts and their relationships represents conceptual knowledge from the software test area. In another context, we have developed the METKIT CAI System which enables us to handle such types of knowledge on the computer [13]. The system has been developed in ESPRIT II Project METKIT (Metrics Education Toolkit) and supports different types of access to conceptual knowledge. In the METKIT Project, the system was used to provide knowledge about measurement as a means of software quality assurance. The idea of using models was used here to facilitate the understanding of software metrics. The use of the system in this area has led to very encouraging results.

The system is based on a specific structuring of conceptual knowledge [8, 12]. The structuring means are very simple: sets, elements, relations, and descriptions. Sets and elements represent concepts, relations their relationships, and so-called explanations contain detailed information. There are relations between sets as well as between elements. Each set, each element, and each relation are assigned an explanation. Sets and relations as well as elements and relations define networks. The system allows sets, elements, and relations to be defined and modified, and explanations to be edited. In addition, it provides two types of access, on the one hand via alphabetic sorting of the names of sets and elements and, on the other, via a graphic representation of the networks.

To model knowledge about test concepts, we distinguish the aforementioned sets of objects, models, and test concepts, as well as the relations between objects and models, and between models and test concepts respectively (see Figure 12.1). The access via the graphic representation of these relationships can be used, for example, to define test concepts for a specific object. Starting from an object, we may ask for its context and receive the models which are inferable from it. A further question about the context of a model leads to the test concepts defined on it. Starting with a test concept, we may also search for objects for which it is usable. The graphic representation of the relations enables us to see the context of an object, a model, or a test concept directly (see Figure 12.2).

12.7 SUMMARY

The testing of large software systems is still very expensive, and generally does not lead to reliable propositions about their correctness. Since it is not the aim to test as much as possible, we must attempt to use the test expenditure as optimally as possible. The thesis here is that the expenditure of testing can be reduced by a goal-oriented selection of test concepts. Goal-oriented means that suitable test concepts are selected depending on the respective test object and the test goal.

As a basis for such a selection, it is suggested that test concepts be defined not directly on the objects considered in the software development process but on formal models which are interpreted as abstract representations of those objects. Modelling has proved effective in many areas. The approach using models supports the exact definition of test concepts and provides a solid basis for their examination. In this way, the understanding of test concepts can be facilitated and their advantages and disadvantages are identified more easily.

By interpreting a model as an abstract representation of objects, findings of the theory underlying the model can be used as propositions about the objects. Since this is independent of specific languages, the propositions apply to whole classes of objects, namely to all objects for which the model is accepted as an abstract representation.

By means of the METKIT CAI System, the approach suggested here can be used for a systematic analysis and definition (including suitable documentation of test concepts. The handling of knowledge about concepts and their relationships on the computer enable us to build and extend knowledge step by step. New test concepts and new models can be inserted as easily as new object types. The model approach also enables us to consider test concepts from other areas (e.g. VLSI design).

ACKNOWLEDGEMENTS

The author wants to thanks Susanne Flacke, Angelika Linden and Dirk Meyerhoff for many stimulating discussions which have contributed to the ideas presented here and, in addition, Ursula Bernhard for her translation of a previous German version of this text.

REFERENCES

[1] Bache, R. and Müllerburg, M. 1990. Measures of Testability as a Basis for Quality Assurance. *IEE/BCS Software Engineering Journal,* 5 (2), March, pp. 86–92.

[2] Chow, T.S. (ed.) 1985.*Tutorial Software Quality Assurance*. IEEE Computer Society Press, Los Angeles.

[3] Franck, R., Spillner, A. and Herrmann, J. 1990. Methods and Tools for Integration Testing of Large Software Systems. In *Proc. 2nd European*

Conference on Software Quality. European Organisation for Quality Control (EOQC).

[4] Harrold, M.J. and Soffa, M.L. 1991. Selecting and Using Data for Integration Testing. *IEEE Software*, March, pp. 58–85.

[5] Howden, W.E. 1976. Reliability of the path analysis testing strategy. *IEEE Transactions on Software Engineering*, **SE-2** (3), September, pp. 208–15.

[6] Howden, W.E. 1987. *Functional Program Testing and Analysis*. New York: McGraw-Hill, Inc.

[7] Linnenkugel, U. and Müllerburg, M. 1990. Test Data Selection Criteria For (Software) Integration Testing. In *Proc. of The First International Conference on Systems Integration*, April, pp. 707-17. IEEE.

[8] Meyerhoff, D. and Müllerburg, M. 1992. Structured Hypertext Applied to Software Measurement. In *Proc. of 12th World Computer Congress (IFIP'92)*, September. IFIP.

[9] Miller, E.F. and Howden, W.E. (eds) 1978. *Tutorial: Software Testing and Validation*. IEEE. IEEE Catalog No. EHO 138-8.

[10] Müllerburg, M. 1989. Fundamental concepts of software testing. Revised version of the paper On Fundamentals of Program Testing. In *Proc. of the 1st European Seminar on Software Quality*, European Organisation for Quality Control (EOQC), 1988, pp. 290–305.

[11] Müllerburg, M. 1990. Software Testing: A Stepwise Process. In *Proc. of the 2nd European Conference on Software Quality*. European Organisation for Quality Control (EOQC).

[12] Müllerburg, M., Meyerhoff, D. and Flacke, S. 1991. Enhancing Accessibility of Metrics Knowledge. In *Proc. of EUROMETRICS 91*, pp. 369–379. EC2.

[13] Müllerburg, M., Meyerhoff, D. and Flacke, S. 1992. The METKIT System at the Age of One. In *Proc. of EUROMETRICS 92*. EC2.

[14] Myers, G.J. 1979. *The Art of Software Testing*. London: John Wiley & Sons.

[15] Prather, R.E.1987. On hierarchical software metrics. *Software Engineering Journal*, March, pp.42–45.

13 Usability Assessment and Measurement

Nigel Bevan and Miles Macleod [1]
National Physical Laboratory

13.1 WHY DOES USABILITY MATTER?[2]

Most computer software in use today is unnecessarily difficult to understand, hard to learn, and complicated to use. Difficult to use software wastes the user's time, causes worry and frustration, and discourages further use of the software. Why is the usability of most computer software so poor, and what are the benefits that more usable software could bring to the employer and supplier?

Benefits to the employer include:

- Usable software increases productivity and reduces costs. Difficult to use software is time-consuming to use, and not exploited to full advantage as the user may be discouraged from using advanced features. Difficult to learn software also increases the cost of training and of subsequent support.
- Usable software increases employee satisfaction. Difficult to use software reduces motivation and may increase staff turnover.
- In Europe, employers have an obligation to meet the requirements of the Display Screen Equipment Directive (CEC 1990) which requires software in new workstations to be 'easy to use' and to embody 'the principles of software ergonomics' (Bevan, 1991b).

Benefits to the supplier include:

- Software suppliers are increasingly facing a market where users demand easier to use software, and legislation and standards are putting pressure

---

[1] This chapter includes a description of tools to measure usability produced by participants in the ESPRIT MUSIC project (see Rengger 1991; Wietoff, Arnold and Houwing 1991; Gunsthövel and Bösser 1991; and Kirakowski, , Porteous and Corbett 1992), and material based on ISO 9241-11 produced by members of ISO TC159/SC4/WG5/SG2 and edited by N. Bevan (see Brooke, Bevan, Bringham, Harker and Youmans 1990).

2. Author: Nigel Bevan

on employers to provide usable software. End-users are becoming more discerning. Promotional programmes, such as 'Usability Now!' in the UK, are making purchasers more conscious of the benefits of usability, and more inclined to give greater weight to ease of use when making purchases.

- Usability is increasingly providing suppliers with a market edge, as can be seen in recent advertising campaigns by Microsoft and Amstrad which have promoted ease of use as a major selling feature.
- International standards for usability and the user interface are nearing finalisation, will increasingly be cited in public procurement, and provide a means to meet the requirements of the European Display Screens Directive (Bevan 1991a).

13.1.1 Why is software so difficult to use?

Given the potential benefits to the supplier, employer, and end user, why is so much software so difficult to use? A major problem is that in spite of recent acknowledgement that usability is an important software quality (e.g. ISO 9126), it has remained a fuzzy concept which has been difficult to evaluate and impossible to measure. As a consequence it is often not explicitly identified as part of the user requirements and does not form part of the product specification. Even when ease of use has been identified as a desirable property, how can a product developer with the responsibility for developing a product to specification, on time, and within budget justify spending the extra resources required to produce a usable product? An additional problem is that dealing with usability requires skills in human factors, and is difficult to integrate with many existing design processes.

What is required is a common understanding of what constitutes usability and how it can be specified and measured. This has been one of the major objectives of the development of ISO 9241-11: Guidance on specifying and measuring usability (Brooke et al., 1990), which will be published as a Draft International Standard in 1993.

13.1.2 Benefits of measuring usability during design

In parallel with this activity, the ESPRIT MUSiC project has been developing a set of methods for specifying and measuring usability which are consistent with the approach taken in the standard (see section 6 below). The objectives of measuring usability during design are to ensure that the delivered product reaches the minimum required level of usability, and to provide feedback during design on the extent to which the objectives are being met, and on details of potential usability defects in the product.

13.2 USABILITY FEATURES AND ATTRIBUTES[3]

13.2.1 Can usability be measured by features and attributes?

The ideal way to specify and measure usability would be to specify the features and attributes required to make a product usable, and measure whether they are present in the implemented product. This is the approach taken with other software qualities such as functionality, efficiency and portability, and it enables quality to be designed into a product.

The problem with usability is that it is very difficult to specify what these features and attributes should be. There have been many attempts to describe them, including dialogue principles, guidelines and checklists, and analytic procedures.

13.2.2 Dialogue principles

High level principles for user interface design are contained in ISO 9241-10 (ISO 1992b) 'Dialogue principles' (which is based on an earlier DIN standard). These principles are: suitability for the task, suitability for learning, suitability for individualisation, conformity with user expectations, self-descriptiveness, controllability, and error tolerance.

ISO 9241-10 gives applications and examples of each principle. For example, one application of controllability is 'If interactions are reversible and the task permits, it should be possible to undo the last dialogue step'. An example of this is 'The dialogue system offers the possibility to access deleted objects'.

These principles have broad application, and are particularly relevant in interpreting the requirement in the European Display Screens Directive (CEC, 1990) that 'the principles of software ergonomics shall be applied' to the operator/computer interface. However, it has proved impossible to formally assess compliance to these types of general principles. In particular it is difficult to decide whether and to what extent they apply in borderline cases. This means that they cannot be used as a basis for measurement.

13.2.3 Checklists and guidelines

There are many user interface guidelines which can improve usability when applied in design. Some guidelines are in terms of user interface features (e.g. provision of help, screen layout of a menu), and others state higher level attributes (e.g. consistency, flexibility). There are a number of collections of guidelines for the design of user interfaces. The best known is by Smith and Mosier (1986), and this formed the starting point for more rigorous guidelines

---

[3] Author: Nigel Bevan

which are being published by ISO as international standards (consisting primarily of recommendations) (ISO 1993a). The most ambitious example of a complete specification of features is probably the Menu Dialogue guidelines in ISO 9241-14 (ISO 1993d). These are in the form of 112 conditional recommendations. Only those guidelines which are applicable have to be followed, for instance, 'If the ordering of option usage is known, options should be placed in that order in the menu'.

Other more general checklists include those by Ravden and Johnson (1989) where users fill in detailed checklists about the acceptability of various aspects of the interface thus highlighting particular types of problems; and EVADIS (Oppermann et al. 1989, 1992) where usability specialists evaluate the usability of the system for predefined tasks by assessing whether it meets detailed requirements given in checklists.

Some procedures for the assessment of the usability of software (e.g. McGinley and Hunter 1992) also use adherence to guidelines as a basis for assessment.

There are also more detailed style guides. For example, when a graphical interface is appropriate, the IBM CUA Guide to User Interface Design (IBM 1991a, 1991b) provides detailed advice on how the features can be most effectively implemented.

13.2.4 Limitations of guidelines and checklists

Guidelines have the advantage that they can be applied early in design, and adherence to most guidelines can be assessed merely by inspection of the product without user testing. However, guidelines have a number of limitations:

- Detailed and specific guidelines are likely to be appropriate only for specific systems and specific types of users. However, guidelines and principles expressed in general terms are difficult for developers and evaluators to interpret – they can mean very different things to different people. (This is eloquently demonstrated by Grudin, 1989).
- There is no guarantee that any particular set of guidelines is exhaustive and deal with all relevant aspects of the user interface.
- Many alternative design solutions can be equally compatible with guidelines, but changing an interface feature to be compatible with one guideline often makes it incompatible with another. There is no easy way to trade off the benefits of different guidelines.
- The effectiveness with which guidelines are applied depends on the skill of the designer in interpreting and applying them and making any necessary trade-offs.
- Some usability attributes are context-dependent properties of interaction which can only be evaluated when a product is actually used by representative users for representative tasks.

- Evaluating whether a product is consistent with guidelines can be very time-consuming. For instance, applying the menu guidelines standard to a complete product requires that every menu in a product is checked for conformance with every applicable recommendation.
- Following guidelines does not ensure that a product reaches any particular level of usability. In particular the structure of dialogue design is just as important as the more easily assessable surface features. In many cases the usability of a product will be improved by redesigning the interface to be consistent with guidelines, but a much bigger improvement to the usability can often be made by considering whether the task can be carried out more effectively by a more fundamental redesign (e.g. avoiding the use of menus to search for information by supplying a unique key which gives direct access).
- Guidelines often attempt to generalise across a wide range of characteristics of users, tasks, and environments, and it is very difficult to specify rigorously the limits of the context in which a guideline is applicable.
- Where guidelines are expressed in general terms, their interpretation may rely so much on expert opinion that objective evaluation is simply not possible.
- When guidelines are used for evaluation the result is a checklist showing which parts of a product conform to which recommendations. While this can be used to identify potential problems with the interface, it cannot be turned into measures as there is no way of weighting the importance of the different recommendations.

13.3 ANALYTICAL EVALUATION[4]

More formal analytical approaches to evaluation can produce measures which give predictions about usability. The methods require at least a partial specification of the system and its user interface, and employ some kind of theoretical representations of the user. They can be quite simple and of limited scope – for example the Keystroke Level Model (K-LM) (Card, Moran and Newell 1980) – or more complex and wide-ranging, such as SANe (Gunsthövel and Bösser, 1991). Being based on specifications, they can be conducted early in the design cycle. Analytic methods only model limited aspects of users, tasks and software, and the results tend to focus on quite detailed aspects of the design, such as menu design and specific dialogue sequences. While they cannot assure usability, they can be very effective at identifying significant problems early in design.

The Keystroke-Level Model is one of the oldest and simplest methods for

---

4 Author: Miles Macleod

theoretical evaluation of how easy it is to perform a task via a given computer interface. The K-LM is explicitly limited to predicting time for expert, error-free task performance. As its name suggests, a K-LM analysis describes interaction at the level of individual keystrokes and mouse movements: the input which an expert user has to make into the system in order to perform the task. It also makes a simple allowance for mental operation time at specific points in the interaction. By adding together predicted times for individual keystroke-level actions, the K-LM provides a means of predicting the time it will take expert users to perform individual tasks if they do not make any mistakes.

More sophisticated analytic models can be employed, early in design, to test specifications for specific aspects of usability for users who have different degrees of skill and knowledge. These models represent at some level the processes of system and the cognitive processes or abilities of the user. They work by generating predictions of the complexity of thought and action which are demanded of the user in performing specified tasks. They require a cognitive model of the user, and a specification of the user system interface. Their aim is to reduce the need for design changes later in development, when alterations are more difficult and expensive to make. Currently available methods require substantial expertise to deliver useful predictions, although some recent methods are easier to apply, such as the more recent version of Cognitive Complexity Theory (Kieras 1988) and SANe (Gunsthövel and Bösser, 1991). The SANe toolkit has been developed partly within the MUSiC Project. SANe is one of the MUSiC tools for measuring usability and is described in more detail in below.

13.4 CONTEXT OF USE[5]

13.4.1 Usability depends on the context of use

It is not meaningful to talk simply about the usability of a product, as usability is a function of the context in which the product is used. The characteristics of the context (the users, tasks, and environment) may be as important in determining usability as the characteristics of the product itself. Changing any relevant aspect of the context of use may change the usability of the product. For instance, the user interface may be improved by conforming to good dialogue design practices, or the fit between the user and the rest of the overall system may be improved through means such as selection and training or good task design. A product which is usable by trained users may be unusable by untrained users. Aspects of the working environment such as lighting, noise, workstation design might be improved.

5 Author: Nigel Bevan, based on ISO DIS 9241-11 (1993) and Maissel et al. (1991)

13.4.2 Relationship of the dialogue principles to the context of use

The context of use is relevant whenever designing for or evaluating usability. For instance, it is necessary to identify the relevant characteristics of the intended users, tasks, and environments before applying the dialogue principles for design or evaluation.

Some dialogue principles are closely related to particular aspects of the context of use. 'Suitability for the task' deals with design issues which are closely associated with the task characteristics. When applying this principle, particular consideration should be given to those tasks which particular types of user may need to perform to meet the goals of the user organisation. 'Suitability for learning', 'suitability for individualisation', and 'conformity with user expectations' deal with design issues which are closely associated with the user characteristics. When applying these principles careful consideration should be given to the needs of different types of intended users when performing intended tasks in particular situations.

13.4.3 Usability is the quality of interaction in a context

While it should in principle be possible to predict usability from an analysis of the characteristics of the product, the users, the task, and the environment, it is rarely possible in practice. Although these factors in combination determine the usability of a product used in a particular context, the only thing which can be accurately measured is the consequence in terms of the quality of interaction. Usability is a property of the overall system: it is the quality of interaction between a user and other parts of the overall system. The quality of interaction can be measured by the extent to which the intended goals of use of the overall system are achieved (effectiveness); the resources such as time, money, or mental effort that have to be expended to achieve the intended goals (efficiency); and the extent to which the user finds the overall system acceptable (satisfaction). The overall system consists of the users, tasks, equipment (hardware, software, and materials), and physical and social environments which influence the interaction.

Usability in this sense is defined in ISO 9241-11 (ISO 1993c) as 'The effectiveness, efficiency and satisfaction with which specified users achieve specified goals in particular environments'. The remainder of this chapter explains and extends the approach to usability taken in ISO 9241-11 (Brooke et al. 1990).

The relationship between the factors is illustrated in Figure 13.1.

13.4.4 Usability attributes of a product and usability of an overall system

The usability of an overall system encompasses all factors which may influence use of a product in the real world, including organisational factors, such as working practices and the location or appearance of a product, and individual differences between users, such as those due to cultural factors and prejudice. This broad approach has the advantage that it concentrates on the real purpose of design of a product – that it is usable by real users carrying out real tasks in a real technical, physical, and organisational environment.

The term usability is sometimes used more narrowly to refer specifically to the usability attributes of a product, e.g. the definition of usability as a software quality in ISO/IEC 9126 (ISO 1991): 'a set of attributes of software which bear on the effort needed for use and on the individual assessment of such use by a stated or implied set of users'.

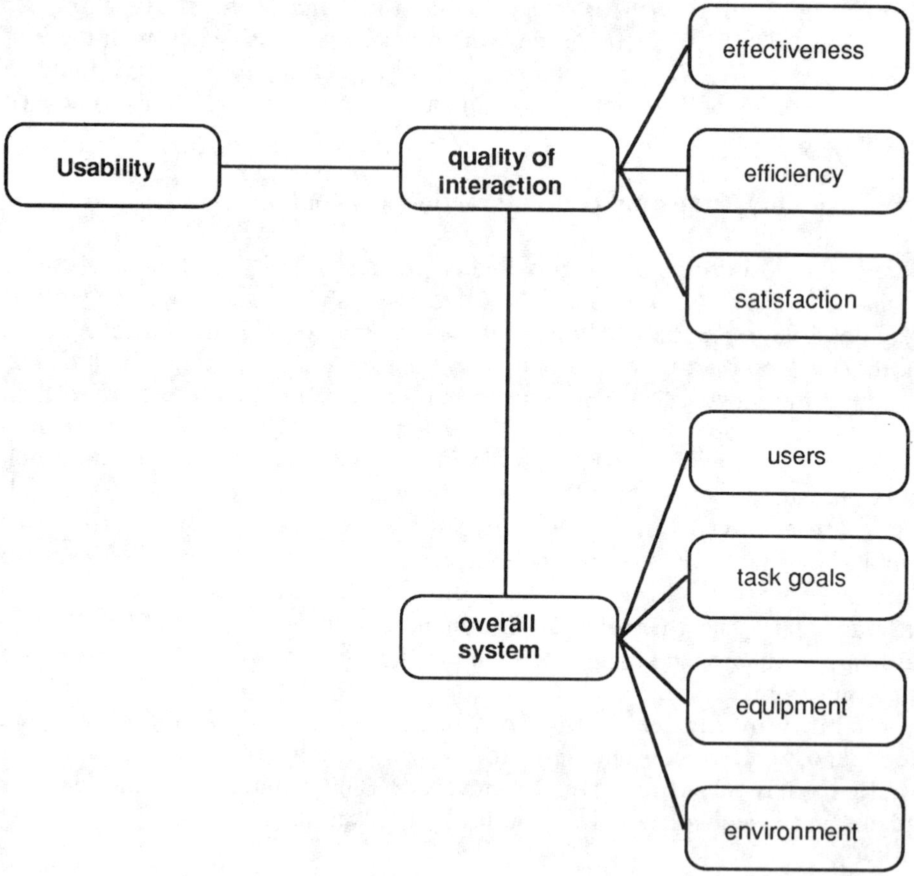

Figure 13.1 Usability factors

The relationship between the definitions is that the product-centred definition is concerned with the usability attributes of the software which will determine usability in a specific context. The usability attributes in the product contribute to the effectiveness, efficiency, and satisfaction with which specified users achieve specified goals in particular environments. But the effectiveness, efficiency, and satisfaction will also depend on other software qualities such as functionality, reliability, and system efficiency, in addition to the relevant aspects of the context of use. The usability attributes of a product are thus only one contribution to the usability of an overall system.

The term usability means different things to different people. Usability can be viewed in different ways for different purposes, focusing on one or more of the following views:

- the product-centred view of usability: that the usability of a product is the attributes of the product which contribute towards the quality of interaction
- the overall system view of usability: that the usability of an overall system is the combination of characteristics of the user, product, task, and environment which cause a particular quality of interaction
- the quality of interaction view of usability: that usability is the quality of interaction between a user and a product in the context of an overall system
- the outcome of interaction view of usability: that usability can be measured as the effectiveness, efficiency, and satisfaction with which specified users achieve specified goals in particular environments.

The designer and specifier of a product need to start with the overall system view to identify the context in which the product will be used. All the components of the overall system that influence the quality of the interaction must be described if it is to be fully specified or evaluated. Given this context, the developer will be concerned with maximising usability and diagnosing defects by taking the product view. Both specifier and developer will wish to improve the quality of interaction. Since this cannot be directly assessed they can use measures of the outcome of interaction to specify usability and measure whether desired levels are achieved.

13.5 SPECIFYING AND MEASURING USABILITY[6]

13.5.1 Context of measurement must match context of use

When usability is measured, it is important that the conditions for a test of usability are representative of important aspects of the overall context of use. Unless evaluation of usability can take place in conditions of actual use, it will

---

[6] Author Nigel Bevan, based on ISO DIS 9241-11 (1993) and Rengger (1993).

USERS	EQUIPMENT/TASK	ENVIRONMENT
PERSONAL DETAILS User types Audience and secondary users SKILLS & KNOWLEDGE Product experience System knowledge Task experience Organisational experience Training Keyboard & input skills Qualifications Linguistic ability General knowledge PHYSICAL ATTRIBUTES Age Gender Assumed physical capabilities Physical limitations and disabilities COGNITIVE ATTRIBUTES Intellectual ability Attitude	EQUIPMENT BASIC DESCRIPTION Product identification Product description Main application areas Major functions SPECIFICATION Hardware Software Materials Other Items TASK CHARACTERISTICS Task breakdown Task name Task goal Task frequency Task duration Frequency of events Task flexibility Physical and mental demands Task dependencies Task output Safety criticality	ORGANISATIONAL STRUCTURE Hours of work Group working Job function Work practices Assistance Interruptions Management structure Communications structure ATTITUDES & CULTURE IT policy Organisational aims Industrial relations JOB DESIGN Job flexibility Performance monitoring Performance feedback Pacing Autonomy Discretion TECHNICAL ENVIRONMENT CONFIGURATION Hardware Software Reference materials PHYSICAL ENVIRONMENT WORKPLACE CONDITIONS Atmospheric conditions Auditory environment Thermal environment Visual environment Environmental instability WORKPLACE DESIGN Space and furniture User posture Location WORKPLACE SAFETY Health hazards Protective clothing/equipment

Table 13.1 Example of breakdown of context

be necessary to decide which attributes of the actual or intended context of use are to be represented in the context used for evaluation. When specifying or evaluating usability it is therefore important that the context selected is representative of the important aspects of the actual or intended context of use. Particular attention should be given to those attributes which are judged to have a significant impact on the usability of the overall system.

Using a breakdown of the context such as the example given in Table 13.1, information needs to be collected under each of the headings on the context in which the equipment is actually used (or is intended to be used).

13.5.2 Choosing tasks, users, environments

The choice of appropriate types of user, tasks, and environments depends on the objectives of the evaluation and how the product is expected to be used. For a general-purpose product it may be necessary to specify or measure usability in several different contexts, which will generally be a subset of the possible contexts and of the tasks which can be performed.

Care should be taken in generalising the results of any measurement of usability to another context which may have significantly different types of users, tasks, or environments. Also, if usability is measured over a short period of time it may not take account of infrequent occurrences which could have an impact on usability, such as intermittent system errors.

The nature of the product and tasks being specified or evaluated will determine the range of the measures and the breadth of the context which may influence the measures. For instance, the usability of a new cut-and-paste feature will be influenced by a comparatively limited and well-defined context, while a new time-management system will be influenced by a wide context which may include other users and organisational issues. For the cut-and-paste feature, efficiency might be based on the mental effort or time required to successfully complete tasks, while for the time-management system, time and overall financial cost might be relevant resources.

13.5.3 Choosing usability measures

A description of the quality of interaction should consist of appropriate measures of user performance (effectiveness and efficiency), and of user satisfaction. Because the relative importance of components of usability depends on the context of use and the purposes for which usability is being described, there is no general rule for how measures can be combined. It is normally necessary to provide at least one measure for each of the components of quality of interaction, and it will often be necessary to repeat measures in several different contexts.

13.5.3.1 Effectiveness

Measures of effectiveness relate the goals or sub-goals of using the system to the accuracy and completeness with which these goals can be achieved.

For example, if the desired goal is to transcribe a two-page document into a specified format, then accuracy could be specified or measured by the number of spelling mistakes and the number of deviations from the specified format, and completeness by the number of words of the document transcribed divided by the number of words in the source document.

13.5.3.2 Efficiency

Measures of efficiency relate the level of effectiveness achieved to the expenditure of resources. The resources may be mental or physical effort, which can be used to give measures of human efficiency, or time, which can be used to give a measure of temporal efficiency, or financial cost, which can be used to give a measure of economic efficiency.

From a user's perspective, the time he or she spends carrying out the task, or the effort required to complete the task are the resources he or she consumes. These two types of resources produce two different definitions of efficiency:

$$\textbf{Temporal efficiency} = \frac{\textbf{Effectiveness}}{\textbf{Task time}}$$

$$\textbf{Human efficiency} = \frac{\textbf{Effectiveness}}{\textbf{Effort}}$$

Temporal efficiency can be measured using the MUSiC Performance Measurement Method (section 13.6.4), while human efficiency can be derived from measures of cognitive workload (section 13.6.6).

From the point of view of the organisation employing the user, the resource consumed is the cost to the organisation of the user carrying out the task, for example:

- The labour costs of the user's time
- The cost of the resources and the equipment used
- The cost of any training required by the user.

In this case, efficiency can be stated as:

$$\textbf{Economic efficiency} = \frac{\textbf{Effectiveness}}{\textbf{Total cost}}$$

For example if the desired goal is to print copies of a report, then efficiency could be specified or measured by the number of usable copies of the report printed, divided by the resources spent on task, such as labour hours, process expense, and materials consumed.

13.5.3.3 Satisfaction

Measures of satisfaction describe the comfort and acceptability of the overall system to the people who use it and to other people affected by its use. Measures of satisfaction may relate to specific aspects of the system or may be measures of overall satisfaction.

Satisfaction can be specified and measured by attitude rating scales such as SUMI (section 13.6.5), but for existing systems attitude can also be assessed indirectly, for instance, by measures such as the ratio of positive to negative comments during use, rate of absenteeism, or health problem reports. Measures of satisfaction can provide a useful indication of the user's perception of usability, even if it is not possible to obtain measures of effectiveness and efficiency.

13.5.3.4 Relative importance of measures

The choice of appropriate measures and level of detail is dependent on which characteristics of the context of use may influence usability and the objectives of the parties involved in the measurement. The importance each measure has relative to the goals of the overall system should be considered. Effectiveness and efficiency are usually a prime concern, but satisfaction may be even more important, for instance, where usage is discretionary.

13.5.4 Derived measures

Some usability objectives will relate to the effectiveness, efficiency and satisfaction of interaction in a particular context. But there are often broader objectives such as learnability or flexibility. These can be assessed by measuring effectiveness, efficiency and satisfaction across a range of contexts.
The learnability of a product can be measured by comparing the usability of one user over time, or comparing the usability of a product for experienced and inexperienced users. (One of the prerequisites for learnability is that the product implements the dialogue principle 'suitability for learning', which refers to the attributes of a product which facilitate learning.)

Flexibility of use by different users for different tasks can be assessed by measuring usability in a number of different contexts. (One contribution to flexibility in use is that the product implements the dialogue principle 'suitability for individualisation', which refers to attributes of the product which facilitate adaptation to the user's needs for a given task.)

Usability can also be assessed separately for subsidiary tasks such as maintenance. The software quality of maintainability can be assessed by the usability of the maintenance process: in this case the task is software maintenance, and the user is the software maintainer.

13.6 MUSiC METHOD

13.6.1 MUSiC project

MUSiC (Metrics for Usability Standards in Computing) is an ESPRIT project which is developing methods and tools for the specification and measurement of usability. Tools have been developed for measuring four aspects of usability: user performance, user satisfaction, cognitive workload and analytic metrics which can predict usability. In addition, there is a Context Guidelines Handbook to identify the key characteristics of the users, tasks, and environments, and an Evaluation Design Manager to guide the choices being made when planning and carrying out an evaluation.

13.6.2 Context Guidelines Handbook

Usability evaluation and measurement must take place in an appropriate context which matches the context in which the product will be used. A systematic method for describing the context of use and specifying the context of measurement has therefore been developed by the MUSiC project. In cases where it is not feasible to match all of the components of the context of measurement to the context of use, particular care must be taken not to over-generalise from the results of the study. A description of the context of measurement is an essential part of the report of any evaluation.

The Context Guidelines Handbook incorporates a Context of Use Questionnaire and a Context Report Table, with practical instructions on how to use them to describe a product's context of use, and to specify an appropriate context of measurement.

The critical components of the context which could affect the usability during an evaluation can be identified by the following procedure (Maissel et al. 1991, Macleod et al. 1993):

Consider the characteristics under each heading to decide whether or not they could affect usability. (Each decision will have to be made based on knowledge of HCI and ergonomics, and experience of any similar product evaluations.) These decisions should be made without concern for the design of any evaluation.

Next decide how each of the items which will, or might, affect usability will be represented in the context of use for evaluation. The components can either be controlled, monitored, or ignored.

Components which are controlled are those characteristics which are fixed or kept within specified ranges, for example, selecting subjects with specific levels of product experience, or carrying out the usability measurement of a product in fixed lighting conditions.

Controlled components may be manipulated to introduce a number of experimental conditions to the evaluation. For example, having two experimental task conditions based on the provision or denial of a help manual. It may be necessary to use a larger number of subjects in each experimental condition in order to draw firm conclusions based on statistical tests.

Components which are monitored are not controlled or selected in any systematic way, but they will be monitored so as to avoid extremes or account for outliers in the data. For example, when subjects are not selected in order to guarantee equal proportions of males to females, but their gender is noted.

If a component is ignored, no attempt is made to control or monitor the value of the component. For example, in an air-conditioned office the temperature of the environment might be ignored.

13.6.3 User-based performance measurement[7]

13.6.3.1 MUSiC performance measurement method

Observing the use of a system gives valuable information about usability, unobtainable by other means. Analysis of what is observed, with the help of a video recording, provides a highly effective means of evaluating usability. To obtain valid and reliable results, the people observed should be representative users performing representative work tasks in appropriate circumstances, and the analysis should be methodical. The MUSiC performance measurement method – developed at the National Physical Laboratory, UK – provides a validated method for deriving performance-based usability metrics. The people observed and the tasks they perform are selected as a result of a context of use study, assisted by the MUSiC Context Guidelines Handbook. As part of the analysis, task output must also be assessed. The method is fully documented in the MUSiC Performance Measurement Handbook (Rengger et al. 1993), and is supported by a software tool (DRUM) which greatly speeds up analysis of the video and helps manage the evaluation.

The performance measurement method gives measures of the effectiveness and efficiency of system use by evaluating the extent to which specific task goals are achieved, and the times taken to achieve task goals. It also gives measures of time spent unproductively (for example, overcoming problems and seeking help), plus diagnostic data about the location of such difficulties.

These measures enable comparison of prototypes of alternative designs with earlier versions of a system, or with competing products. The diagnostic information helps identify where specific problems are encountered and where improvements need to be made.

13.6.3.2 Video-assisted usability analysis and DRUM

DRUM, the Diagnostic Recorder for Usability Measurement , is a software tool

[7] Author: Miles Macleod

developed at NPL within the MUSiC Project (Macleod and Rengger 1993). It supports the MUSiC performance measurement method, and also has wider applicability. Video recording offers considerable advantages for usability evaluation. Video clips of end-users working with a system provide convincing evidence for designers and developers of the usability of their system, and of specific problems. However, analysis is required to convey this information effectively, as an unanalysed interaction log contains too much low-level detail.

Video analysis has previously been very time-consuming, with analysis times of ten hours for every hour of video being typical. It can now be performed much more quickly using DRUM – two or three hours to analyse one hour of video. DRUM supports the management and analysis of usability evaluations, including the derivation of usability metrics, and the identification of evaluator-defined critical incidents for diagnostic evaluation. DRUM assists in many aspects of the evaluator's work:

- management of data through all stages of an evaluation
- task analysis to assist identification and analysis of specific events and usability problems
- video control, and creation of an interaction log of each evaluation session
- automated find and video replay of any logged event
- analysis of logged data and calculation of metrics.

DRUM was produced after extensive requirements capture from usability analysts and study of pre-existing evaluation support tools. It has been iteratively developed since 1990 in collaboration with industry to meet the identified needs of usability testing. DRUM has a graphical user interface, on-line context-sensitive help, and a comprehensive user manual (Macleod et al. 1992). It runs on Apple Macintosh and drives a variety of video machines.

DRUM's support for task analysis allows evaluators to predefine, at a suitable level of analysis, the events they wish to log (hierarchically organised if required). This subsequently enables the evaluator to build up time-stamped records of observed events, avoiding difficulties of data analysis which can be encountered with capture of data at the low level of keystrokes and mouse events (Theaker et al. 1989, Hammontree et al. 1992). Initial logging of events can be carried out in real time, if so desired. Most logging is generally carried out retrospectively. Comments can be added to log entries at any time, and entries can be edited. Full control of the video is provided by DRUM, including a variable speed shuttle control. Once any event has been logged, it can be automatically located on the video and reviewed. DRUM gives easy access to previously created logs and other evaluation data files from its database.

The DRUM metrics processor calculates and delivers usability measures and metrics which can be inspected and grouped within DRUM, or exported to a statistics package for further analysis.

13.6.4 Measures of the task performance of users[8]

13.6.4.1 Task effectiveness

In the MUSiC performance measurement method the effectiveness with which a user uses a product to carry out a task is comprised of two components: the quantity of the task the user completes, and the quality of the goals the user achieves (Rengger et al. 1993). Quantity is a measure of the amount of a task completed by a user. It is defined as the proportion of the task goals represented in the output of the task. Quality is a measure of the degree to which the output achieves the task goals.

As quantity and quality are both measured as percentages, task effectiveness can be calculated as a percentage value:

$$\textbf{Task effectiveness} = \frac{(\textbf{Quantity x Quality})}{\textbf{100}}\ \%$$

13.6.4.2 Efficiency

In the Performance Measurement Method, the efficiency of the user is defined as:

$$\textbf{User Efficiency} = \frac{\textbf{Effectiveness}}{\textbf{Task Time}}$$

Efficiency iS measured in a particular context. The values have little meaning unless there are efficiency benchmarks against which to compare them. For instance, the efficiency measures can be used to compare the efficiency of:

- two or more similar products, or versions of a product, when used by the same user groups for the same tasks in the same environments
- two or more types of users when using the same product for the same tasks in the same environment
- two or more tasks when carried out by the same users on the same product in the same environment.

In each of these examples the relative efficiency of a test condition can be quoted as a percentage of any of the others.

13.6.4.3 Productive period

The MUSiC performance measurement method defines the productive period of a task as the proportion of the time a user spends on the task progressing towards

[8] Author: Ralph Rengger, National Physical Laboratory, Teddington, Middlesex, UK.

the task goals, irrespective of whether the goals are eventually achieved.

Unproductive periods of the task are periods during which users are seeking help (Help time), searching hidden structures of the product (Search time) and overcoming problems (Snag time). Productive time is therefore defined as the Task time remaining after Help, Search, and Snag times have been removed.

The Productive period of a user is the Productive time expressed as a percentage of the Task time:

$$PP = \frac{\text{Task time} - (\text{Help time} + \text{Search time} + \text{Snag time})}{\text{Task time}} \times 100\ \%$$

13.6.4.4 Measures of learning

The rate at which a user learns how to use particular products in specified contexts can be measured by the rate of increase exhibited by individual metrics when the user repeats evaluation sessions. Alternatively, the efficiency of a particular user relative to an expert provides an indication of the position on the learning curve that the user has reached.

The MUSiC Relative User Efficiency metric is defined as the ratio (expressed as a percentage) of the efficiency of any user and the efficiency of an expert user in the same context.

$$\text{Relative user efficiency} = \frac{\text{User efficiency} \times 100}{\text{Expert efficiency}}\ \%$$

$$\text{Relative user efficiency} = \frac{\text{User effectiveness}}{\text{Expert effectiveness}} \times \frac{\text{Expert task time}}{\text{User task time}} \times 100\%$$

13.6.4.5 Grouped results

When measuring the usability of a product by the MUSiC performance measurement method the results from a group of users with similar characteristics are combined to provide mean usability measures.

Testing of groups of up to ten users is generally found to be a practical proposition as the cost and time for testing larger groups is often prohibitive. However, even with ten users, if there are major differences in the characteristics of the users, then there will be a large variance associated with the mean values of the metrics.

13.6.5 User satisfaction – SUMI[9]

To measure user satisfaction, and hence assess user-perceived software quality, University College Cork has developed the Software Usability Measurement

---

[9] Authors: Jurek Kirakowski and Murray Porteous, University College Cork, Human Factors Research Group, Department of Applied Psychology, Cork, Ireland.

Inventory (SUMI) as part of the MUSiC project. SUMI is an internationally standardised 50-item questionnaire, available in English, German, Dutch, Spanish, and Italian. It takes approximately 10 minutes to complete. At least ten users who are typical of the sorts of people who will be using the software are required to get accurate results with SUMI. The results which SUMI provide are based on an extensive standardisation database based on a full range of software products such as word processors, spreadsheets, CAD packages, communications programs etc. SUMI results have been shown to be reliable and to discriminate between different kinds of software products in a valid manner.

SUMI provides three types of measures: an Overall Assessment, a Usability Profile, and Item Consensual Analysis which gives more detailed information. For the Overall Assessment and the Usability Profile, output is given in a standard format on a scale of 0 to 100 with a mean of 50 and a standard deviation of 10, so that most software products will score somewhere between 40 and 60.

13.6.5.1 Overall assessment

This a general global assessment of usability and it is given by a single numerical figure. The global assessment is useful for setting targets and making quick comparisons between many products or versions of the same product.

13.6.5.2 Profile of perceived usability

This breaks the overall assessment down into five sub-scales:

Affect, Efficiency, Helpfulness, Control, and Learnability.

The sub-scales represent the dimensions with which end-users structure their judgement when they assess the usability of software.

The sub-scales were identified, confirmed, and validated by factor analysis of large amounts of data collected during the development of SUMI and its predecessors, and by discussion with software engineers, human factors experts, end-users, etc. Items which make up these sub-scales have been drawn from a large sample item pool, and have been selected on the basis of their discriminatory power.

13.6.5.3 Item consensual analysis

Item consensual analysis lists out those items on which the software being rated was significantly better or worse than the standard of comparison. This gives an indication of specific aspects of the software which people consistently like or dislike. It is possible to go back and interview users to find out why they gave these ratings. This gives diagnostic information of potential usability defects in the software.

13.6.6 Cognitive workload[10]

Cognitive workload is particularly important in safety-critical tasks. Furthermore, there is a human tendency to strive for an optimal level of performance more or less independent of the technology used. Adequate usability measures should, therefore, reflect aspects of mental effort as well as just performance. Measures of cognitive workload are indirectly derived from the mental effort people invest in their task, rather than directly from the task requirements.

Within the MUSiC project, valid and reliable measures of cognitive workload have been developed by Delft University of Technology (Wiethoff et al. 1991). Cognitive workload can be measured either by objective or by subjective means.

Objective measures are measures that are relatively independent from personal judgements relating to task complexity and are not directly under the conscious control of the subject. The strength of objective measures is that they are unobtrusive and taken whilst the subject is performing the task as well as responding quickly to changes in mental effort.

Subjective measures, on the other hand, are measures obtained by asking people how difficult they find a task, with the help of questionnaires. In this case, measures can only be taken after a task has been finished subjects can consciously control the outcome of the evaluation.

13.6.6.1 Objective measures

A measure of mental effort is Heart Rate Variability which indicates how much the heart rate varies over time. The variation is influenced by blood pressure regulation, temperature regulation, and respiration. In particular it has been shown that the variability related to blood pressure regulation is reduced when people invest mental effort. This variation can be distinguished from the other influences by the distinctive frequency band in which this variation shows itself. Under some circumstances respiration can exert an influence on this frequency band and so it is also necessary to record respiration. The heart rate variability measure is derived directly from the pulse of the heart, so only the occurrence of heartbeats need be recorded. Heart rate itself may increase in situations in which people invest more mental effort, but may also be influenced by other factors such as stress, movements, etc.

Heart rate is measured by applying three light, easy to attach, electrodes on the chest, connecting them by special cables to an amplifier, and attaching this to a recording system. The electrodes are non-intrusive – within moments of attaching the electrodes, the user rarely continues to notice their presence. Respiration is measured by a transducer held in place by a band, attached around

---

[10] Authors: Bert Arnold, Edo Houwing,.Marian Wietoff, Technische Universiteit Delft, Kaanalineg 2B, Postbus 5050, 2600 GB Delft, Netherlands.

the chest and abdomen of the user. The bands are easy to attach with tape over the individual's clothes and do not hamper movements of the individual.

13.6.6.2 Subjective measures

In addition to objective measures, cheaper and easier to use tools are needed in many instances for both laboratory and field experiments.

The Subjective Mental Effort Questionnaire (SMEQ) was developed at the University of Groningen and Delft University of Technology. The SMEQ contains just one scale and has been carefully designed in such a way that individuals are supported in rating the amount of effort invested during task performance. The SMEQ has been administered in various laboratory and field studies with high validity and reliability values.

The Task load Index (TLX) was developed by the Human Performance Group at NASA Ames Research Center. The TLX is a multi-dimensional rating procedure that provides an overall workload score based on a weighted average of ratings on six sub-scales. Three sub-scales relate to the demands imposed on the subjects in terms of:

- mental: the amount of mental and perceptual activity required by the task
- physical: the amount of physical activity required by the task
- temporal: the time pressure felt due to the task.

A further three sub-scales relate to the interaction of an individual with the task:

- performance: the individual's perception of the degree of success
- effort: the degree of effort an individual invested
- frustration: the amount of insecurity, discouragement, irritation and stress.

The TLX is an internationally widely used and acknowledged technique.

13.6.7 Analytic measures[11]

The Westfälische Wilhelms-Universität has developed analytic measures of aspects of the usability of interactive IT systems based on system specifications and on a computer model of user interaction (Bösser 1991).

Analytic measures of usability are measures which describe aspects of usability from the analysis of formal representations of interactive IT systems. Appropriate formal descriptions are often available during the requirements analysis and design phases of system development projects.

The SANe user interaction model is based on the dynamic model of the user interface, and on a model of user tasks. User procedures (the way in which the

---

[11] Author: Tom Bösser, Institut für Allgemeine & Angewandte Psychologie, Westfälische Wilhelms - Universität Münster, Spiekerhof 40143, D-44 Münster, Germany.

user solves the tasks with a specified system) can be generated by simulation. Measures (a total of 25) describe the following aspects of usability quality: efficiency of use, learning requirements, cognitive workload, adaptedness of the system to the tasks, and robustness.

The SANe user interaction model is based on a cognitive model of human skills (Skill Acquisition Network) and can include empirical estimates of performance parameters for human interaction depending on the use of specific interface objects, such as keyboards, pointing devices, or speech interfaces.

13.6.7.1 Applications of SANe

Different scenarios imply different usage of analytical measures of usability. The following scenarios are defined in the SANe method:

- compare alternative designs in respect to usability quality
- follow versions of a system through a development project and track usability quality
- identify shortcomings and deficiencies
- assure conformance to quality requirements defined by DIN/ISO standards and the European Directive on health and safety relating to display terminals
- support procurement projects where the best system for a defined usage context is required.

Analytic measures are most appropriate in the context of the development of application-specific systems, and are most effective in a user-centred development process involving rapid prototyping, design iterations, and the use of CASE tools and interface builders.

The SANe method has been used in the domains of office systems, process control, telecommunications and IT applications in vehicles. Very large applications were analysed and evaluated successfully. With applications which have evolved over long periods of time and were poorly documented, reverse engineering had to be performed with SANe which provided a highly useful accurate documentation of the dynamic model.

13.6.7.2 Derivation of measures

Analytic measures of usability are based on psychologically meaningful cognitive models and on principles of computational complexity. The dynamic model of the user interface defines the state-space in which user behaviour occurs, and tasks are defined as goal states in this space. User procedures are paths traversing this space, leading from an initial to a goal state.

Often the information required to construct a dynamic model of the user interface is readily available in design documents. The task model is developed as part of requirements analysis. Software tools support a highly efficient procedure of model development, debugging, simulation and rapid prototyping, evaluation and documentation.

Use of the SANe method in a user interface development project tracks usability quality of the merging product through all phases of development at small additional cost.

A number of studies have shown that in the comparative analysis of systems analytic measures give good predictions of empirically measurable aspects such as performance, learning cost, and decision complexity.

Analytic measures include aspects such as robustness or memory load which are not directly measurable. It has been shown that these measures allow meaningful interpretation and indicate desired features of systems.

13.6.7.3 SANe tools

The SANe toolkit is a development environment including syntax-directed graphical editors for dynamic models and task models, linking, simulation, and evaluation. Import/export and translators are available to CASE tools, interface builders for MOTIF and OPENLOOK, and to 'Hyper' programming environments.

MiniSANe implements the same analytical measures, but is based on form-filling and does not include the syntax-directed editors and simulation capabilities.

13.7 CONCLUSIONS

The MUSiC methodology is the first comprehensive approach to the measurement of usability. It reinforces the principles in ISO 9241-11, and provides a practical method for specifying and measuring usability during design.

The MUSiC project recommends that the following steps are taken to incorporate usability into design:

- identify business objectives related to usability
- identify critical success factors for usability
- identify appropriate usability goals for these critical success factors
- include usability goals in the requirements specification
- measure usability during development to ensure that goals are met
- feed back information on usability defects into design.

Not all usability measures are required in every situation. The number and type of measures used should depend on the business objectives and the resources available. There are often practical constraints:

- to obtain feedback on usability prior to building a prototype, if the interface is fully specified, use SANe (if cost-effective)

- to obtain the users' perception of the usability of a product already in use, use SUMI (if cost-effective)
- to evaluate the usability of a product or prototype, use the Evaluation Design Manager and/or Context Guidelines to design a usability study (if cost-effective)
- to obtain the users' perception of the usability, include SUMI
- to obtain objective measures of usability and diagnostic feedback, select performance measurement tool(s) according to cost-effectiveness
- to obtain information about cognitive workload, select cognitive workload tool(s) according to cost-effectiveness.

Usability as operationalised by MUSiC encompasses all factors which contribute to the users' view of quality. Other software qualities contribute to this global objective. In this sense usability is the critical software quality for successful and cost-effective use of software.

ACKNOWLEDGEMENTS

The MUSiC project is part funded by the Commission of the European Communities. The work at the National Physical Laboratory was jointly supported by the Department of Trade and Industry.

REFERENCES

Bevan, N. 1991a. Standards relevant to European Directives for display terminals. In Bullinger (1991).

Bevan, N. 1991b. Enforcement of HCI? *Computer Bulletin*, May 1991.

Brooke, J., Bevan, N., Brigham, F., Harker, S. and Youmans, D. 1990. Usability statements and standardisation – work in progress in ISO. In *Human Computer Interaction - INTERACT'90* D. Diaper et al. (ed.), Elsevier.

Bullinger, H.J. 1991. *Proceedings of the 4th International Conference on Human Computer Interaction*, September 1991. Stuttgart: Elsevier.

Card, S., Moran, T.P. and Newell, A. 1980. The Keystroke-Level Model for User Performance Time with Interactive Systems. *Communications of the ACM*, **23**, (7) (July) pp. 396–410.

CEC 1990. Minimum Safety and Health Requirements for Work With Display Screen Equipment Directive (90/270/EEC). *Official Journal of the European*

Communities, No. L 156, 21/6/90.
Grudin, J. 1989. The Case Against User Interface Consistency, Communictions of the ACM **32** (10), 1164–73.

Gunsthövel, D. and Bösser, T. 1991. Predictive metrics for usability. In Bullinger (1991).

Hammontree, M.L. et al. Integrated data capture and analysis tools for research and testing on graphical user interfaces. In *Proc. CHI'92*, pp. 431–32. ACM Press.

IBM 1991a. SAA CUA Guide to user interface design. IBM Document Number SC34-4289-00.

IBM 1991b. SAA CUA Advanced interface design. IBM Document number SC34-4290-00.

ISO 1991. ISO 9126: Software product evaluation – Quality characteristics and guidelines for their use.

ISO 1993a. ISO 9241: Ergonomic requirements for office work with visual display terminals.

ISO 1993b. ISO DIS 9241-10: Dialogue principles.

ISO 1993c. ISO DIS 9241-11: Guidelines for specifying and measuring usability.

ISO 1993d. ISO DIS 9241-14: Menu dialogues.

Kieras, D.E. 1988. Towards a Practical GOMS Model Methodology for User Interface Design. In Helander, M. (ed.), *Handbook of Human-Computer Interaction*, pp. 135–57.

Kirakowski, J., Porteous, M. and Corbett, M. 1992. How to use the software usability measurement inventory: the user's view of software quality. *Proceedings of European Conference on Software Quality*, 3–6 November 1992, Madrid.

McGinley, J. and Hunter, G. 1992. SCOPE catalogue of software quality assessment procedures 3: usability section. SCOPE project deliverable.

Macleod, M., Drynan, A. and Blaney, M. 1992. *DRUM User Guide*. UK: National Physical Laboratory, DITC, Teddington.

Macleod, M., Thomas, C., Dillon, A., et al. 1993. *Context guidelines handbook, Version 3*. UK: NPL, Teddington.

Macleod, M. and Rengger, R. (Submitted for publication 1993) The Development of DRUM: A Software Tool for Video-assisted Usability Evaluation. UK: NPL, Teddington.

Maissel, J., Dillon, A., Maguire, M., Rengger, R. and Sweeney, M. 1991. *Context guidelines handbook.* MUSiC Project Deliverable IF2.2.2, UK: NPL, Teddington.

Oppermann, R., Murchner, B., Paetau, M., Pieper, M., Simm, H. and Stellmacher, I. 1989. *Evaluation of dialog systems.* Germany: GMD, St Augustin.

Oppermann, R., Murchner, B., Reiterer, H. and Koch, M. 1992. *Software-ergonomische Evaluation Der Leitfaden EVADIS II.* Berlin: Walter de Gruyter.

Ravden and Johnson 1989. *Evaluating the usability of human-computer interfaces.* Chichester: Ellis Horwood.

Rengger, R., Macleod, M., Bowden, R., Blaney, M. and Bevan, N. 1993. *MUSiC Performance Measurement Handbook.* UK: NPL, Teddington.

Smith, S. L. and Mosier, J. N. 1986. Guidelines for designing user interface software. MITRE Corporation, Bedford, Mass. ESD-TR-86-278.

Theaker, C. J. et al. 1989. HIMS: A Tool for HCI Evaluations. In *Proc. HCI'89 Conf.*, Nottingham, UK, 5–8 September pp. 427–39. Cambridge University Press.

Whiteside, J., Bennett, J. and Holzblatt, K. 1988. Usability engineering: our experience and evolution. In *Handbook of Human-Computer Interaction*, M. Helander (ed.). Elsevier.

Wiethoff, M., Arnold, A. G. and Houwing, E. M. 1991. The value of psychophysiological measures in human-computer interaction. In Bullinger (1991).

14 Test Automation Using an In-house Testing Tool: a Case History

Mark Fewster
Performance Software Ltd

14.1 BACKGROUND

14.1.1 The products and testing activities

The product range comprises over 120 programs, 2.5 million lines of non-comment code statements, and is ported to all leading industry workstation hardware platforms. The main programs are graphical; user interaction is both keyboard and mouse-driven.

The people who developed or changed the software would perform their own tests. Next, an independent test group, skilled in the use of the product, performed an evaluation of the software before undertaking integration and system tests.

14.1.2 The problems with manual testing

Integration and system testing were done manually and would be repeated for each platform. In 1989 these typically consumed 38 man-weeks effort for every release on every platform. In that year the product was delivered on four platforms over a nine-month period. The length of this period was attributed mainly to the manual testing 'bottle-neck'. The increasing size and complexity of the product meant that each release required more testing effort. This together with the increasing number of platforms (nine are planned for 1991) meant a more efficient way of testing was required.

Since the product had been supported on more and more platforms, it is not meaningful to compare the total test effort release on release. It is useful to consider the average test effort per platform. The graph shows the average effort per platform for three releases. This takes into account not only the manual test effort but also the evaluation effort and administration overheads. Because the tests were done manually (and often from a vague test specification) the tests would often find more generic bugs (i.e. bugs present on all platforms) in the second and subsequent platforms – proving that they were effectively random tests being performed differently every time.

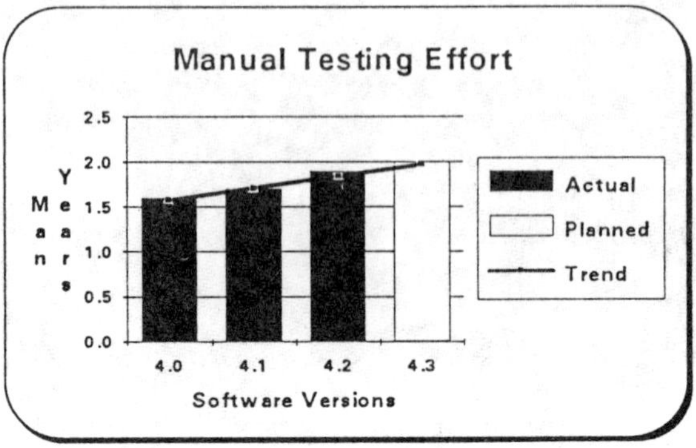

Figure 14.1

14.2 SOLUTIONS

14.2.1 Multi-solution strategy

The requirement was to reduce the cost of testing without reducing the test coverage. In addition to test automation other solutions were implemented in parallel: outside consultancy; training in testing techniques; and better deployment of testing staff.

14.2.2 Test automation tools

A decision had to be made between buying in a tool or developing one in-house. Buying in a tool would mean that test automation could start right away if a suitable tool could be found. Developing a tool in-house would use precious development effort, not only for the implementation but also for maintenance. There was a little experience of automatic testing, albeit on a very small scale. (Two development groups used Unix shell scripts to 'automate' some unit tests. These scripts were based on the same one, an attempt at a generic test script, but each had been 'customised' to meet the specific needs of individual test sets.)

A brief market survey of commercially available testing tools did not reveal any that met all the requirements. It has to be said that the survey was not very thorough. At that time, nobody was aware of any available catalogue of testing tools such as Graham(1991), Software Quality Engineering (1990), and *The STARTS Guide* (1987). However, there was a strong belief that developing some basic test tools would be straightforward. The decision was taken to develop an in-house tool.

14.2.3 Tool functionality

The automatic test harness tool was required to control a series of tests on different programs and software units.

Each test was defined by its input data, instructions on how to run the test, and the expected output data. The tool required that the programs to be tested were capable of being driven solely from data held in files – it was fortunate that most of the programs did have this capability. The comparison process was performed by different programs depending on the format of the data to be compared. Some formats could use a simple comparison, reporting every difference between the two files. More complex comparison programs were required for files that contained legitimate differences.

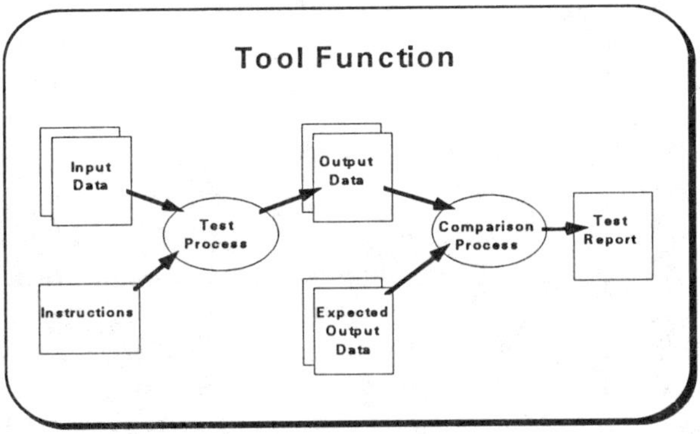

Figure 14.2

Expected output data was not pre-specified manually, instead a reference testing approach was used where the initial test output was manually verified and then used as a reference point for automatic comparison of all further runs.

A test report was generated giving the status of each test run. This also contained details of the versions of software, the machine used, the elapsed times, etc.

14.2.4 Development effort

The test harness tool and a few 'standard' comparison tools were developed in just under a year with nearly four man-years effort. A lot of use was made of prototypes before the detailed requirements could be confirmed. Towards the end of this development period, the test group undertook to automate the integration tests. This was completed with about nine man-months effort. Not all the required tests could be automated – it was still necessary to perform some manually. This was because the programs being tested did not allow access to their internal data structures, often the final result data was insufficient to be sure the test had worked.

14.3 PILOT TRIAL

14.3.1 First use of tool

The automated integration tests were used to test a release. The automatic tests took one man-week, additional manual tests took two man-weeks. The automatic tests could be run in about ten hours but a lack of comparison tools meant that manual effort was required to verify the results. Without automation, integration test took ten man-weeks on every platform. With automation this had been reduced to three man-weeks. Further reductions were possible.

14.4 FULL AUTOMATION

14.4.1 The new goal

Having made a significant impact on integration test, the next step was to automate system test. However this was a much larger undertaking, 28 man-weeks of manual tests to be condensed into tests that could be run automatically.

Unfortunately not all the manual testing was supported by detailed test specifications. Some areas of functionality, when system tested, would be 'exercised' by the test group as they saw fit. Similarly there was little official test data. Manual testing relied on each tester either knowing where suitable data could be found or generating it on the spot. Also, most of the data was platform specific – there was no mechanism for transferring certain types of data between platforms.

This situation was perhaps not as bad as it sounds for many of the testers had been involved with testing for some time and knew just where to find past test data. However, this did mean that we had not only to automate the tests but also define what it was that had to be automated. This complication made it imperative that the testers were involved in the test automation.

14.4.2 Development effort

To automate system test took five man-years over an elapsed time of about a year. Of this effort one man-year involved enhancements to the test tool, the rest was developing the test data.

It was decided to combine the automated integration tests with those being developed for system test. With manual testing, passing the integration tests was effectively the entry criteria for starting system test. For automated testing there seemed little value in retaining the two sets separately since either could be run in a matter of hours rather than weeks. A lot of the integration test result validation had been done manually so these tests themselves needed further work. (By now we had a richer set of comparators that enabled us to automate the test result validation.)

14.4.3 Technical problems

14.4.3.1 Programs not designed for testability

The development groups often proved unwilling or unable to make changes that would enable better testing of their applications. Fortunately, the decision to develop our own test harness tools saved a lot of anguish. It was sometimes possible to implement a temporary work around within the test tool itself by building into it knowledge of the program to be tested.

Few of the programs had been designed with automatic testing in mind. Over a two and a half year period many improvements were made.

14.4.3.2 Cross-platform differences

Despite designing the test data to be 'portable', it came as something of a surprise just how different the test results were on different hardware platforms. It was known that binary files would be of little use as test result data as this can never be compared across platforms. (It is necessary to compare the test results from one platform with the expected result data from a different platform, since it is neither desirable nor practical to hold expected result data for each platform.) However, there were many subtle differences in the ascii files generated by the same tests on different platforms. Most of these could be handled intelligently with existing comparators, but it did take effort that was not planned. The most difficult of these differences were with the graphical output data, e.g. differences in the order items were drawn.

14.4.3.3 Debug information

When the automated testing of the applications started in earnest, debugging the failed tests soon became a time-consuming task. Large tests were inefficient since the person debugging would often rerun the test a number of times with monitoring tools and have to wait until the test reached the point of failure before work on tracing the fault could start .

Debugging also suffered from test automation because the person debugging had to do more work to identify the problem. Previously, a tester would find a fault and then experiment with different input data or actions to try to pinpoint it. The findings were then presented to the person responsible for fixing the problem. With automated tests, the problem fixer was left to unravel why the test had failed (this often required an understanding of what the test was trying to do) and then pinpoint the fault. This problem was made worse by the early versions of the test harness tool which had been designed specifically for finding defects, not helping with analysing them. A number of test-tool enhancements were identified and implemented to ease this problem.

14.4.3.4 Platform architecture

The different hardware platform architectures caused some problems. The most obvious of these was the different processor speeds. The test tool has the ability to abort tests that either 'hang' or run into an infinite loop. This was achieved by declaring as part of the test definition its expected run time. This varied ten fold across the different platforms so tests could be aborted prematurely or machine time can be wasted waiting for the test tool to abort a test that 'died' some hours earlier.

14.4.4 Non-technical problems

14.4.4.1 Too much change too soon

Too much change was undertaken too soon. Perhaps the most significant change (apart from the test automation itself) was the reorganisation that resulted in the testers being moved into the development groups. Had they been left in their own group, fewer people would have become involved at a time when we were still sorting out teething problems and these could have been dealt with more efficiently and with much less anguish.

The reorganisation also meant that some development people were required to do testing that had previously been done by a tester. This was met with resistance – resistance to testing and to the tool. This was partly addressed by the test training. One engineer said of the course, 'Beforehand I thought "oh no! not a testing course!" but I was pleasantly surprised with how enjoyable testing now seems.'

14.4.4.2 Implied automation of development testing

The original goal, to attain 100% test automation, was widely publicised but perhaps not qualified sufficiently well. There was an implication that development testing (unit or module testing done by the development staff) was to be automated. The result of this was for some developers to take a quick look at the test tools, see one or more problems and then backoff. There was not sufficient resource to introduce them all to the tool in a more helpful way.

14.4.4.3 Teething problems caused delays

Because of the number of people involved within the first few weeks of testing, the number of problems and difficulties people found with the new approach to testing seemed enormous. Most of the problems were fairly simple to correct, but the task of communicating the solution to everyone involved proved difficult. The tool became a good excuse for every problem people had. Many problems blamed on the test tool were found to have nothing to do with it! Automatic testing had taken on a very general meaning, which was that any problems encountered while testing with the test tool could be blamed on the tool itself! Most managers never 'wised-up' to this – and they still believe the test tool caused their projects to run behind schedule and over budget!

14.5 THE RESULTS ACHIEVED

14.5.1 Test effort per product release

With the first major release of the product to undergo automatic testing, the average effort per platform was about 48% of what would have been expected with manual testing. This average fell as further platforms were tested.

With all the teething problems the first platform showed no real gains. Subsequent platforms used 60%, 50% and 35% of what would have been expected with manual testing. The test effort for the ninth platform was expected to be around 25%.

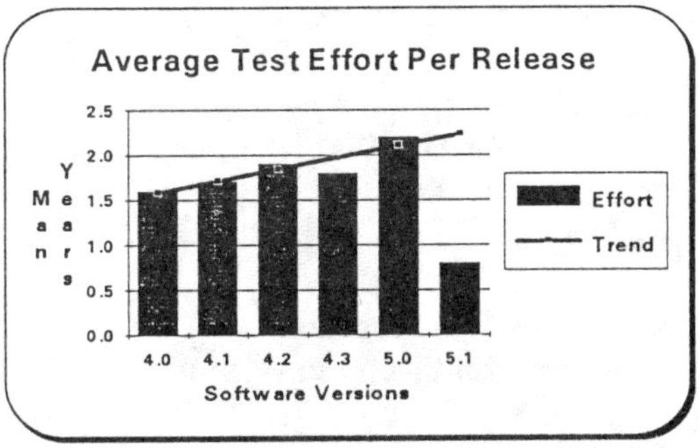

Figure 14.3

It turned out that the effort required could not be reduced any further. This is because the software that is being tested has defects in it! The first pass of testing usually finds a good few problems. Once these are fixed the second pass finds some more. It is this repetition of testing that keeps the test effort high. This does have one advantage however: any small improvement to the test automation is repaid several times over.

A total of eight man-weeks manual testing was being planned for each of the remaining platforms. It was thought that this could be reduced to four man-weeks if the software had fewer bugs at the start of testing. So 79% test automation was achieved although, in theory at least, this could have been as much as 89%.

14.5.2 Lessons learned

14.5.2.1 Need management commitment

This is very important but it has to be planned. In retrospect, the pros and cons of test automation were not explained enough to the managers. An initial 'sales campaign' explained to all the technical staff the aims and benefits of test automation. On its own this was not enough. They should have been repeatedly asked their views to check their understanding. It was all too easy to assume that management would see and understand the problems as the implementors did. There would have been benefit in reading Bouldin (1989) if only it been known of at the time.

14.5.2.2 Makes debug effort more visible

For the first time ever, testing of a major product release was suspended awaiting bug-fixed software from the development groups. Never before had the testers caught up with the developers! Testing and debugging have become more distinct activities.

14.5.2.3 Need to design for testability

There is no substitute for the freedom to choose which data is recorded at which points in time during a test. Not only does this make testing more precise and meaningful but it considerably eases the task of tracing faults. Many of the tests had to 'make do' with whatever data the program could offer when it could offer it. This lead to difficulties in finding out why tests had failed and made debugging much harder work.

14.5.2.4 Need training in testing techniques

The training proved successful not only in encouraging new techniques but also in changing people's attitudes towards testing. There is also a lot to learn about how to design tests for automation. Some will be general and some will be application specific.

14.5.2.5 Tests should be short

At the start of the system test automation there was concern over the overheads associated with a lot of small tests. It was known that long tests (i.e. individual tests that take hours to run) were not desirable, but it was thought that a lot of short tests would incur unacceptable overheads (principally for run-up and run-down times of programs under test, and result comparison times).

It is now clear that tests that run for more than a few minutes have the greater potential for time wasting than several shorter tests. There are several reasons for this. Firstly, because of the different platform architectures, the test time out period is usually a lot larger than is necessary. This can lead to several hours being wasted on just a handful of aborted tests. Secondly, long tests have the potential of finding many defects, but usually only one at a time. These tests have to be rerun after each bug fix. Thirdly, the time spent debugging a problem found by a long test can be several times that for a short one.

14.5.2.6 Control cost of maintaining test data

A lot of the automated test effort was spent reworking the test data. The unexpected differences in test results between platforms forced the creation of platform-specific test data for a time. The job of merging the different versions later on took several man-weeks but was necessary to prevent the expected maintenance effort being repeated for each platform.

14.5.2.7 Test-stopping bugs dtop tests!

This seems obvious – but the impact of it was not clear before we started the testing. The danger of leaving code untested because a test ended before it completed is all too real. To minimise this, tests must be short and failed tests thoroughly investigated.

Some bugs that caused tests to abort before they were complete took on a high priority for fixing even though they may not have affected the end-user. If the decision is taken not to fix the bug, there is then the choice of abandoning the test (and risk leaving software untested), changing the test so it can carry on (if this is possible), or reverting to manual testing for that test.

14.5.3 Benefits achieved

14.5.3.1 Test effort per platform quartered

The average test effort per platform for the first four platforms was cut by three-quarters. While the first platform used only 4% less effort than would have been expected for manual testing, the subsequent platforms improved on this significantly. The last platform achieved about an 80% reduction.

14.5.3.2 Consistency of regression testing

The repeatability of the automated tests is reassuring. Automated tests for bug fixes were implemented; this should guarantee that bugs found in one product release would never appear again (something that didn't happen often but was very embarrassing when it did).

14.5.3.3 Deskilled test running

Less experienced testers and developers have been able to assist with testing that is normally the domain of experienced testers. This allowed better use of valuable skills.

14.5.3.4 Bug fixes fully regression tested

Bug-fixed releases were more rigorously regression tested than would have been practical with manual testing. This found more defects (caused by the fixes) that would have otherwise reached the end-user.

14.5.3.5 Improved time to market

The product had been delivered on more hardware platforms and in the shortest period of time than had ever been achieved before. Also a new hardware model was supported earlier because it could be tested quickly and with little effort. Again, this would have been delayed weeks, if not months, without automated testing.

14.5.3.6 Improved cross-platform quality

The consistency of regression testing gave greater confidence in the different platform releases – what worked, worked on all platforms.

14.5.4 The payback

Over the two and a half years since the test automation project was started five man-years was spent developing and maintaining the test tools and a further five man-years developing the test data. Significant benefits weren't seen until after all this effort had been put in. Six months into automated system testing the 'break even' point was reached. Beyond that, man-years of manual test effort was being saved every three or four months.

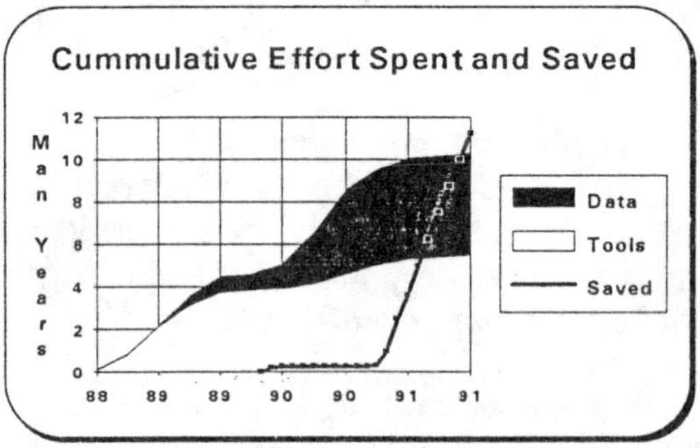

Figure 14.4

The graph above shows the cumulative effort for developing the test tools and the test data. The 'savings' line is the actual and estimated benefit of the test automation programme. Work started in July 1988; the 'break even' point (considering major product releases only) occurred in July 1991.

14.6 SUMMARY

Manual testing had become a bottleneck in the product life cycle and was becoming increasingly costly. Furthermore, the requirement to support more hardware platforms would accelerate the cost. Automatic testing was chosen as the principle solution.

A trial of the test tools was successful and so encouraged an aggressive target to automate the whole of system testing. Many problems were encountered:

- Programs not designed for testability – several changes were necessary before some programs could be automatically tested.

- Cross-platform differences – many unexpected differences between the test results on different platforms caused a lot of rework of the tests.
- Debug information – debugging an automated test proved difficult. Both the test tools and test data required improvements to aid debugging.
- Too much change too soon – organisational changes occurred in parallel with the introduction of test automation. These and other technical changes made it harder work.
- Teething problems caused delays – there was no contingency in the plans to deal with problems with the new approach to testing.

The main benefits achieved are:

- Test effort cut – the first platform showed little improvement but now teething problems have been overcome subsequent platforms are achieving an 80% reduction in total test effort.
- Consistency of regression testing – repeatability of automated tests is reassuring.
- Bug fixes fully regression tested – bug-fix releases were more rigorously tested. This found further defects (caused by the fixes) that would have otherwise reached the end-users.
- Improved time to market – the time between product releases on different platforms was reduced.

The effort spent developing the tools and test data was matched by the savings gained through the reduction in test effort after only six months of testing. From then on savings of man-years of manual test effort is possible every three to four months. This does not take into account the many other benefits, some of which are described above.

The automated testing programme was considered a success and is being continued. Increasing benefits should be expected as tool use is increased, but the initial results have already proved the value of the strategy.

ACKNOWLEDGEMENTS

Thanks are due to Dorothy Graham (Grove Consultants) for her encouragement and support.

REFERENCES

Bouldin, B.M. 1989. *Agents of Change: Managing the introduction of automated tools*. Yourdon Press Computing Series. Englewood Cliffs, N.J.: Prentice-Hall.

Graham, D.R. 1991. Computer-Aided Software Testing: The CAST Report. Unicom Seminars Ltd. Uxbridge, Middlesex, UK.

Myers, G. J. 1979. *The Art of Software Testing*. New York: John Wiley & Sons.

SQE 1990. *Testing Tools Reference Guide, the catalogue of software quality support tools and services*. Jacksonville, FL: Software Quality Engineering.

The STARTS Guide 1987 2nd edn. A guide to methods and software tools for the construction of large real-time systems. Prepared by industry with the support of the DTI (UK Department of Trade and Industry) and NCC, The National Computing Centre, Manchester, UK.

15 Automated Testing: Building and Implementing a Repeatable Test System

Ian Weavers
Standard Chartered Bank

15.1 COST OF TESTING

In Figure 15.1 below the first release is the first time you implement a particular application. From the figures that we've gathered from around the bank, we've found that for the first release 40% of the total cost of development is actually spent testing. For subsequent releases, the amount of time spent on development goes down dramatically, because you've made the big investment, you've got the functionality out there, and you're making minor or local enhancements.

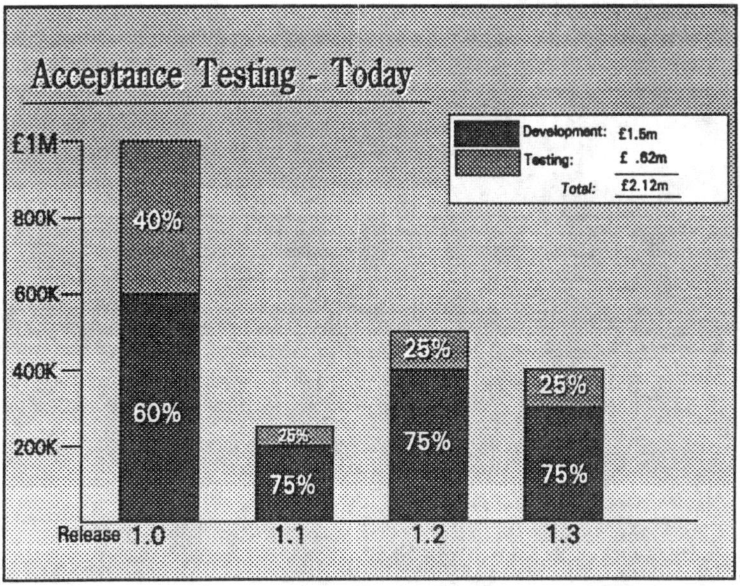

Figure 15.1

What is interesting, and was of concern to us, is that the amount of testing done in subsequent releases was firstly, less than that done in the first release and, secondly, was a constant proportion of the development effort. The implication was that we were only testing the actual changes being made. We were not testing for the 'knock-on' effect of these changes and, since the initial development testing ratio was 60:40 and in subsequent releases it was around 75:25, the testing we were doing was less rigorous than in the first release. The dangers of not testing for knock-on effect were highlighted last year in the BBC Radio 4 Science Now programme. Around sixty programmers were given a system and a change specification which could be implemented by a one-line code modification. Only four achieved the change with no 'knock-on' effects. One programmer caused twenty-seven subsequent errors.

The IEEE surveyed the cause of defects. This survey indicated that over 50% of defects are in existing features and caused by the implementation of new features.

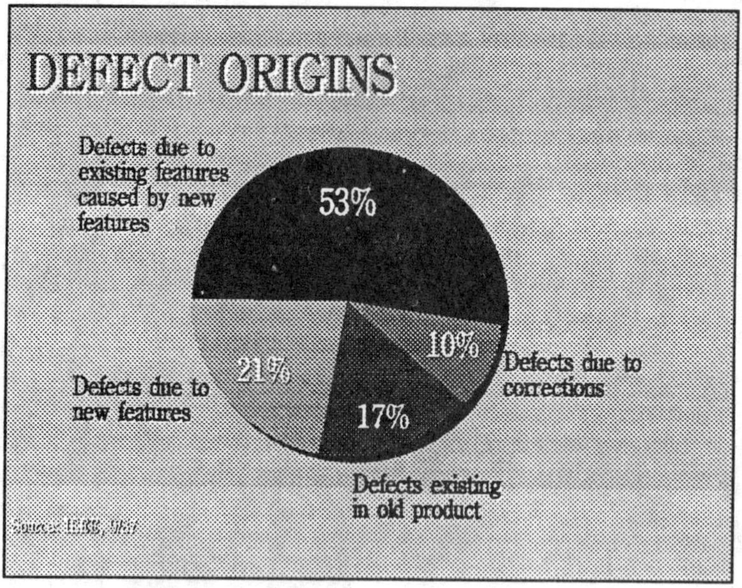

Figure 15.2

Why would we get a 53% rate of defect due to the incorporation of new features? Because developers are not testing for the knock-on effect but only testing the enhancements – not their impact on existing functionality.

If we ask ourselves what is the cost of testing, we also have to ask what are the costs of these defects. Because these are all in production, how much do the defects cost the business?. Here we get into risk management because one defect may not cost us anything at all or cause us any harm at all, then another error may bring the system down and cause us to lose business.

If we were to do testing properly, we should expend as much effort testing each subsequent release as the effort we expended testing the first release.

We realised that we could not afford this much testing, but the consequence of not testing properly was that we were finding too high a proportion of errors in production.

15.2 WHY DOES TESTING COST SO MUCH?

Testing is expensive because it is labour intensive, it's an iterative process and a high level of skill is required. Systems are getting more and more complicated and testing isn't a trivial exercise. One has to have a lot of business knowledge about how the different transactions relate to each other, and a lot of technical knowledge to simulate what the production people do every night running the systems. Quite often one gets dragged into using production data to do testing. Now this can be useful because it's real live data one's using but it can be very expensive in terms of volumes.

I worked on a project where we were using production data and we decided to analyse the data that we were putting through the system. We found that we were putting 50,000 transactions through this system and that most of the cases were going down the same path, with only about 200 going down different paths. The other 49,800 went down one of the paths the other 200 cases went down. We therefore got rid of the other 49,800 and just used the relevant 200 cases. The benefit was that our batch runs went through in a few seconds as opposed to a few hours. Quite often production data is used to test a system because we don't know any other way, and yet it costs us an awful lot of money.

Also, if one has to check the results of 50,000 transactions going through a test it's going to take an awful long time to do so.

More importantly, at the end of the test we have a short lived asset because we tend to throw it all away. The next time we have to test we have to repeat the whole exercise from scratch. Why do we throw it all away? There are a number of reasons:

- we have not documented the individual test cases
- the test cases are no longer valid for the new functionality
- test cases are date dependent
- the testing team has changed.

Generally, we don't think beyond the particular exercise in which we are involved, i.e. to test the system now as quickly as possible. All the effort is wasted because when we're finished we start all over again for the next release.

To parallel this to programming, it's the same as developing a program to deliver user requirements, testing that program, putting it into production, and throwing away the source code. If we ever needed to change the program we could just write it again. If you think about it that's what we do with testing.

15.3 THE INDUSTRY'S VIEW

The industry says we should attack this testing problem with tools. There are a number of tools on the market designed to assist with testing and Standard Chartered has bought most of them. In many cases we've bought several different versions of most of them in different places around the world. Our collection of testing tools is pretty impressive, yet none of these tools have really made any difference to the overall amount of time it actually takes to test a system. The industry said we should go and buy tools so we did, but it really hasn't made any difference.

The industry also says we need techniques to tackle testing. A particularly prevalent technique is to second users on to development projects. We did this to help to reduce the direct cost charged from IT because users don't pay twice for their own staff. Also the users do get involved in the system at an earlier stage, so you have actually some people involved that will be using the system once it is in production. The problem is that many times these users don't actually move back to the business – they soon become IT people.

Risk analysis is all about making the decision 'Do I need to test?' Having changed only one line of code do I need to retest the whole system or do I take the risk that I got it right? Industry data does not, however, support risk analysis as a successful technique. Quite often we tend to kid ourselves that we are actually making good risk decisions. The quality of the risk analysis is often dependent on the level of the individual's knowledge of the system. So if I'm changing program X and I know that program Y is not affected then I don't have to test program Y. The problem with risk analysis is that it is not consistent because it's so dependent on the individual's knowledge.

The next technique the industry says we should use is the preservation of our test data. If you keep all your test data you can use it again next time you have to test the system. The problem with this is that most organisations don't have standards for preserving test data. Once you've actually embarked on the testing exercise you are working to fixed deadlines. Now you are going to find two types of errors – errors in the system and errors in the test data you put together. How often do we go back and change the test data in our documentation? Most of the time we don't, thus invalidating the effort of preserving test data.

We might also preserve the physical test data – the database backup of the test, so we know we've got all the test data. But this is only in machine-readable format and nobody knows what's actually in this, the database, because we haven't documented it anywhere else. What you tend to find is that your disk packs are littered with dumps of databases from many years of testing. You keep them because they were important. What happens in my experience is that when DASD gets a bit tight somebody sends out a catalogue list around the department with a covering memo saying 'Does anybody know what this big database is – if you don't know we are going to delete it?'. People don't know what it is so we end up deleting many years of valuable data solely because we haven't catalogued it properly.

Saving output is very important. We produce a lot of output and the industry says we should keep this because it matches up with out test data. We had one project in the bank that was producing so much output that we hired a temporary clerk whose job it was to collect the output each morning from the printers, punch holes in it, put it into binders, and put it on a shelf. This was a very important and responsible job. It was test output so we had to keep it. Eighteen months later, the department hired another temporary clerk to throw all the documentation away. It had never been looked at. If you file thousands and thousands of sheets of paper is anyone ever going to read it?

The industry says we should do all the above, and more. We tried them all and, like testing tools, they really did not make any difference.

15.4 THE CLASSIC APPROACH

We can broadly break up the development cycle into analysis/design/(code), unit test, system test, and user acceptance test. As you move, in time, through the cycle fewer and fewer people are involved, but, the elapsed time for each phase of testing increases. If you look at the testing tools available to us today, the majority are aimed at unit testing and only some are aimed at system testing. Practically none are aimed at acceptance testing and those that are, are certainly not designed for use by business analysts and users – who are exactly the people who perform acceptance testing.

In the classic approach to the improvement of testing, the tool suppliers and the buyers, typically systems development managers, have concentrated on unit testing productivity. This has a marginal beneficial effect on elapsed time for the total project or, to put it another way, of increasing the likelihood of delivering the project on time. With only a small percentage of the total development cycle used in unit testing, very significant productivity gains here have only a marginal impact on the total. Alternatively, productivity gains can be used to unit test more systems. This does not help because all we are now doing is feeding more systems into the manual bottleneck of acceptance testing.

Unit testing tools have been, and continue to be, successfully justified on reduced system costs. The users, however, don't care about this justification.

If there is a revenue stream dependent on the implementation of a system, the business can't get the revenue stream until the users get the system. Therefore the system is on the critical path for getting the revenue stream. So if cutting the cost of the system doesn't speed up the delivery of the system the users aren't interested. Speed/time is more important than system cost.

Users want their systems delivered faster because the sooner they get their system the sooner they can recognise the revenue. The real pressure is to deliver faster rather than to deliver cheaper.

Therefore, despite the investment in tools, we continue either to throw resources at the latter stages of development or to skimp on testing. In both cases, quality decreases, costs increase, and the users still do not get their system any sooner.

15.5 A NEW APPROACH

The real challenges are to deliver systems more quickly by reducing the elapsed time, to improve quality by improved test coverage, and to reduce cost by reusing previous test cases.

The way we have achieved this at Standard Chartered is to focus our attention on user acceptance testing as this was a manually dominated task and took the longest in elapsed time. The key to this approach was to consider any software test as an asset which would be capitalised, then we used the industry tools and techniques to build and maintain the asset and to ensure that users did not need to become technicians in order to use the asset.

In order to design and build the asset we had to define its characteristics. These can be grouped together under three main headings:

Economic

- minimum execution time – preferably overnight
- minimum machine resource
- least necessary technical expertise
- fewest number of people – never more than five
- minimum consumable resources – only exceptions should be printed

Evolutionary

- must have a life over more than one release of the system
- must be understandable – well documented
- maintainable and adaptable – able to run in different environments
- extendable – can build on/merge in other tests

Operational

- easy to run and rerun by users
- gives consistent results – the same test run twice gives the same results

- covers usable functionality – the same system can be used by two separate functions
- clear indication of unexpected results – don't hide them amongst reams of expected results
- rapid access to results/inputs – to determine cause of unexpected results.

With these characteristics in place, we were in a position to identify both the benefits to be achieved from the asset and its fundamental design criteria.

We then proceeded to the technical design of what we have come to term the Repeatable Test System (RTS).

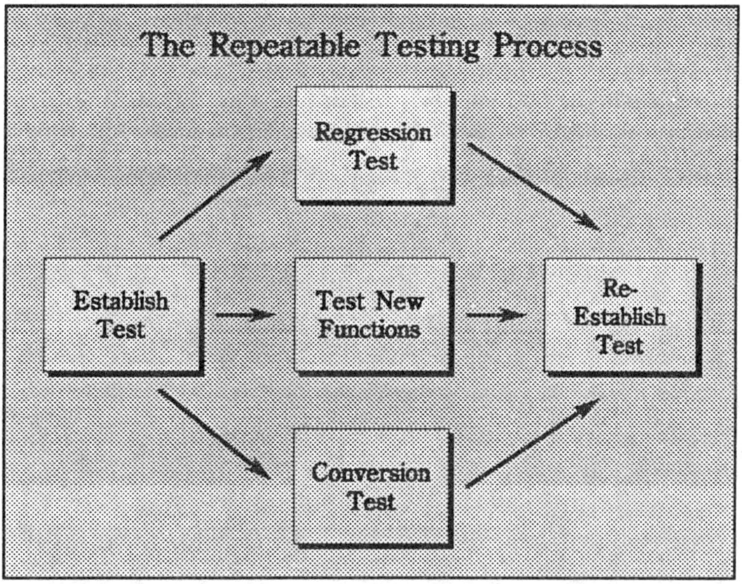

Figure 15.3

In building the physical asset, we wanted to follow Standard Chartered's system strategy of using, wherever possible, industry recognised and accepted packages from credible worldwide suppliers. With four data centres around the world – three in the Far East and one in the UK – we were also looking for flexibility and a phased approach to implementation. The big bang approach was never going to work for us and, as we discovered, would not have worked if we had only been running one data centre.

Following a detailed review of the market, we decided to use products from two companies, Compuware and Legent, as the core of our Repeatable Test System. The products we use are Playback, a capture/replay/comparison tool, and File-AID, a file and data management tool, both from Compuware; and Endevor, a software management tool from Legent.

Even with these products in place, we were still faced with our own development effort As mentioned above, these and other tools in the market are designed for technicians, so we were faced with development of a user-friendly common systems environment so everyone that needs to run the system has the same user-friendly interface. In addition, we had to build in automatic JCL creation in order for the users to be able to run one test followed by another test without having to worry about the combinations of batch and on-line applications. Equally importantly, the users also needed the ability to determine for themselves the transaction rates and number of users so that they could effect their own concurrency and stress testing.

15.6 BENEFITS

Through careful selection of the initial application against which we would use RTS, we were able quickly to start to demonstrate tangible benefits to the users.

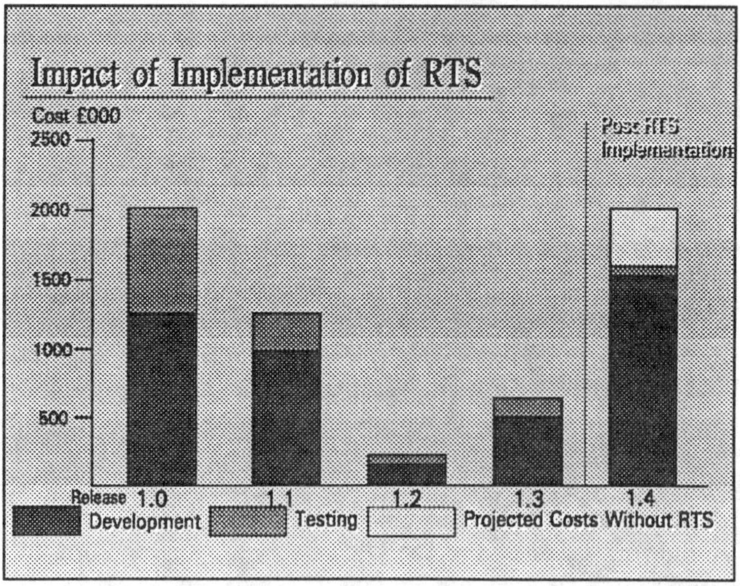

Figure 15.4

Most recently, we have used RTS on a full release of one of our treasury systems (above). The identified savings were a reduction in estimated acceptance testing costs from £430,000 to £53,000. Whilst the cost saving is important, we have also reduced the overall development cycle on this release by 20% (acceptance test reduction of over 80%), thus delivering on the key user requirement of speed/time. We also know that because we have used RTS, our testing has been far more exhaustive than we were used to and, with this knowledge, we are confident that the quality of the system delivered is much greater than before. The initial indications bear this out, but we will have to wait until the next release is implemented before we can truly put a figure on the quality improvement.

Besides these huge tangible benefits, we have also identified not insignificant intangibles:

- greater user involvement, enabling users to control their own destiny
- less use of technical resource as users start their own jobs, control their own test data restoration, etc.
- less resource usage in terms of paper, CPU time, and overtime
- greater confidence in the delivered system
- an overall improvement in morale.

15.7 THE FUTURE

RTS has already proven its benefit and we are actively implementing it across all our other systems and applications. We have, however, yet to measure quantifiably the benefits from improved quality and, hence, reduced maintenance and redevelopment. We know they are there; we just don't know the scale.

Despite all the benefits, we are aware that user acceptance testing is just one of the tasks in the whole testing process.

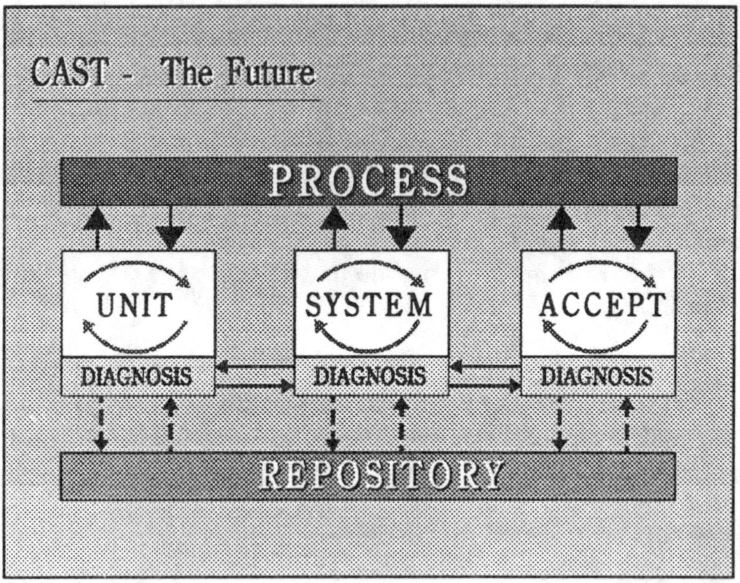

Figure 15.5

Standard Chartered are developing process management testing models, to work with Compuware's tools set. When this is in place, we will have effective control of the complete testing process and will have truly implemented Computer Aided Software Testing (CAST).